The East Timor Question

THE EAST TIMOR QUESTION

The Struggle for Independence from Indonesia

Edited by
Paul Hainsworth &
Stephen McCloskey

Foreword by John Pilger
Preface by José Ramos-Horta

I.B.Tauris *Publishers*
LONDON ● NEW YORK

Published in 2000 by I.B.Tauris & Co Ltd
Victoria House, Bloomsbury Square, London WC1B 4DZ
175 Fifth Avenue, New York NY 10010
www.ibtauris.com

In the United States and Canada distributed by St Martin's Press
175 Fifth Avenue, New York NY 10010

ISBN 1-86064-408-2

A full CIP record for this book is available from the British Library
A full CIP record for this book is available from the Library of Congress

Library of Congress catalog card: available

Typeset in Baskerville 10/12pt by The Midlands Book Typesetting Company,
Loughborough, Leicestershire
Printed and bound in Great Britain by MPG Books Ltd, Bodmin, Cornwall

CONTENTS

Acknowledgements

The editors wish to recognise the constant support and co-operation received from the following organizations and individuals throughout the writing and compilation of this book: Paul Barber and his colleagues in Tapol, the Indonesia Human Rights Campaign; the British Coalition for East Timor; the Catholic Institute for International Relations; Hugh Dowson; the East Timor *Action* Network in the United States of America, which continually disseminates valuable updated information on East Timor and Indonesia; Tom Hyland, and the staff and volunteers of the East Timor Ireland Solidarity Campaign in Dublin; Mairead Maguire and the members and supporters of the East Timor Solidarity Campaign in Northern Ireland. These organizations and other East Timor networks throughout the world are a prime example of how civil society can make a decisive contribution to alleviating serious human rights situations like that in East Timor. Thanks are also due to Gerard McCann, and the staff and Management Board of the One World Centre in Belfast, who offered constant encouragement and interest in this project, and were a ready source of information. The offices and staff of Amnesty International in Belfast, Dublin and London were also enormously helpful with material, particularly in the context of a rapidly changing situation in East Timor and Indonesia. A debt of gratitude is owed to José Ramos-Horta for providing us with a preface to the book at a time of immense uncertainty and upheaval in East Timor, and John Pilger for his typically forthright and compelling foreword which reflects his longstanding support for the East Timorese. At I.B.Tauris, Dr Lester Crook was a patient and supportive Commissioning Editor, and Managing Editor Steve Tribe offered challenging and useful comments on the manuscript. Finally, we thank Luciano Da Conceicao, José Lopes, Boaventura Moreira and Dino Gandara Rai, four of the many East Timorese forced to flee their country during Indonesia's occupation and currently resident in Dublin, for their constant inspiration and support throughout.

Notes on Contributors

Jim Aubrey is the executive spokesperson for Australians for a Free East Timor and director of Humanity First, a human rights consultancy. He has directed campaigns against the Timor Gap Treaty and the Australia-Indonesia security agreement, and is the author of a book recently published by Random House entitled *Free East Timor*.

Carmel Budiardjo, a former political prisoner in Indonesia, is the founder and chair of Tapol, the Indonesia Human Rights Campaign. Her recently published autobiography is entitled *Surviving Indonesia's Gulag*.

Estêvão Cabral is an East Timorese postgraduate student at the University of Lancaster and organizer/editor of FITUN. Formerly active in the internal resistance movement, Cabral is the Fretilin representative for Britain. He has also completed a PhD on East Timor.

Peter Carey is a fellow in modern history at Trinity College, Oxford, and a worldwide authority on East Timor. Amongst his recent publications are *East Timor at the Crossroads: The Forging of a Nation* and *East Timor: Third World Colonialism and the Struggle for National Identity*.

Adrian Guelke is professor of politics at Queen's University Belfast, where he is director of the Centre for Ethnicity and Conflict. He has published widely on Northern Ireland, South Africa and international politics.

Paul Hainsworth is a senior lecturer in politics at the University of Ulster. He is also a founder and chair of the East Timor Solidarity Campaign, Northern Ireland, as well as being an activist in Amnesty International's (UK) human rights campaign for Indonesia and East Timor. He has published widely on European and East Timorese politics.

Pedro Pinto Leite is a senior lecturer in law at the University of Leiden (Holland) and coordinator of IPJET, the International Platform of Jurists for East Timor, which recently published *International Law and the Question of East Timor*, with the Catholic Institute for International Relations.

Stephen McCloskey is the coordinator of the One World Centre for Northern Ireland, a resource base for global and developing-world studies. He has recently completed a distance-learning MSc in environmental and development education through South Bank University in London and is secretary of the East Timor Solidarity Campaign, Northern Ireland.

Andrea Needham is one of the Seeds of Hope group which successfully disarmed a Hawk aircraft before it could be sold to Indonesia. In a subsequent court case, the Seeds of Hope women were famously acquitted in 1996.

Hugh O'Shaughnessy is an investigative journalist who has worked for the BBC, *The Independent*, *The Observer* and other media outlets. A specialist and activist on East Timor, O'Shaughnessy recently published *East Timor: Getting Away with Murder*.

Jen Parker is one of the Seeds of Hope group which successfully disarmed a Hawk aircraft before it could be sold to Indonesia. In a subsequent court case, the Seeds of Hope women were famously acquitted in 1996.

John Pilger is a renowned journalist and broadcaster who has written widely on the issue of East Timor and produced television documentaries on the territory, including *Death of a Nation: The Timor Conspiracy*, which was first broadcast in 1994 and updated in 1999. His most recent book is *Hidden Agendas*, published in 1998 by Vintage.

José Ramos-Horta is the vice-president of the National Council of Timorese Resistance (CNRT) and the joint recipient of the 1996 Nobel Peace Prize.

Charles Scheiner is the director of the East Timor *Action* Network (ETAN), which has established 'chapters' or local branches throughout the USA. ETAN is also a member of the International Federation for East Timor.

Maureen Tolfree is an activist for East Timor. Her brother, Brian Peters, was killed in 1975 in the Balibo incident at the time of the Indonesian invasion. She is a patron of Britain's Stop the Hawks – No Arms to Indonesia Coalition, and a co-sponsor of the British Coalition for East Timor.

Eilís Ward lectures on women and politics in the Department of Politics, Trinity College, Dublin, where she has recently completed her PhD on civil society and Irish foreign policy (with a strong emphasis on East Timor as an issue). She has also published on refugee policies and on the women's movement in Ireland.

Jo Wilson is one of the Seeds of Hope group which successfully disarmed a Hawk aircraft before it could be sold to Indonesia. In a subsequent court case, the Seeds of Hope women were famously acquitted in 1996.

Foreword

John Pilger

A silence enveloped East Timor for 16 years after it was invaded by the Indonesian military. There were no Kosovo-type headlines, no public appeals by the major charities, no questions in Parliament that anyone can remember. Yet no place on earth was as defiled and abused by murderous forces, in collaboration with the 'international community', as East Timor. What has happened there is one of the great and, until recently, unrecognized crimes of the twentieth century. I write that carefully; not even Pol Pot succeeded in killing, proportionally, as many Cambodians as the Indonesian dictator Suharto and his fellow generals have killed in East Timor. According to a comprehensive study commissioned by the Australian Parliament, 'at least' 200,000 East Timorese, a third of the population, have died under the Indonesian occupation. The word genocide is often misused. This was genocide.

Western governments secretly documented the unfolding of the genocide from well before the first Indonesian paratroopers landed in Dili on 7 December 1975. 'I saw the intelligence that came from hard, firm sources,' Philip Liechty, the CIA desk officer in Jakarta at the time, told me. 'There were people being herded into school buildings by Indonesian soldiers and the buildings set on fire. There were people herded into fields and machine-gunned, and hunted in the mountains simply because they were there. None of that got out [and yet] Suharto was given the green light [by the USA and its allies] to do what he did ... without continued US logistical military support, the Indonesians might not have been able to pull it off.' Suharto's resource-rich Indonesia, said President Richard Nixon, was 'the prize of South-East Asia'.

In 1989, Bishop Carlos Filipe Ximenes Belo, the head of the Catholic Church in East Timor, appealed directly to the world in a letter to the United Nations secretary-general. 'We are dying as a people,' he wrote. He received no reply. It was not until 12 November 1991, when a British cameraman, Max Stahl (a pseudonym), recorded on videotape Indonesian troops shooting and beating to death scores of unarmed young people in the Santa Cruz cemetery in Dili following a peaceful demonstration, that the rest of the world glimpsed the horror and the struggle of East Timor.

My own filming trip to East Timor, made under cover with the late David Munro in 1993, produced images and meetings I shall never forget. Working with an old aeronautical map (we couldn't locate any other, such was East Timor's isolation), we travelled through the Matabean mountains, with everywhere silhouettes of crosses rising above us: crosses on peaks, crosses in tiers on the hillsides, crosses beside the road. The inscriptions told of whole communities killed in the space of a few days. From Tata Mai Lau, the highest peak, 3048 metres above sea level, a Calvary line of crosses reached all the way down to where the pope had said mass in 1989, in full view of a crescent of hard, salt land beneath which lay countless human remains.

What astonished us on that trip was the resilience of the East Timorese resistance. Mathematically, it should have been wiped out; but it lived on, as we found, in the hearts and eyes of almost everyone: eyes that reflected a defiance and courage of a kind I had not experienced anywhere else. And it is this spirit and determination that fuelled the opposition to the Indonesian machinations aimed at undermining the right of the East Timorese to self-determination.

The resisters were mostly young people, raised during Indonesian rule, who kept alive the nationalism minted in the 1970s and its union with a spiritual, traditional love of country and language; it was they who confronted the soldiers and the local death squads paid and trained by the military, who buried the flags and maps and drew the subtle graffiti of a sleeping face resembling the tranquil figure in Matisse's *The Dream*, reminding the Indonesians that, whatever they did, they would one day reckon with a Timorese reawakening. Independence has been their victory and that of their tireless leaders, at home and in exile: men of remarkable calibre, like Xanana Gusmão, José Ramos-Horta and Carlos Belo.

The foreign friends of the East Timorese, who are represented in the following pages, can also take credit. However, for them the task of rebuilding an entire society – after the bloody and destructive pro-Jakarta militia/military backlash of post-referendum East Timor – remains urgent. It is to redirect the power of the West, the misnamed international community, away from destruction towards construction, from exploitation towards genuine help. The British government prior to the referendum the distinction of being the largest supplier of weapons and armaments to the Indonesian army, sending everything from Hawk fighter-bombers to machine guns. Even as Foreign Secretary Robin Cook was outlining his 'ethical' foreign policy, he was secretly approving licences for arms contracts with

Jakarta. José Ramos-Horta then called on the Blair government to freeze these shipments. But it refused, until finally caving in to international pressure during the intense phase of widespread human rights abuses which followed the referendum. Even then, only a temporary suspension on arms sales was imposed. Arms sales policy and licensing must be fundamentally changed if the East Timorese and other peoples are to be genuinely free of repression and human rights violations presided over by politicians and orchestrated by the military. The freedom of the East Timorese people, which is their basic human right, supersedes all other interests. The East Timorese now deserve nothing less than a maximum effort to assert their independence as a nation state.

Preface

José Ramos-Horta
1996 Nobel Peace laureate and vice-president of
CNRT (the National Council of Timorese Resistance)

This book has been written at a crucial time in the East Timorese people's fight for self-determination and against a background of genocide against them, perpetrated by the Indonesian political and military authorities. In April 1999, I expressed my concerns about the future of East Timor to the Secretary-General of the United Nations, Kofi Annan and, by way of a preface to the book, I would like to reiterate these as East Timor prepares for the referendum on its constitutional status on 30 August 1999.

As I wrote to the Secretary-General: 'I know you are conscious of the enormous injustice and betrayal that befell the East Timorese people. The violence unleashed against this small nation with active complicity of the major powers stands as one of the greatest crimes of our times.' We are at a critical historical juncture with freedom and justice within our grasp. However, after 23 years of a brutal colonial occupation, the 'Indonesian military authorities remain defiant and are bent on denying the people of East Timor their hard-won rights. This is also a test of wills between the United Nations and the forces of intolerance and violence. I welcome the agreement brokered by the UN Secretary-General that paves the way for a vote on the future of East Timor on 30 August 1999.

However, I have expressed my deep concerns regarding this precarious agreement that does not contain the essential guarantees of security that are *sine qua non* conditions for a truly democratic process free of coercion and terror. The Indonesian side has prevailed in its refusal to reduce its military presence in the territory and in its unwillingness to disarm the gang of criminals it has armed and fostered. It continues to carry out a systematic campaign of murder and destruction with total impunity. Our people, terrorized for 23 years, are expected to vote on their future with 'protection' provided by the very same army and gangs of criminals that have turned the country into a hell far worse than contemporary Kosovo and apartheid South Africa.

The 30 August vote will prove to be a farce and the credibility of the United Nations will be seriously damaged if firm preventive measures are not considered now. It is necessary that the Security Council is seized of the question. After all, there are two Security Council resolutions on the question of East Timor that remain to be implemented. In particular:

- the presence of the Indonesian army, an army of occupation, must be reduced to a maximum of 1000 and they must be confined to a designated area;
- similarly, the Falintil (the resistance) should be confined to designated areas;
- the paramilitaries and the gang of militias must be totally disarmed;
- only the United Nations should provide security.

Failure to implement these measures is a recipe for disaster. The inability or unwillingness of the powers that be to compel the Indonesian army to comply with the United Nations Security Council and General Assembly resolutions calling for a total withdrawal of its troops from East Timor threatens the entire peace process, and will only prolong the conflict well into the next century.

Again, as I communicated to Kofi Annan:

I am conscious Mr Secretary-General of the enormous difficulties you face. I believe that you are equally conscious that the difficulties, intransigence, and arrogance do not come from our humble people. I am also fully aware that you have been doing your utmost to move this process forward and that the apparent flaws in the New York agreement were the price you had to pay in order to enable the United Nations to gain access to East Timor. My concerns and strong reservations are not therefore born of distrust in your leadership. Quite the contrary, you have my full confidence and respect. They are meant only to alert you to the risks and dangers ahead so that no stone is left unturned to ensure maximum security and fairness for this historical mission. Success in East Timor will have profound positive impact on the credibility of the United Nations that we all cherish.

If we fail to guarantee a fair and democratic process, there should be no illusion that the people of East Timor will give up their struggle. Examples abound of traditionally peaceful communities and political movements changing tactics when their non-violent strategy is not rewarded. And Indonesia and the world community can expect that the new generation of East Timorese will seek other forms of struggle in the same positive manner as other betrayed nations have done.

At the time of writing, the conditions in East Timor are not conducive to the holding of a free and fair referendum, with the militias armed and active. However, the fact that the referendum is being called at this time is a tribute to the brave struggle and work of the East Timorese people inside and outside the territory. The international solidarity community has also played its part here, and this book is a testament to that. I commend it, therefore, to readers.

Editors' note: This preface was obviously written before the August 1999 referendum in East Timor, and the violent and destructive militia/military backlash that followed. It is clear, though, from José Ramos-Horta's words, that the East Timorese were always vulnerable to risks and danger, and paid a heavy price for exercising their vote. The book is dedicated to the people of East Timor and their future.

1

Introduction: East Timor – From European to Third World Colonialism

Stephen McCloskey

Background to the conflict

The troubled history of East Timor has been marked by levels of conflict, poverty, exploitation and – for almost a quarter of a century – genocide, which are exceptional, even in the context of the Third World. As with most other Third World countries, East Timor's past, and indeed its future, is bound up with the strategic and material interests of Western powers, and until October 1999, East Timor was one of the few developing countries yet to accede to full self-determination and independence. If East Timor can be considered a microcosm of Third World expropriation by developed countries, then the territory's occupation by Indonesia in 1975 was also an example of how corrupt administrations in developing countries can assume the aggressive colonial practices normally associated with Western imperialism. The combination of Western duplicity and self-interest with a brutal Third World dictatorship consigned East Timor to almost 25 years of 'systematic killing, gratuitous violence and primitive plunder'.[1]

The island of Timor is located some 480 km north of Australia and has an area of 32,300 square kilometres (roughly equal to that of the Netherlands),[2] and was divided in 1859 to facilitate the territorial designs of the Dutch and Portuguese. West Timor developed a distinctive social character under the control of the Dutch – which included the practice of Protestantism – and fell under the auspices of Jakarta following the Indonesian proclamation of independence in 1945. As the furthest outreach of the Catholic Portuguese colonial empire, the more 'Latinized' East Timor remained under Lisbon's control after partition, continuing an occupation which spanned over 400 years, broken only by the occupying forces of the Japanese army during the Second World War. As Taylor states: 'By the time that the Japanese surrendered, some 60,000 Timorese, or 13 per cent of the population had died as a result of the war', despite Portuguese East Timor's neutrality during the conflict.[3] The extent of Timor's human sacrifice in support of Australia's war effort is a source of bitter irony in the territory given Canberra's *de facto* and (on 14 February 1979) *de jure*[4] recognition of Indonesia's annexation of East Timor, a position that only began to unravel following the economic and political ferment which gripped Indonesia in the late 1990s.

In the context of the Third World, the post-war era was generally characterized by the fragmentation of colonial empires and withdrawal of direct forms of administrative control, which were superseded by more insidious, but no less effective, measures to effect 'Western' economic control of the southern hemisphere. The establishment of the World Bank and International Monetary Fund (IMF) in 1945, as multilateral institutions designed to promote international trade, for example, has resulted in a 'new colonialism' of developing countries, most evident in the crippling debt crisis which has enveloped the Third World.[5] East Timor, however, remained a remote Portuguese colonial outpost until the 1970s, partly because of the comparatively more benign character of the colonial regime, and also due to the largely passive resistance of the East Timorese, which helped to sustain their traditional Maubere (East Timorese) culture and society. The independence movement in East Timor developed at a later stage than in other Portuguese colonies but, by the mid-1970s, a clandestine national liberation organization attracted broad support throughout Timorese society.[6] The opportunity presented in April 1974 by the political upheaval of the 'Carnation Revolution' in Lisbon facilitated the emergence of new political parties in East Timor, that were intent on influencing the territory's future direction.

Independence and re-colonization

Following events in Lisbon in 1974, the changed political scene in East Timor saw the emergence of three main parties: the UDT (Timorese Democratic Union), 'led by members of the colonial administrative élite',[7] initially favoured federation with Portugal but eventually supported independence; Fretilin (the Revolutionary Front for an Independent East Timor), a formerly clandestine independence movement which was legalized in September 1974; and a third much smaller party, Apodeti (the

Timorese Popular Democratic Association), was established with the encouragement and support of the Indonesian consulate in Dili, and favoured full integration with Indonesia. In January 1975, a Fretilin-UDT coalition – supported by the Portuguese – was formed, with the main aim of establishing an independent East Timor. This coalition, however, was undermined by Indonesian intelligence agencies, which convinced the UDT leadership that Fretilin was plotting an uprising to impose a 'communist-styled' regime on the island. Such claims were intended to play on the fears of UDT supporters and, as Pilger has pointed out, the idea that Fretilin 'would turn East Timor into a base for communist insurgency was absurd... Above all, they were nationalists who wanted their people to control their own destiny, trade and resources.'[8]

The Indonesian military, however, was intent on eroding confidence in the liberation movement by dividing the main political parties, and thereby manufacturing a premise its their full-scale intervention in East Timor. In July 1975, Fretilin won 55 per cent of the vote in local council elections,[9] and this prompted the Indonesian military leadership to orchestrate a UDT *coup d'état*, launched on 11 August, to check the Front's growing popular support. The coup plunged East Timor into civil war and cost some 1500 lives, although by September 1975 Fretilin controlled all the territory. East Timorese troops in the Portuguese colonial army had decisively supported Fretilin in the civil war and also facilitated the establishment of Falintil (Armed Forces for the National Liberation of East Timor), a pro-independence military wing. The Portuguese government, which 'wanted the army out of Timor',[10] withdrew its administration from Dili during the civil war, abnegated its responsibilities to the Timorese, and ignored Indonesia's clear manipulation of the political scene in the territory.

On 28 November 1975, Fretilin declared the Democratic Republic of East Timor, and received recognition of its status from 12 nation-states, though importantly not the Portuguese government, which maintained its position of acquiescence to Indonesia. The fact that Lisbon withheld recognition of the Timorese republic meant that the United Nations (UN) continued to recognize Portugal as the legitimate administrative authority in East Timor throughout Indonesia's occupation of the territory. Moreover, Lisbon's status as the *de jure* governing power in East Timor enabled the Portuguese authorities – albeit belatedly – to promote the cause of East Timor in the UN and European Union (EU), and also represent the Timorese in direct negotiations with Indonesia over the future of the territory. However, the Portuguese did not intercede on behalf of the East Timorese in 1975 when Indonesia 'launched a secret intelligence operation, code-named Operasi Komodo, aimed at destroying the burgeoning independence movement'.[11] The intentions of the Indonesian military were made clear when five Australian-based television journalists (two Britons and three Australians) were murdered at Balibo on 16 October, in what a recently published Australian government report described as 'the start of a general offensive by the Indonesian military to annex East Timor' (see Chapter 4).[12] The muted response to the Balibo killings – and to the subsequent murder of a sixth journalist, Roger East – from Western governments, with access to intelligence reports on Indonesian troop movements, convinced General Suharto that a full-scale invasion had their approval. Indeed, on 7 December, just hours after US President Gerald Ford and his Secretary of State, Henry Kissinger, completed an official visit to Jakarta 'where they probably learned of, and endorsed Suharto's expansionist plans',[13] the full-scale invasion of East Timor was launched.

Occupation and resistance

Since 1975, over 200,000 Timorese – one-third of the pre-invasion population – have died at the hands of the Indonesian military and, as Pilger suggests, 'Proportionately, not even Pol Pot in Cambodia killed as many people'.[14] The massive human rights violations in East Timor which followed Indonesia's invasion included random massacres, extra-judicial killings, starvation, deaths from preventable disease, torture, forced movement of population, coerced sterilization of women, rape and imprisonment without legal redress. The repeated human rights excesses of the Indonesian state and Jakarta's illegal occupation of East Timor were condemned in ten UN resolutions, and yet the dominant UN member states consistently failed to galvanize an appropriate response to enforce the resolutions – unlike, for example, the resolve shown during the Iraqi invasion of Kuwait in 1990. Until the collapse of the Indonesian economy in 1997 and subsequent political turmoil created by popular unrest, Jakarta had enjoyed diplomatic support from Western governments based on favourable trading relations. The weakness of the UN position on East Timor can be sourced to Western support for General Suharto's overthrow of Indonesia's 'communist' President Sukarno in a bloody coup in 1965 when, as Budiardjo states, 'at least half a million people were killed' (see Chapter 5). Regarded as a bulwark against communism in South-East Asia, Suharto was valued as an ally by the West because of the strategic importance of Indonesia in the region, combined with Jakarta's pursuance of an ultimately disastrous neo-liberal economic programme. Moreover, Suharto's methods of internal repression within Indonesia and East Timor necessitated a regular supply of weaponry from member states of the UN, including Britain, the USA and Australia (see Chapters 8, 9 and 10, respectively).

When Suharto claimed East Timor as the '27th province' of Indonesia on 2 June 1976, following the approval of annexation by a fraudulent 'people's assembly' comprised totally of UDT and Apodeti members, the international community again refused to intervene directly on behalf of the Timorese. The UN decolonization committee, however, condemned the annexation as illegal, and – Western Sahara aside (see Chapter 12) – East Timor was the largest non-self-governing territory on the UN General Assembly's decolonization list until 1999. In the absence of international assistance, however, the Fretilin guerrillas, faced by overwhelming military opposition, waged an unorthodox yet effective campaign against the Indonesian forces, which sustained the independence movement. In 1978, Fretilin ordered the mass surrender of civilians within the Indonesian-controlled cities. In an attempt to 'Timorize' the conflict and create division among the East Timorese, the Indonesian military armed and equipped new local recruits, who later, under orders from Fretilin, 'rebelled and re-joined the revolutionary forces'.[15] In 1983, the Fretilin leader, Xanana Gusmão, signed a cease-fire agreement with General Purwanto, the commander of the Indonesian forces in East Timor. Following the visit to East Timor in July by an Australian parliamentary delegation, which viewed the territory 'firmly in an Indonesian context',[16] Leonardus Murdani, commander-in-chief of the Indonesian armed forces, unilaterally broke the cease-fire. On 17 August, a new military offensive was launched in East Timor, called Operasi Persatuan (Operation Unity), thereby dispelling any suggestion that Suharto's regime was interested in negotiations with the Fretilin resistance.

From 1980, Suharto introduced a resettlement programme in East Timor whereby 'voluntary' migrants were relocated to the territory under the guise of relieving overpopulation in islands such as Java and Bali. The overriding aim of this insidious process was to neutralize the independence movement in East Timor and further 'de-Timorize' the territory through the eradication of indigenous culture, language and religion. In 1992–93, a total of 662 Indonesian families were resettled in East Timor, and whilst there were no precise statistics available, most observers placed the number of voluntary transmigrants 'in the vicinity of 150,000'.[17] The exploitation of East Timor's resources, as evidenced by the transmigration programme, was taken further in 1989 when Indonesia and Australia signed the Timor Gap Treaty to extract and profit from East Timor's oil and gas reserves (see Chapter 10), a contract which also involved 12 multinational corporations based in Britain, the Netherlands, Japan and the USA. The 'business-as-usual' approach to relations with Suharto's Indonesia encompassed both Western governments and private capital, as the genocide in East Timor continued unabated.

The 1991 Dili massacre and exposure of genocide

The dominant media interests in the West largely ignored developments in East Timor in the 15 years which followed Indonesia's invasion in 1975 (see Chapter 3). Echoing the positions of Western governments, the mainstream media chose to either deliberately disregard or downplay the extent of human rights abuses in the territory, as strategic and commercial matters took precedence. As Scheiner suggests (see Chapter 9) on the USA:

> Throughout the 1970s and 1980s, the US media and Congress continued to ignore East Timor. Between the day after the 1975 invasion and the 1991 Dili massacre, East Timor was covered precisely once among 100,000 US network television news pieces. East Timor rarely made the newspapers, and was almost totally absent from public view.

The Western media's silence on the situation in East Timor was eventually broken through a combination of dogged resistance and courage on the part of the Timorese, the campaigning activities of Timorese exiles and solidarity organizations in Western countries, and the persistence of a small group of journalists and broadcasters – such as Max Stahl, Hugh O'Shaughnessy, David Munro, Noam Chomsky, and John Pilger – who ensured that East Timor eventually became a global concern.

The late 1980s witnessed the increased mobilization of Timorese students, who protested against the ongoing human rights violations in the territory. When Pope John Paul II visited the Timorese capital Dili in 1989, a group of students unfurled a pro-Fretilin banner some 20 metres from the altar where mass was celebrated. It is estimated that of the 80,000 who attended the ceremony, some 13,000 were members of the Indonesian security forces,[18] prepared to react to pro-independence protests in the full glare of the international media. Student protesters who shouted slogans denouncing the Indonesian regime were immediately arrested and some reporters covering the pope's visit had their equipment confiscated. The Timorese recognized the importance of maximizing the opportunities presented by high-profile visits to their country as a means of publicizing and exposing the brutality of Indonesia's occupation. A planned visit by a Portuguese parliamentary delegation in November 1991 offered such an opportunity, and the East Timorese organized pro-independence demonstrations as they awaited the delegation's arrival. The visit was cancelled, however, because of Jakarta's objections to the inclusion of Jill Jolliffe, an Australian, investigative journalist, in the Portuguese press corps.

On 28 October 1991, one day after Lisbon announced the cancellation of this visit, a Timorese student, Sebastião Gomes, was killed by Indonesian troops whilst taking refuge in the Motael Church in Dili.[19] On 12 November 1991, hundreds of Timorese attended a memorial service for the student and joined a funeral procession to his grave. As the mourners gathered in the enclosed Santa Cruz cemetery, they were cut down by the Indonesian military using US-supplied M-16 automatic weapons. According to authoritative sources, 271 Timorese were killed at Santa Cruz, 382 were wounded, and a further 250 'disappeared', many of whom are presumed to have been subsequently killed by the Indonesian military.[20] Although there had been similar massacres perpetrated by the Indonesian military in the past, the carnage at Dili was to significantly undermine Jakarta's international standing, as East Timor became a major source of embarrassment to the Indonesian government and its supporters. The Dili massacre, unlike previous atrocities, had been captured on film by Max Stahl, a British journalist, who managed to smuggle footage of the Indonesian military action to the outside world and thereby accelerated the process of making East Timor an international issue. In commenting on the significance of Stahl's coverage of the Dili massacre, Hugh O'Shaughnessy (see Chapter 3) suggests that: 'Whether the Indonesian authorities knew it or not, Stahl's film was the death knell for the continued dominance of Indonesia in East Timor.'

Stahl also contributed to *Death of a Nation: The Timor Conspiracy*, the John Pilger/David Munro 1994 documentary on East Timor, which further exposed the oppression of the Timorese. An updated version of this film, *The Timor Conspiracy*, screened on 26 January 1999, prompted some 200,000 people to phone an information line flagged up at the end of the programme, with a total of 1400 calls received per minute.[21] The impact of these broadcasts has also been clearly manifested in the global network of campaign and solidarity organizations which have taken up the cause of East Timor, and contributed to the process of raising public awareness about the human rights situation in both East Timor and Indonesia. The campaign groups exerted considerable pressure on transnational organizations such as the EU and UN and on national governments to implement the ten UN resolutions which condemn Indonesia's occupation of East Timor, and to respect Timorese rights to self-determination. A celebrated example of the effective lobbying work of solidarity organizations has been the success of the East Timor Ireland Solidarity Campaign (ETISC) in persuading successive Irish governments to promote the cause of East Timor in the EU and UN (see Chapter 11).

International pressure on Indonesia in regard to its occupation of East Timor increased in 1996 when the Nobel Peace Prize was jointly awarded to Bishop Carlos Ximenes Belo, head of the Catholic Church in East Timor, and José Ramos-Horta, the special representative of the CNRM (the National Council of Maubere Resistance – reconstituted in 1997 as

CNRT, the National Council of Timorese Resistance). The Nobel Committee pointedly recognized the representatives of East Timor's religious and civil society for their 'sustained and self-sacrificing contributions for a small but oppressed people'.[22] The committee made it clear, in the citation for the 1996 Peace Prize, that it regarded Indonesia as being responsible 'for systematically oppressing the [East Timorese] people',[23] and this further exposed Jakarta's human rights record to international scrutiny. In his Nobel lecture, Ramos-Horta reserved particular criticism for the Western powers that had sustained Indonesia's occupation of his homeland: 'We find it repulsive that Western countries that more loudly make rhetorical speeches about human rights are the ones that manufacture weapons that have killed more than 200 million people in the developing world since World War II.'[24]

As Britain superseded the USA in the 1990s as Indonesia's largest supplier of armaments (see Chapters 7 and 8), both Belo and Ramos-Horta recognized the importance of stemming the trade in arms with Jakarta, particularly as Western-supplied weaponry had been used for purposes of repression in East Timor. The 'removal of all heavy weapons' from East Timor was part of a three-phase CNRM peace plan outlined by Ramos-Horta in his Nobel lecture, which included a referendum on self-determination for the Timorese (see Chapter 14). The significant role that East Timor played in the political demise of President Suharto forced Indonesia's subsequent, transitional administration to reconsider its position on the territory, and agree to hold a referendum on the future of Timor in August 1999.[25]

Suharto's downfall

In the 1990s, Indonesia's economic programme of rapid growth through increased exports and inward investment saw the archipelago emerge as one of the Asian region's so-called tiger economies. Although annual growth rates ranged from 6 to 8 per cent in the early to mid-1990s, Indonesia's foreign debt continued to spiral, which led to 27 per cent of the population living in absolute poverty.[26] President Suharto's regime could withstand international criticism for internal repression as long as the economy continued to flourish and the Indonesian security forces could contain popular dissent to his leadership. The 1997 parliamentary elections in Indonesia were held amid accusations of political 'cronyism', complaints about the illegal enrichment of Suharto's family circle, repression of the limited number of political movements in opposition to the ruling Golkar (Golongan Karya) party, and severe censorship of the press. Although a restricted electoral system returned a parliamentary majority for the Golkar party,[27] which elected Suharto to his fifth term as president in March 1998, the Indonesian economy was in a severe downward curve, reflecting the political mismanagement at the heart of the administration.

The cumulative events which forced Suharto's downfall gathered momentum in 1997, with extensive forest fires which severely damaged Indonesia's environment and that of neighbouring countries, including Malaysia and Singapore. In April 1997, a stock market crisis resulted in the Indonesian currency (rupiah) losing 50 per cent of its value as a slump in market confidence enveloped South-East Asia, with other countries in the region similarly experiencing financial crises and facing the risk of hyperinflation.[28] The economic turmoil in Indonesia forced a sharp increase in food and fuel prices, which resulted in increased poverty levels and mass demonstrations throughout the archipelago. Between October 1997 and March 1998, 2 million workers were made unemployed and the social unrest extended to ethnic violence as protesters vented their anger against the regime through attacks on minority groups, particularly the Chinese community.[29] The fledgling pro-democracy forces and trade unions, which had emerged in Indonesia in the early 1990s, recognized the growing popular unrest as an opportunity to dislodge Suharto from office. The pro-democracy movement was aided by the fact that Suharto seriously misjudged the gravity of the situation confronting him, as illustrated by the fact that his new cabinet included his eldest daughter and other business partners – a sign of his intentions to maintain the old political order. Suharto's disregard for the plight of those most affected by the economic crisis and their protests outraged students throughout Indonesia, who emerged at the forefront of the campaign against the President.

On 12 May 1998, four students were killed at Trisakti University by the Indonesian military, followed by sustained rioting targeted at the Chinese community, which claimed a further 1200 lives (see Chapter 5). The May riots destabilized the country and brought events to a head as the military intervened decisively to end President Suharto's 32-year dictatorship. The ABRI (Armed Forces of the Republic of Indonesia)[30] commander-in-chief, General Wiranto, threatened severe military action if a 1-million-strong demonstration planned for 20 May were to proceed. The mass rally was abandoned and Wiranto – who wielded considerable political influence at this point – brokered a handover of power between Suharto and his Vice-President, B. J. Habibie, on 21 May 1998. Suharto's position as president had been secured by the military throughout his three-decade tenure in office, and it was the former president's inability to maintain the *status quo*, contain popular unrest and ensure economic stability that prompted the military leadership to manoeuvre him from office.[31]

Key themes

Few conflict situations in the developing world generated a greater public response and provoked a more sustained campaign within Western civil society than that in East Timor. This book examines some of the key aspects of Western complicity in the invasion and subsequent annexation of East Timor, and the West's prioritization of strategic interests over human rights concerns in the territory. Through the compilation of insightful and informed contributions from some of the foremost commentators and activists on East Timor, the book provides up-to-date analysis of the contemporary situation in the territory, including developments within Indonesia following the downfall of President Suharto in May 1998, which led to its first tentative steps towards democracy. The range of experiences reflected in the book – from academics, human rights activists, journalists, campaigners, NGO representatives and East Timorese spokespersons – provides a diversity of perspectives relating to the struggle for independence in East Timor.

Carey and O'Shaughnessy (Chapters 2 and 3 respectively) relate personal experiences of the oppression wrought on the East Timorese by Indonesia's occupying forces. Carey, an academic and campaigner for East Timor, details the multi-layered command structure of the 'ubiquitous' Indonesian military and reveals the level of impunity with which the armed forces perpetrated human rights abuses in the territory. O'Shaughnessy outlines the difficulty experienced by journalists in reporting the situation in East Timor, particularly in the first 15 years of the conflict, when the Western media was, at best, indifferent to the plight of the East Timorese. An award-winning journalist and campaigner, O'Shaughnessy witnessed the use of Hawk aircraft in East Timor – a fact regularly denied by the Indonesian and British governments – and he condemns those Western regimes which 'conveniently kept silent about the atrocities' committed in the territory.

The theme of Western complicity with Jakarta is taken up by Scheiner and Aubrey (Chapters 9 and 10), again experienced campaigning activists for East Timor in the USA and Australia respectively. Aubrey provides an insight into Canberra's long-term material and diplomatic support of, Suharto's Indonesia, maintained despite East Timor's massive contribution to the Australian resistance to the Japanese army in the Second World War. As the only country to have provided *de jure* recognition of Indonesia's occupation of East Timor, Australia is rightly condemned by Aubrey. The USA similarly gave priority to strategic and commercial interests in South-East Asia, through its support of Indonesia, over the protection of human rights in East Timor. Significantly, both Aubrey and Scheiner reveal recent shifts in the respective positions of Canberra and Washington in the post-Suharto era that undoubtedly contributed to Indonesia's decision to facilitate a referendum in August 1999. Australia, however, has yet to launch a full independent enquiry into the Balibo incident on 16 October 1975, when five television journalists were murdered by invading Indonesian forces in East Timor. Maureen Tolfree's brother, Brian Peters (see Chapter 4), was one of two Britons killed at Balibo – an incident which signalled the Indonesian invasion – and she movingly recounts her long struggle to uncover the full truth surrounding her brother's death, including the complicity of Western governments in keeping the facts conveniently hidden.

During the Conservative administrations of Thatcher and Major (1979–97), British aid to Indonesia quadrupled while the overall aid budget decreased. The immoral and cynical use of overseas aid as a trade sweetener was an important aspect of the Conservative government's unqualified support of Indonesia, which developed to the point that Britain became the number-one arms supplier to Indonesia. Paul Hainsworth (Chapter 8), a campaign activist and academic, analyses the perspectives and performance of the new Labour government elected in May 1997, and questions the current administration's claims of pursuing an 'ethical foreign policy' in the context of Britain's arms sales to Jakarta. The high expectations of the Labour administration in foreign affairs have yet to be realized, although Hainsworth does acknowledge some positive steps taken.

The book contains a number of contributions from internationally recognized campaigners for East Timor (Aubrey, Budiardjo, Cabral, Carey, O'Shaughnessy, Pilger, Ramos-Horta, Scheiner and the Seeds of Hope women), which reflect the global dimension to the East Timor issue and reveal how individuals and campaign groups can perform an important educational role in civil society. As an experienced commentator and activist on East Timor based in Ireland, Ward (Chapter 11) examines the remarkable role which the ETISC (East Timor Ireland Solidarity Campaign) has played in influencing Irish government policy on Indonesia and East Timor. This fact was reflected in a visit to East Timor in April 1999 by David Andrews, the former Irish Minister for Foreign Affairs, 'believed to be the first by a European Foreign Minister to the former Portuguese colony since it was annexed by Indonesia in 1976'.[32] The Irish government's official delegation to East Timor and Indonesia included Tom Hyland, head of the ETISC, thereby indicating the level of influence which the campaign group has had on the government's position on the territory. During his visit to East Timor, David Andrews personally witnessed[33] the activities of anti-independence militia groups. The militias were mobilized after the January 1999 announcement of a referendum in East Timor, and were responsible for widespread human rights abuses in an effort initially to stall the consultation process and later, following an overwhelming vote for independence, to prevent the mandate being implemented. Journalists accompanying the Irish delegation witnessed militia attacks on pro-independence supporters, and as David Andrews stated: 'We saw for ourselves that the army and police were letting this all happen.'[34] Moreover, allegations of collusion between the Indonesian military and paramilitary groups were supported by the eyewitness accounts of journalists in East Timor and, as Conor O'Clery suggested in the *The Irish Times*, 'few doubt that the militias are the creation of the Indonesian army intelligence unit, Kopassus'.[35]

The positive role of the Irish government in contributing to the reconciliation process in East Timor was recognized by the European Union when it appointed David Andrews as a special envoy to the territory following his visit in April. The present Irish government's diplomatic efforts on behalf of the East Timorese represent a continuation of the position adopted by the previous administration, which is examined by Ward in some detail. She particularly focuses on the attempts of the Irish government to lobby for a more committed EU common position during its European presidency in 1996, and acknowledges the difficulties which smaller European nations have in shaping EU policy. The limitations of political lobbying are also considered by Needham, Parker and Wilson (Chapter 7), who were collectively involved in a famous action to disarm a British Aerospace (BAe) Hawk aircraft that was awaiting export to Indonesia. The aim of the action was to raise awareness of the arms trade between Britain and Indonesia, and publicize human rights atrocities in East Timor. The courage of the four women directly involved in the action, and of their support team, is very evident in their story. Furthermore, the fact that they successfully defended themselves when tried for criminal damages created British legal history. The Seeds of Hope women inspired Timorese activists (and arms-trade opponents) throughout the world with the success of their action, and publicly challenged the British government's sanctioning of arms sales to Indonesia.

The recent history of East Timor has been intricately meshed with that of Indonesia, and Budiardjo and Cabral (Chapters 5 and 6) present informed accounts of recent events within the archipelago, and also of how Jakarta reported the East Timorese conflict both internally and externally. Budiardjo is a long-standing campaigner for democratic reform in Indonesia, and is the founder of Tapol, the highly respected Indonesia Human Rights Campaign. In her analysis of the present situation in Indonesia, Budiardjo states: 'The multiplicity and complexity of Indonesia's current political and social problems can be traced to the three decades of Suharto's stranglehold on power, and the extremely violent way in which he seized control in 1965.' Budiardjo contends that the post-Suharto/Habibie era offers Indonesia an opportunity to create a culture of democracy and openness in civil society, but maintains that the role of the military could still be to the forefront in determining the country's future. This theme is reinforced by Cabral, the Fretilin representative for Britain, who presents a detailed analysis of the propaganda methods used by the Indonesian government throughout the conflict in East Timor. Cabral insists that 'the Indonesian propaganda machine has continued to undermine political parties, solidarity groups, media and individuals sympathetic to the cause of East Timor'. This practice extended to attempts to discredit the Timorese leaders, Xanana Gusmão and José Ramos-Horta, in an effort to undermine the independence movement in East Timor. Cabral thus urges that such propagandist methods must be deconstructed in the context of a democratic Indonesia.

Chapters 12 and 13 (Leite and Guelke) draw lessons for East Timor from other conflict situations and consider the importance of legal redress for victims of human rights abuses. As General Secretary of IPJET (International Platform of Jurists for East Timor), Leite considers East Timor in a comparative perspective with Western Sahara, a territory which is on the UN decolonization committee's list of non-self-governing states, a status shared until recently by East Timor. Both East Timor and Western Sahara were colonized by neighbouring Third World states – Indonesia and Morocco – which were themselves colonized by European powers, the Netherlands and France respectively. Leite questions the effectiveness of the UN in the Saharan situation, where Morocco has used the issue of electoral eligibility successfully to undermine a UN-sponsored referendum mission established to settle the future of Western Sahara. Leite considers the chequered record of the UN in Western Sahara and East Timor to be a direct consequence of its members' pursuit of selfish political, economic and strategic interests; this has allowed both situations to deteriorate since the mid-1970s.

Guelke (Chapter 13) discusses the reconciliation process from a South African perspective and examines the important role which the international community played in dismantling the apartheid regime in his country. Guelke also discusses recent references to Xanana Gusmão as the 'Mandela of Timor',[36] given his leadership of the Fretilin resistance movement, long-term imprisonment, and current role as president of the CNRT. There is also the strong possibility that Gusmão, like Mandela, will become president of his country following Indonesia's withdrawal from East Timor. Guelke's overall assessment of the possible links between South Africa and East Timor is that: 'Both cases stand out as fundamental and unambiguous violations of the principle of self-determination, as it has been interpreted by the international community.' Guelke speculates, too, about the possibility of establishing a 'South Africa-style' truth and reconciliation commission in East Timor as part of the settlement to the conflict.

In Chapter 14, Hainsworth considers significant developments in the post-Suharto era and discusses the future political direction for East Timor in the light of the 30 August UN-sponsored referendum, which saw an overwhelming 78.5 per cent (from an almost 99 per cent turnout) of East Timorese vote for independence.[37] He emphasizes the need for a massive social and economic reconstruction effort in East Timor following the widespread devastation wreaked by pro-Indonesian militias in the wake of the referendum result, which included the forced displacement of the vast majority of the East Timorese people. Hainsworth also argues for the introduction of a judicial process in East Timor – given the brutal legacy of Indonesia's 24-year genocidal occupation – to ensure legal redress for the East Timorese as they begin to contemplate building a peaceful future. He suggests that the international community has a responsibility to set a clear example to states such as Indonesia – proven guilty of widespread human rights abuses – that they will be held legally responsible for their actions.

In considering the complicit role of Western powers in supporting Indonesia's occupation of East Timor, this book also reflects on how the governing interests of dominant world states have superseded the implementation of the norms and conventions of international law. The lessons to be drawn from East Timor include the need to ensure that the principles and values which underpin multinational human rights conventions are respected and enforced without favour and in all contexts where abuses are committed. The genocide which marked Indonesia's occupation of East Timor could have been prevented with the concerted and fulsome implementation of the UN resolutions which condemned Jakarta's actions. More positively, this book serves as a testimony to civil society organizations which embraced the cause of East Timor and ensured it became an international issue which negligent Western states and a compliant mainstream media could no longer ignore. The challenge for international bodies, governments and NGOs in the new millennium is to ensure that situations like that in East Timor are never allowed to recur. This responsibility also lies with Indonesia's new rulers (see Chapter 14) in the post-Suharto era.

References

1   John G. Taylor, quoted in *The New Internationalist*, No 253, March 1994, p. 6, edited by John Pilger under the title 'East Timor: the silence and the betrayal'. For a full account of the background to, and impact of, the Indonesian invasion see Taylor, John G., *Indonesia's Forgotten War: The Hidden History of East Timor* (London, 1991, Zed Books). The title reflects the fact that for 15 years after the 1975 invasion, the situation in East Timor was largely ignored by the Western media.

2   Carey, Peter, 'East Timor: Third World colonialism and the struggle for national identity', *Conflict Studies*, No. 293/294, October/November 1996, Research Institute for the Study of

Conflict and Terrorism, London, p. 1. See also Carey, Peter, *East Timor at the Crossroads: The Forging of a Nation* (London, 1995, Cassell). For more background information on East Timor's history, culture and society, see *The World Guide 1999–2000* (London, 1999, New Internationalist Publications Ltd), pp. 229–230.

3 Taylor, *Indonesia's Forgotten War*, p. 14.

4 Chinkin, Christine, 'Australia and East Timor in international law' in *International Law and the Question of East Timor* (London, 1995, CIIR/IPJET), p. 277.

5 For a useful account of the debt crisis in the developing world, see Somers, Jean, 'Debt: the new colonialism' in Regan, Colm *et al.*, *75:25, Ireland in an Increasingly Unequal World* (Dublin, 1996, Dóchas). This text provides an overview of key development issues in local and global contexts.

6 *The World Guide 1999–2000*, p. 229.

7 *The New Internationalist*, p. 6.

8 *Ibid.*

9 Carey, *Conflict Studies*, No. 293/294, p. 4.

10 Taylor, John G., 'Decolonisation, independence and invasion' in *International Law and the Question of East Timor* (London, 1995, CIIR/IPJET), p. 41.

11 *The New Internationalist*, p. 6.

12 The report, published in January 1999 by the Australian government's Department of Foreign Affairs and Trade (DFAT), accepts that Indonesia's *de facto* invasion of East Timor began on 16 October 1975. See Hugh Dowson's articles on the report in *Timor Link*, a quarterly newsletter published by the Catholic Institute for International Relations (CIIR), No. 46, February 1999, and also the newsletter of the British Coalition for East Timor, February 1999.

13 Described as the 'big wink', see *The World Guide 1999–2000*, p. 229.

14 *New Internationalist*, p. 5. See also *Conflict Studies*, No. 293/294, p. 12. As Carey suggests, 'since their December 1975 invasion, the Indonesians were directly responsible for the deaths of between a quarter and a third of the local population, one of the worst levels of mortality of any society in post-war history'. Carey bases these figures on statistics produced by the Timorese Catholic Church.

15 *The World Guide*, p. 229.

16 *Indonesia's Forgotten War*, p. 138.

17 Pinto, Contancio and Jardine, Matthew, *East Timor's Unfinished Struggle: Inside the Timorese Resistance* (Boston, MA, 1997, South End Press), p. 245. The number of transmigrants began to dwindle following an announcement by President Habibie in January 1999 that a referendum on the future of East Timor would be held in August. For an analysis of the post-Suharto era and the transitional Habibie administration, see *Tapol Bulletin*, No. 151, March 1999, published by Tapol, the Indonesia Human Rights Campaign.

18 *The World Guide*, p. 230.

19 See *Timor Link*, No. 22, February 1992, p. 1 and a Tapol press release on the incident reproduced in *FITUN Bulletin*, No. 5, November 1991. Gomes (18) was unarmed when he was killed trying to resist Indonesian troops as they raided the Motael church.

20 See *Conflict Studies*, No. 293/294, p. 20.

21 British Coalition for East Timor, newsletter, February 1999. The audience reaction to the film, as illustrated by these figures, challenges the notion of 'solidarity fatigue'. *Death of a Nation: The Timor Conspiracy* was first broadcast by Central Television in 1994.

22 *East Timor – Nobel Peace Prize: Lectures Delivered at the 1996 Nobel Peace Prize Awarding Ceremony* (Lisbon, 1997, Editions Colibri), p. 31.

23 *Ibid.*

24 *Ibid.*, p. 137.

25 *Tapol Bulletin*, No. 151.

26 *The World Guide*, p. 307.

27 Ibid. In the May 1997 elections, Golkar won 74 per cent of the vote and 325 out of 400 seats in the new parliament, which included 12 of Suharto's relatives.

28 *The World Guide*, p. 307.

29 *Ibid.*

30 The ABRI (Angkatan Bersenjata Republik Indonesia – the Armed Forces of the Republic of Indonesia) were separated from Polri (the Indonesian police force) on 1 April 1999. The ABRI were subsequently renamed Tentara Nasional Indonesia (TNI). Polri was given the role of providing security before and during the referendum on the future of East Timor held on 30 August 1999. For further details on TNI and Polri, see *Tapol Bulletin*, No. 153, July 1999, and *Timor Link*, No. 47, June 1999.

31 For a detailed account of the events which led to Suharto's downfall see *Tapol Bulletin*, No. 151, and also Budiardjo (Chapter 5).

32 *The Irish Times*, 16 April 1999.

33 *The Guardian*, 19 April 1999.

34 *Ibid.*

35 *The Irish Times*, 19 April 1999.

36 After Gusmão was transferred from prison to house arrest and became more accessible to the international media, such comparisons became more common, although they probably stemmed from a meeting between Mandela and Gusmão in 1997. See 'Timor's "Mandela" says forget about the past and build a future', David Shanks's interview with Gusmão in *The Irish Times*, 9 March 1999 and 'The Mandela of Timor' in *Timor Link*, No. 46, February 1999.

37 *The Irish Times*, 17 September 1999.

2

A Personal Journey through East Timor

Peter Carey

Introduction

'And what is a teacher?' enquired the guard at the Indonesian checkpoint on the East Timor border as we showed our passports. 'Look, a teacher does this.' My son wrote as though on an imaginary blackboard. 'Ah yes, we know what you do – you are an artist and you have come to East Timor to teach your son sketching!' That suited me just fine – a fictitious identity courtesy of the Indonesians. What more could one want? They had even written my name wrongly in their dusty ledger, mistaking my middle name for my surname. So, welcome Peter Ramsay, artist, to the land of violence and make-believe.

Timtim (Timor Timur), Jakarta's '27th province', was – at the time of my visit – in its 22nd year of Indonesian occupation. A former Portuguese colony (the most distant and neglected of all Lisbon's overseas possessions), it was invaded on 7 December 1975 by Indonesia to prevent its independence under the left-leaning Revolutionary Front for an Independent East Timor (Fretilin). It has since suffered one of the heaviest population losses in post-war history, with nearly a third of the original pre-1975 inhabitants – 200,000 out of 700,000 people – being killed by war, famine, disease and neglect.[1] This would be the equivalent of Scotland losing its entire population north of Stirling, a form of genocidal 'Highland clearance' carried out by an army of 'Butcher' Cumberlands. In Indonesia, the duke's spiritual descendants were richly rewarded: every Indonesian soldier who served in East Timor drew double pay and had opportunities for personal advancement, especially the officers. President Suharto's son-in-law, Major-General Prabowo Subianto, the youngest two-star general in the Indonesian army and former commander of the élite special forces (Kopassus), was just one whose career was assisted by his East Timor experience. Units of his much-feared former regiment – known locally as the Rajawali (eagle) and Nanggala (magical ploughshare weapon) companies – could be seen everywhere. Armed with Heckler and Koch automatic weapons – courtesy of British Aerospace (BAe), which purchased the German company in 1994[2] – they patrolled in civilian dress in unmarked Toyota Landcruisers with smoked-glass windows.

The hours of darkness were their favourite time, as I discovered nearly to my cost. At eight o'clock on a moonless night, I was travelling back with my 16-year-old son and a local priest from the extreme eastern point of the island, a famous beauty spot. Noticing lights to the left of our vehicle, I turned to the priest to ask about their provenance. No sooner had the reply 'Kopassus' (special forces) left his mouth than a figure dressed entirely in black (jump-suit zipped up the front with the peaked cap of the Rajawali unit shading his moustached face) loomed out of the darkness, powerful halogen torch in hand. Up in front, just visible behind a large palm tree, was another Kopassus soldier, covering our pick-up truck with his automatic rifle. 'What are you doing out on the road so late, Father?' The priest had already warned us that too tardy a return might raise suspicions that we had been in contact with the Falintil (Forças Armadas de Libertação Nacional de Timor-Leste/Armed Forces for the National Liberation of East Timor) guerrillas. 'Just returning from a swim, *Pak*' (literally 'father' – the honorific title given to all Indonesian occupying forces, known colloquially, and with disdain by locals, as the Bapak[s]). Now we had some explaining to do, for these were only recently deployed Kopassus troops, just arrived from their base at Batujajar in West Java, tense and trigger-happy in an all-too-hostile land. The priest, however, was a well-known figure and we had a perfect alibi since we were expected in the next village to collect a sick parishioner for treatment at the mission centre. Even then, nothing was left to chance: our jump-suited friend followed us into the village and, with his commanding officer present (a young engineer captain), proceeded to monitor our conversation with the Timorese village head. During this exchange, he let slip some interesting facts: not only had he served in East Timor before during the infamous Operation Security (Operasi Keamanan) in 1982, when almost the entire able-bodied male Timorese population between the ages of 15 and 50 had been forced to act as 'beaters', crossing the island in long lines from west to east to flush out the Falintil/Fretilin fighters (an operation which had caused many deaths);[3] but he had also received training in Australia, having participated in the

'Kangaroo 95' (June–July 1995) joint exercises with the Australian army and commando units of the Australian Special Boat Squadron (SBS). There could have been no more vivid illustration of the way in which Western military establishments, in particular those of the British, Australians and Americans, had provided direct assistance to the Indonesian armed forces in their illegal occupation of East Timor.

While our conversation ended with handshakes all round, it was quite different for Timorese who fell into Kopassus clutches. Mere suspicion of involvement with the guerrillas or the civilian clandestine resistance could have meant a death sentence. In the same area where I met the jump-suited commando, I received news that two Timorese suspects had been tied to a post and starved to death in an undisclosed location near the south coast. Kopassus techniques of 'disappearing' suspects had become ever more sophisticated – many were buried in shallow graves right under their camps – it was increasingly hard for agencies like the International Committee of the Red Cross (ICRC) to trace victims. At the same time, Kopassus interrogation methods were often designed to leave few marks on the bodies of their victims: black plastic bags drawn tight over the head to induce temporary suffocation (with water sometimes poured over the outside to give the impression of drowning) was a favourite practice. Even Timorese who worked for the Indonesian administration were tortured in this fashion: a sub-district head (*camat*) near Lospalos had been taken from his house at night on three separate occasions to undergo the black-bag treatment. This experience had shaken him so badly that he had confided to our friend, the local priest, that another torture session would be beyond endurance. Flight to the provincial capital, Dili, which the priest offered to facilitate, seemed the only way to escape further persecution. At least there, arrest and imprisonment would not necessarily have spelt death at the hands of the Kopassus torturers.

Indonesian force deployment: rival command structures and security levels

What was most depressing for me in East Timor was to discover the ubiquitousness, impunity and multi-layered nature of the Indonesian military presence. Known to local Timorese as the 'green snakes', Indonesian soldiers were everywhere – patrolling in full battle-dress in broad daylight, their green camouflage uniforms blending uneasily into the lush vegetation of the late rainy season countryside. In the coffee-growing town of Ermera (population 40,000-plus), some 35 km to the south-west of Dili, near where the Falintil commander, Konis Santana, was said to be conducting operations, no fewer than five new infantry battalions, each with around 700 men, had been deployed, at least three of them from Sulawesi (Celebes) – two of them crack units attached to the Army Strategic Reserve (Kostrad) – and the others from Central and East Java.[4] Indeed, so intense was the security presence at the time of my visit that locals told me they dared not go too far into their coffee gardens for fear they might be suspected of having contacts with the guerrillas. Given the fact that these regular Indonesian army 'territorial' troops were rotated every eight months, it was extremely difficult for the local Timorese to establish good working relations with them. No sooner had contacts and understandings been reached than new battalions came in and the process had to begin all over again. The problems caused by the large numbers of troops on the ground – official Indonesian sources admitted to over 15,000 but there may have been double that number – and the bewildering number of different levels of military and paramilitary presence compounded the problems for the local inhabitants.[5] In Ermera, for example – along with other sensitive areas, like Baucau, Viqueque, Lautem and Lospalos, where the armed resistance was especially active – there were at least five levels of security, each answerable to their own separate command structures.

Starting at the village level, there were first the local – often Timorese – Koramil (Kommando Rayon Militer/sub-district military command) troops, who acted as the provincial garrison force. These were assisted by Hansip/Wanra (Pertahanan Sipil) (also known as Ratih – Rakyat Terlatih/Trained People's Force) or civil defence units, which were nearly all locally recruited. Then there were the special Timorese battalions (744 and 745), which operated alongside the Indonesian special forces and were often deployed on important missions.[6] Beside them were the police and village 'guidance' officials, usually NCOs seconded from the Indonesian police and army – the so-called Binpolda and Babinsa – who were there to 'assist' (in fact, 'direct') the local village heads (*kepala desa*) in security matters, and who often wielded more power than the village heads did. In every village, there were also intelligence agents. Often these were soldiers disguised as merchants who sold things from house to house to enable them to listen in to people's conversations and uncover political activity, which was then reported back to the police and the military.[7]

In 1995, a new surveillance initiative was launched by Major-General Prabowo (then deputy commander of Kopassus, and post-December 1995 the commander).[8] This was the Garda Paksi (Penegak Integrasi/Upholders of Integration Guard), which was recruited locally from Timorese youth. Resistance sources in Lisbon referred to them as 'Timorese collaborators, generally unemployed, with a low-level of educational achievement', some of whom hailed from pro-integration Apodeti (Associacão Popular

Democrática Timorense/Timorese Popular Democratic Association) families.[9] The unit was principally targeted at the East Timorese Clandestine Front, the civilian arm of the resistance which carried off some striking propaganda coups against the Suharto regime, most notably the November 1994 APEC (Asia-Pacific Economic Cooperation forum) sit-in at the US embassy in Jakarta. According to the resistance, the Garda Paksi were given basic military training at the Indonesian army base in Aileu some 30 km to the south of Dili, and were then sent for further training under Kopassus auspices in Java.

Thought initially to number some 3000 (500 of whom were assigned to keep tabs on East Timorese students in Java and Bali) and led by José Catarino de Melo, a well-known East Timorese intelligence agent and a former East Timorese sub-district head (camat) of Ossu near Viqueque,[10] their particular task was to infiltrate the Clandestine Front, whose previous secretary-general, Pedro Nunes (aka Sabalae), and his assistant, Remigio Levi da Costa Tilman, were arrested in June 1995 and tortured to death by Kopassus.[11] One incident during my visit to East Timor in April 1997 provided a vivid illustration of the tensions wrought by the activities of these Garda Paksi in present-day East Timor: the ambush by the Falintil resistance of the local Garda Paksi head near Viqueque on 7 April 1997. This man, Eugenio Soares, who was shot along with five of his colleagues (four of them Hansip members), had apparently made himself deeply unpopular on account of the numerous arrests and torture of suspects which had taken place in the Uatolari district in February 1997, when over 100 had been seized (some dragged out from the sanctuary of the local priest's house and church).[12]

While the Garda Paksi, Hansip/Ratih, Koramil and local Timorese battalion units formed the first level of security in East Timor, the second was provided by the Indonesian police, a large number of whom (some estimates spoke of 2000-plus, or about a quarter of the total deployed in Timor) were drawn from the Brimob (Brigade Mobil or Mobile Brigade; also sometimes known as Perintis), the paramilitary force originally established by the Dutch in the late colonial period (1609–1942) to deal with local rebellions. In 1962 this unit, and all the other police units, were formally militarized and placed under the control of the Indonesian armed forces (ABRI/Angkatan Bersenjata Republik Indonesia).[13] In fact, in East Timor the police chief ranked second to the regional (Korem/Komando Resort Militer) military commander in terms of local security responsibilities, giving the lie to arguments by some Western governments, in particular the British, that the Indonesian police force were separate from the Indonesian military.[14] Relations between the police and the army were not always easy, especially in East Timor, with the regular soldiers looking down on the police as the least prestigious and most corrupt branch of the armed forces – feelings which were shared by the vast majority of Timorese, who referred to them as 'monkeys'.[15] So intense were the rivalries between the army regulars and the police in Timor that violent incidents and tit-for-tat shootings were not unknown. It was even suggested that the ambush which killed 21 policemen outside Baucau on 30 May 1997, following the general election, might have been the work of the army, since their truck was flagged down by a soldier in Indonesian battledress.[16] The only positive aspect of the police presence was that their interrogation methods were, on the whole, less severe than those employed by the army regulars and the special forces (see below), although even here physical violence against suspects was considered the norm.[17]

The third level of security was provided by the regular ABRI infantry battalions and support units, sometimes referred to confusingly as 'territorial' troops. As we have seen, these units were regularly rotated through short (eight- to 12-month) postings, perhaps to prevent them building up too close a rapport with the local people or the Falintil guerrillas, as happened in the 1976–77 period and again in 1983, when individual battalion commanders entered into a series of local cease-fire arrangements with the resistance, often to further their own commercial interests.[18] The system of regular rotation ensured that nearly all ABRI infantry battalions had some fighting experience in East Timor, an experience which had guaranteed not only better rates of pay for ordinary soldiers but also faster rates of promotion for officers. Following the 12 November 1991 Santa Cruz massacre, however, this last prospect became less assured. Two generals lost their commands after Santa Cruz, and other senior officers subsequently found their careers blighted rather than advanced by East Timor service before Indonesia's military withdrawal from the territory.[19]

The fourth level of security was assured by the special forces (Kopassus). Numbering some 4000 in all, a large number – perhaps as many as a quarter of the entire regiment – were regularly deployed in East Timor. Here they served their own independent command structure, one which was not subject to the local district (Kodim/Komando Distrik Militer) authorities, but answerable directly to their regimental headquarters in West Java. Although overall command responsibility – until recently – was assumed by Major-General Prabowo, who himself served several tours of duty in East Timor, including being operational commander at Ossu near Viqueque in the central military district (1989–91), when both he and his troops earned a sinister reputation for violence against the local population,[20] direct operational authority was vested in more recent years (after the 12 November 1991 Santa Cruz massacre) in the Korem commander in Dili, who after 1995 was a special forces officer with close links to

Prabowo.[21] Kopassus also ran the principal military intelligence operation in East Timor – the SGI (Satgas Intelijens/Intelligence Task Force) – which operated the notorious prison and torture/interrogation centre at Colmera, a suburb of Dili, where many Timorese political prisoners were held.[22]

The fifth, and most ubiquitous, level of security was provided by the numerous *agents provocateurs* and intelligence agents (nicknamed *bufo* – clowns – by the locals) who were to be found everywhere in East Timor. As Bishop Belo once put it, East Timor is a society in which 'one half of the population is paid to spy on the other half'.[23] Unlike the other security operations, which covered certain clearly defined areas, the intelligence community spanned the whole of East Timor. Indeed, intelligence work was carried out at every level of security enforcement – the close connections between the Kopassus and the Garda Paksi have already been noted – although how effectively this information was used was quite another matter. Some personal experiences might be helpful here by way of illustration.

Spies, *agents provocateurs* and 'clowns'

Already, on my journey through West Timor, Indonesian policemen in civilian clothes had boarded my bus between the market towns of Kefamenanu and Atambua to find out the purpose of my travels (questions which they had directed at my son – who was sitting away from me at the back of the bus – as well as myself). Recent Muslim-Christian riots in the East Timorese enclave of Oecussi, which had been sparked by an insult to the local priest following a Muslim religious feast (*slametan*), and the subsequent disturbances in Kefamenanu itself, when the main market had been burnt down, may have been one reason for their vigilance.[24] By the time we reached Atambua, where I changed buses for Dili in the mid-afternoon, they had already alighted, but other Indonesian security personnel in mufti seemed to be present on that last leg too. Certainly, our presence was reported to the intelligence services soon after our arrival in Dili later that night, because no sooner had we emerged from the bishop's residence in Lecidere, where we had gone to introduce ourselves, and were making for the Hotel Turismo than we heard a loud bang on the other side of the road: a white Toyota Landcruiser, which had been circling the bishop's house during our visit, had mounted the kerb and was careering along the opposite pavement, the driver having temporarily lost control of the vehicle so intent was he on watching the curious sight of two foreigners with back-packs moving along the darkened Dili waterfront.

Nor was that the only surprise in store for us. I never, for example, received a bill in my name at the Hotel Turismo itself (all receipts for payment being carefully made out to my 16-year-old son!), my registration form having been removed from the front desk soon after our arrival and handed on, I presumed, to the intelligence services. That this had indeed occurred was soon brought home to me on the second day after our arrival in Dili, when two East Timorese 'students' – Ruy (18) and Carlito (23) – accosted us while walking along the same waterfront promenade. These supposed students of tourism (I never discovered if such a subject was ever taught at the local university) immediately gave the game away when I asked them to guess my age. While Carlito hazarded a cautious 'late 30s', Ruy plumped for an unerringly accurate '49'. Just good luck? Hardly! The vanished registration form floated momentarily before my eyes. They had been briefed! Yet what they did with the information which they extracted from us always remained a mystery to me. While they must have surmised that we were not ordinary tourists, no attempt was ever made to search or question us closely – even at the airport on our departure (where our bags were not even scanned). Was this just laziness, or a reluctance on Ruy and Carlito's part to play the role assigned to them by their Indonesian intelligence mentors? Who knows?

Sometimes, the approach adopted was more indirect and subtle. Elliptical conversations seemed to be the order of the day, especially with 'strangers' whom we met – seemingly by chance – while waiting at various bus stations and roadside halts. 'What is the highest mountain in East Timor?' was the opening gambit of one rather well-groomed young man sitting along the shabby shopfront of Baucau bus station. He gave his name as 'Philip' (and certainly knew a thing or two about us, since he asked me why I was contemplating another trip to Venilale when I had never even told him about my original visit there). 'Ramelau! Yes, it must be Foho [Mount] Ramelau!' came my reply. 'I also know something else about it too!' I incautiously went on. 'And what is that?' asked Philip. 'A song! Yes, a song…' 'Don't say that,' cut in Philip. 'It's dangerous!' Then why did he ask me in the first place, when he knew that any mention of Timor's highest mountain would inevitably bring to mind the banned East Timorese national anthem – 'Foho Ramelau'? Was it all an elaborate trap to lead me into compromising indiscretions?

A bold Fretilin handshake, in which the thumb is grasped and bent backwards, was the opening gambit of others. Yet whether one was dealing with a genuine Fretilin supporter or an intelligence agent was quite another matter. 'John of Gaunt! What do you know about John of Gaunt and his relations with Portugal?' was the question posed by another well-turned-out Timorese encountered at the same Baucau bus station. No ordinary bus station this! John of Gaunt? My interlocutor was half-remembering, so he said, the history he had been taught in the 1960s at the exclusive

Portuguese high school in Dili, the Liceu Dr Francisco Veira Machado, and was just so delighted to meet a fellow historian. Could I tell him more about the marriage of John of Gaunt's daughter, Philippa, to King John I of Portugal (reigned 1385–1433), and the making of the Anglo-Portuguese dynastic alliance in the late fourteenth century? 'Sorry, not my period!' I replied. Yet his questions intrigued me. What was he driving at? Was this just intellectual curiosity, or something deeper and more meaningful? Was he trying to tell me something in elaborately nuanced code? Something to do with England and Portugal, our oldest European ally, and the need for our support on the Timor issue? In the end, I never knew. The conversation veered off in a different direction (we were by then on the bus heading for Dili, our words being listened to by adjacent Indonesians), and I was left with a tantalizing sense of unfinished business.

The dangers of openness and honesty for ordinary Timorese was forcibly brought home to me by a final incident on the journey back to Dili. The bus had stopped at Manatuto (birthplace of Xanana Gusmão and the current governor, Abílio Soares), to allow the driver and passengers to eat some food at the Javanese-run roadside noodle restaurant. Inside was a very drunk Indonesian – a North Sumatran Batak – whom rumour had it was an off-duty policeman. As we queued up to buy our meal, he noticed my son and, in a hectoring tone, started to ask questions about me. 'Name? Business? Purpose of journey?' Although drunk, he spoke excellent English. Another coincidence? My son's replies were non-committal. Hoping to avoid a direct encounter, I sat down carefully with my back to him and concentrated on my food. But the Batak interposed himself, swaying unsteadily on his feet right in front of me. 'Name? I asked you your name, right? Well what is it?' Silence. A full minute passed. 'My name is my own business,' I eventually replied. 'Come on! Don't be like that!' The hectoring voice now had an edge to it. I detected a veiled – or not so veiled – threat: 'Don't monkey with me! I have friends in the police station just over the road, and if you can't keep a civil tongue in your head we can teach you some manners.' As a foreigner I could get away with it – just – but if I had been a Timorese it would have been a different story. I had never felt the contrast between occupier and occupied more keenly: this could have been Ireland under the Black and Tans or Nazi-occupied France.

Conclusions

What, then, can one conclude from such a brief eight-day visit? Not much, although each day felt as though one had lived an eternity. The sheer

impunity of the Indonesian military presence was a shock. Given the
weight of international censure of Indonesia since Santa Cruz, I was
expecting Jakarta to have cleaned up its act. The occupation would be
heavy, I thought, but at least now it would be tightly managed and
controlled. But no, the military continued to call the shots unencumbered
by political constraints. The exploitation of natural resources (coffee,
timber and marble) was clearly proceeding apace. Just past Bucoli, on the
road to Baucau, Timorese work gangs were clear-felling sections of the
Walaikama forest (presumably to prevent further guerrilla attacks on military convoys) under the watchful eye of Indonesian soldiers. Meanwhile in
Tibar, the fishing port on the north coast a few kilometres west of Dili (now
destined to become the territory's principal deepwater harbour), Buginese
transmigrants had seemingly taken over the import-export trade, including
the bulk of Ermera's high-quality coffee exports. 'If the UN comes here, we
will shoot them!' was the response of one Indonesian officer to the idea that
international intervention might be a way forward out of the current political impasse.

What was clear was that only effective pressure on Jakarta to desist from
bankrolling a corrupt and self-serving military presence in East Timor, and
on Western governments to stop arming Indonesia and ensure a legitimate
act of self-determination, would alter East Timor's future. Already the
numbers of Indonesian transmigrants (both official and unofficial) had
begun to undermine the balance of Timorese society, bringing Muslims
and Balinese Hindus from inner-island Indonesia into a predominantly
Catholic and animist community. Of the 867,000 inhabitants in East
Timor, fully a quarter were thought to be newcomers.[25] Indeed, with
unemployment rates running as high as 65 per cent amongst East
Timorese youth (compared to 35 per cent amongst transmigrants), frustra-
tions were high and potentially disruptive. But however steep the odds,
East Timorese, both young and old, were still clearly prepared to sacrifice
themselves to achieve a free Timor, the goal that was so brutally denied
them by the Suharto regime and its Western backers in the mid-1970s. We
in the privileged West must ensure that such sacrifice is not in vain – not
least as the struggle for self-determination now enters a difficult and
perhaps decisive phase. As one guerrilla commander prophetically put it,
'let your government know you care. If there is international pressure, if
the [ten] UN resolutions [on East Timor] are implemented, East Timor
[will] be free. Falintil and the clandestine front within East Timor will
continue to fight, but, without help from the outside, we can never hope to
defeat Indonesia with its huge army.'[26] In the post-Suharto era, as recent
developments (see Chapter 14) have shown, international pressure can
effect positive change.[27]

References

1   The most careful analysis of demographic statistics in East Timor in the period 1975–81, when the heaviest population losses took place, can be found in Defert, Gabriel, *Timor Est. Le Génocide Oublié. Droit d'un Peuple et Raisons d'États* (Paris, 1992, L'Éditions L'Harmattan), pp. 147–151 and Fig. 8, which cites a low of 170,000 (based on Indonesian statistics) and a high (based on Church statistics) of 308,000. The pre-invasion population of East Timor numbered around 696,000, see Defert, p. 148.

2   The German-designed MP5 sub-machine guns used by the Indonesian security forces were supplied in 1995 by Heckler and Koch from their Nottingham (UK) factory. So popular are such British-manufactured weapons that the *Asian Defence Journal* has described Indonesia as 'Heckler and Koch' country; see 'Making a killing', *Amnesty*, No. 84, July–August 1997, pp. 18–19.

3   On these 'fence-of-legs' *(pagar betis/*Operasi Kikis) tactics used by the Indonesian army to flush out Fretilin guerrillas in the early 1980s, see Budiardjo, Carmel and Liong, Liem Soei, *The War Against East Timor* (London, 1984, Zed Books), pp. 41–44, 230–231, 238–239; and for a moving personal account of one of these operations which resulted in huge losses of civilian lives in the Aitana region in the eastern sector, see Costa, Cristiano 'Timorese refugee on Indonesian operations in East Timor since 1975', *Tapol Bulletin*, No. 87, June 1988, p. 10; and *Tapol Bulletin*, No. 88, August 1988, p. 19.

4   The three Sulawesi battalions were 700, 713 and 721, the first two Kostrad battalions. On the Menado-based 713, which was for long commanded by the recently appointed army chief-of-staff, Lieutenant-General Wiranto, himself a Kopassus officer who served in East Timor for four years after the 1975 invasion, see *Far Eastern Economic Review*, 22 May 1997, p. 50; and Anderson, Ben, Kahin, Audrey *et al.*, 'Current data on the Indonesian military élite: Selected biographies', *Indonesia*, No. 59, April 1995, pp. 61–62. The other battalions, 459 and 501, were from the Central Java (Diponegoro) and East Java (Brawijaya) Divisions.

5   For official Indonesian figures regarding troop levels in East Timor, see Pell, Claiborne, *Democracy: An Emerging Asian Value*, report to the Committee on Foreign Relations, United States Senate, 104th Congress, 2nd Session, June 1996 (Washington, 1996, US Government Printing Office), p. 11 and appendix entitled 'Military situation', which lists 15,403 men, not including the substantial numbers of special forces/commandos, who were formerly under the direct command of Suharto's son-in-law, Major-General Prabowo Subianto Djojohadikusumo.

6   On the Hansip/Ratih and the locally recruited Timorese battalions (744 based in Dili, and 745 based in Baucau), which also contained many West Timorese (from Atambua) and other Indonesians, see Budiardjo, Carmel and Liong, Liem Soei, *War Against East Timor*, pp. 39–40, 225–226. The Timorese battalions were often used for special operations, for example, the action in late December 1978 led by Major (now Lieutenant-General) Yunus Yosfiah, an Indonesian RPKAD (paratroop) officer then in command of Battalion 744, which led to the death of Fretilin's second president and commander-in-chief, Nicolau Lobato, at Turiscai in the Maubisse hills some 50 km to the south-east of Dili, see *War Against East Timor*, p. 36; and Anderson, Ben, Kahin, Audrey *et al.*, 'Current data on the Indonesian military élite, 1 July 1989–1 January 1992', *Indonesia*, No. 53, April 1992, p. 125, n. 73.

7   See Pinto, Constâncio, *East Timor's Unfinished Struggle. Inside the Timorese Resistance. A Testimony* (Boston, 1996, South End Press), p. 100. For more recent details on the military situation in

28 THE EAST TIMOR QUESTION

East Timor, see 'Indonesia's retreat from East Timor', *Tapol Bulletin*, No. 151, March 1999, pp. 1–6. See also 'Major reshuffle in ABRI', pp. 16–17, in the same issue.

8 Prabowo was implicated in the abduction of 23 pro-democracy activists between late 1997 and early 1998. *Tapol Bulletin*, No. 151, March 1999 reports that, after an army investigation into the abductions, Prabowo was discharged from duties and he left the country, to live in Jordan. See 'Trial of Kopassus abductions a farce', p. 18.

9 CNRM/East Timor National Council of Maubere Resistance, 'East Timor Report', 9 August 1996, website: http://www.cnrmnt.reg.easttimor at pactok.peg.apc.org.

10 *Ibid.*; and on José Catarino de Melo, see Pinto, *Unfinished Struggle*, p. 181.

11 See Carey, Peter, 'East Timor: Third World colonialism and the struggle for national identity', *Conflict Studies* (Research Institute for the Study of Conflict and Terrorism/RISCT), No. 293/294, October–November 1996, p. 24.

12 On the arrests, which led to a strong protest by Bishop Belo to senior Indonesian officers in both Jakarta and Dili, see Commissão Justiça e Paz Diocese Dili, 'Penangkapan/Penahanan di Uatu Lari: Resume Daftar Nama-Nama Warga Masyarakyat yang Ditahan/Ditangkap oleh Aparat Keamanan sejak tgl. 6.2.97 hingga tgl. 10.2.97 (Arrests/detention in Uatu Lari: Resumé of the list of names of members of the community who have been arrested/detained by the security forces from 6.2.97 to 10.2.97)', which lists 59 arrests, the majority of detainees being held in the district military headquarters (Kodim); and 'Timorenses Interrogados', *A Capital* (Lisbon), 16 February 1997, which refers to 109 youths being interrogated in Viqueue on 7 February; on the shootings, see 'GPK Timtim Tembak Enam Orang Hingga Meninggal (Security disrupter gang (Gerombolan Pengacau Keamanan/GPK) in East Timor shoots six people to death)', *Kompas* (Jakarta), 10 April 1997; and Commissão Justiça e Paz Diocese Dili, 'Informação', 7 April 1997.

13 See Cribb, Robert, *Historical Dictionary of Indonesia* (New Jersey and London, 1992, Scarecrow Press), pp. 285–286 (under 'Maréchaussée') and pp. 375–376 (under 'police'). The ABRI were separated from Polri (the Indonesian police force) on 1 April 1999, with the armed forces subsequently being renamed Tentara Nasional Indonesia (TNI). Polri was given the role of providing security before and after the referendum on the future of East Timor held on 30 August. For further details on TNI and Polri, see *Tapol Bulletin*, No. 153, July 1999, and *Timor Link*, No. 47, June 1999.

14 This issue was aired in the report by the British Labour MP, Ann Clwyd, 'British aid to Indonesia: The continuing scandal' (September 1995), pp. 20–28. Many of the criticisms levelled by Clwyd have been addressed in the official National Audit Office report, *Aid to Indonesia* (London, 29 November 1996, The Stationery Office, HC 101 Session 1996–97), pp. 36–39.

15 This was the term I heard a local Timorese use when I went to register with the police in Lospalos during an overnight stay in early April 1997. The fact that many of the police in East Timor hailed from Bali, Lombok and other eastern Indonesian islands (the captain of the Lospalos police was from Lombok), may be one reason why their status was diminished in the eyes of the mainly Javanese military. By 1992, perhaps as many as 70 per cent of ABRI officers were thought to be Javanese, compared with around 55 per cent at the start of Suharto's 'new order' regime in the mid-1960s; see Anderson, Kahin *et al.*, 'Current data, 1 July 1989–1 January 1992', pp. 93–94.

16 See Lloyd Parry, Richard, 'Seventeen killed as East Timor rebels step up attacks', *The Independent*, 2 June 1997; *Tapol Bulletin*, No. 141, July 1997, p. 2. According to the latter source,

17 policemen (including some from Brimob) died when a grenade was thrown into the back of their truck; four others were shot while trying to escape.

17 See the testimony of Michael Davis, a modern history student from Newcastle-upon-Tyne University in the UK, who went to East Timor in August 1996 to conduct research and was taken in for questioning by police intelligence officers in Baucau and Dili, the latter of whom 'refused to believe me when I told [them] that I had not been beaten up by [their] counterparts in Baucau'. See Davis, Michael, 'The role of the younger generation in East Timorese resistance to Indonesian rule', unpublished BA thesis, Newcastle-upon-Tyne University, February 1997, pp. 18–19.

18 See Dunn, James, *Timor. A People Betrayed* (Milton, 1983, Jacaranda Press), p. 309, on the locally negotiated cease-fires in 1976–77; and Taylor, John, *Indonesia's Secret War. The Hidden History of East Timor* (London, 1991, Zed Books), p. 136, on the individual cease-fire initiatives which preceded the general cease-fire (23 March–7 August 1983) negotiated by Colonel Purwanto and Xanana Gusmão. The bartering of high-quality Timorese coffee for rice, sugar, imported medicines and other necessities, was common in the period before the Indonesian capture of the main coffee-producing areas around Ermera in 1977–78.

19 See Anderson, Ben, Kahin, Audrey *et al.*, 'Current data on the Indonesian military élite, 1 January 1992–31 August 1993', *Indonesia*, No. 56, October 1993, p. 126; Anderson, Ben, Kahin, Audrey *et al.*, 'Current data on the Indonesian military élite, 1 September 1993–30 September 1995', *Indonesia*, No. 60, October 1995, p. 106. On the rapid turnover of Korem commanders in Dili since the 12 November 1991 Santa Cruz massacre, and the career difficulties faced by some of them, see note 21 below.

20 For an account of the incident at Bercoli (Berecoli) on 12–15 April 1989, when soldiers of Battalion 328 under Major-General (then Major) Prabowo's command reportedly shot dead 20 civilians, see Taylor, *Forgotten War*, p. 103; and *Tapol Bulletin*, No. 93, June 1989, p. 2. Another incident involving the murder of a top Fretilin commander near Venilale – under cover of a peace negotiation in which Major-General (then Major) Prabowo had used the name of a revered Salesian priest, Fr Locatelli, to secure the Fretilin commander's unarmed attendance – was related to me by a church source during my visit to Venilale in April 1997.

21 After the dismissal of Brigadier-General Rudolf Samuel Warouw on 8 January 1992 in the aftermath of the Santa Cruz massacre, the following officers have served as Korem (pre-1993, Kolakops – Komando Pelaksana Operasi/East Timor Operations Execution Command) commanders in East Timor: Brigadier-General (now Major-General) Theo Syafei (8 January 1992–20 July 1993), a RPKAD (paratroop) officer who later fell into political disgrace with the regime for backing the call for an election boycott (Golput) in May 1997; Colonel (now Major-General) Johny Lumintang (20 July 1993–c. 31 August 1994), an infantry officer who had previously commanded the Airborne Infantry Brigade of the Strategic Army Reserve (Kostrad), and is now head of the Trikora/Kodam VIII Command (Irian Barat and Maluku); Colonel Kiki Syahnakri Y. K. (c. 31 August 1994–27 May 1995), whose career seems to have fallen apart after his departure from East Timor; Colonel Mahidin Simbolon (27 May 1995–late May 1997), previously assistant for intelligence to the Kopassus commander, now attending a course at the National Defence Council (Lemhanas/Lembaga Hankam Nasional); and Colonel Slamet Sidabutar (late May 1997–present), previously commander of Group II of Kopassus based in Surakarta. The last two commanders have had especially close ties with Prabowo, since they hail from his regiment.

22 See Pinto, *Unfinished Struggle*, pp. 148–157; and Cater, Nick, 'Timorese bear the scars of repression', *The West Australian*, 30 September 1995, pp. 18–19, for eyewitness accounts by Timorese of their treatment at the hands of the SGI torturers/interrogators at Colmera.

23 Dixon, Clare, 'Cry of a forgotten land', *The Tablet*, 22 November 1991, quoted in Archer, Robert, 'The Catholic Church in East Timor', in Carey, Peter and Carter Bentley, G., *East Timor at the Crossroads: The Forging of a Nation* (London, 1995, Cassell), p. 131.

24 According to local informants, the disturbances occurred after members of the local Muslim community (estimated at 7000 in Oecussi, or around 20 per cent of the population) had sent a boxed offering of food from the late February (1997) religious feast – which followed the end of the fasting month – to the local priest. Such boxed food offerings are normal for those who are not able to attend such feasts in person. This time, however, the box was found to contain not food, but the gnawed chicken bones and other leftovers from the meal. When the priest opened the box, his Timorese catechist saw what was inside and immediately went to tell the local Catholic inhabitants; a riot ensued, which eventually spilled over into West Timor proper (hence the burning of the marketplace in Kafamenanu in March just before my visit). Many arrests were made, and scores of young people from Oecussi fled over the border to East Timor to go into hiding in Dili and other places. On my return to Kupang on 8 April by the Sempati flight to Surabaya, I witnessed a manacled prisoner being escorted off the plane by a police officer.

25 Figures supplied to me by Universitas Timor Timur sources during my visit to East Timor in April 1997. Compare this with the 1995 figure given in Carey and Carter Bentley, *East Timor at the Crossroads*, p. 13, which estimates the 'newcomer' population at 150,000, or 20 per cent of the total inhabitants of the province. In 1996, in the 15–60 age group 299,177 Timorese were unemployed, as compared to 161,095 non-Timorese. In terms of the private sector, which is dominated by Indonesian/Javanese capital, 95 per cent of all those in employment were non-Timorese compared to 5 per cent Timorese. In the public sector, of those with a university degree, 90 per cent of those employed were non-Timorese, 10 per cent Timorese; of those with a high school (Sekolah Menengah Atas/SMA) diploma, 40 per cent of those employed were non-Timorese, 60 per cent Timorese.

26 See *Timor Link* (Catholic Institute for International Relations/CIIR), No. 39, April 1997, p. 8, quoting Winters, Rebecca and Kelly, Brian, *Children of the Resistance. The Current Situation in East Timor as Seen Through the Eyes of Two Australian Tourists* (Darwin, 1997, Australians for a Free East Timor /AFFET).

27 I would like to acknowledge my thanks to the Oppenheimer Fund of Queen Elizabeth House, Oxford, and the Modern History Faculty of the University of Oxford, for research grants for travel and interviews in East Timor in April 1997. I also wish to express my gratitude to the Catholic Church in East Timor for the unfailing kindness and hospitality of its priests, nuns and lay brothers and sisters.

3

Reporting East Timor: Western Media Coverage of the Conflict

Hugh O'Shaughnessy

At the beginning of the 1990s, the tragic situation in East Timor was familiar to a comparatively small group of people throughout the world. The way in which that generalized ignorance about the territory has been dispelled contains lessons which are relevant to the activities of the media and non-governmental organizations (NGOs) in many similar situations in the developing world. The invasion of East Timor in 1975 had been undertaken by the Indonesians at the height of the Cold War and overseen by the leader of a regime which was judged to be friendly to the interests of the West. Formal protests had been registered and General Suharto had been condemned by the United Nations Security Council on several occasions after the occupation of East Timor by Indonesian troops, but none of the five permanent members of that body chose to take effective action to roll it back. For its part, Portugal – itself returning to calm after the throes of the 'Carnation Revolution' – did not look disposed to pursue what was seen to be a lost cause which it could not put right by military or diplomatic means. Its efforts to publicize the situation – even supposing that the authorities in Lisbon were in a position to know about and analyse it – were therefore minimal. Even if the Portuguese had bent their every effort in an international lobbying campaign, it is questionable how much effect this would have had, given the lack of projection of the Portuguese authorities. Also, among the minority outside the Portuguese-speaking world who were interested in Portugal, many would have regarded the invasion of East Timor as something akin to the relatively peaceful absorption by India of the Portuguese enclaves of Goa, Damão and Diu in 1961.

For a decade and a half, therefore, the dictatorship of General Suharto was secure in the knowledge that friends in Western governments would do their best to prevent his embarrassment by the publication of what was common knowledge in the chancelleries of Europe, the USA and Australia. Nor were the leaders of the Soviet Union and China keen to quarrel with the man who, like themselves, controlled a large and populous country. For 15 years, those administrations which supported Suharto conveniently kept silent about the atrocities that were committed by a regime which was politically and commercially important to East and West alike.

However, throughout the 1990s, the realities of the East Timorese situation became more widely known to the point that East Timor is became common currency of debate in political, diplomatic and business circles worldwide. Few people who consider themselves to be up to date with world events would confess to being completely ignorant of the recent history of the territory: the judgement by Amnesty International and other reputable bodies that some 200,000 people have lost their lives as a result of the invasion and occupation of a territory whose population in 1975 was about 700,000 is a fact that has caught the popular imagination. The international recognition of the Timorese problem was consummated in December 1996 when two leaders of the East Timorese, Bishop Carlos Filipe Ximenes Belo of Dili and José Ramos-Horta, the chief representative of the Timorese resistance abroad in the period of Indonesia's occupation jointly shared award of the Nobel Peace Prize. The overwhelming credit for this change of world attitudes must go to those hundreds of thousands of East Timorese who resisted the Indonesian invaders throughout their occupation with steadfastness, even when their cause looked totally hopeless and they were almost totally bereft of support from outside their small country. In their resistance they have been ably and courageously lead by such figures as their military leaders, Xanana Gusmão and Konis Santana, and by the Portuguese-born Bishop Martinho da Costa Lopes and his successor, Bishop Belo, as well as Ramos-Horta.

The foreign media, the pro-Timorese lobbies and the non-governmental organizations which supported the cause of East Timor can nevertheless share some of the laurels for making known a closely guarded horror story. The revelation of the truth about East Timor's plight was an instance of powerful, effective and ultimately successful cooperation between the media, voluntary agencies and NGOs. It deserves greater study than it has received to date, since such instances of cooperation may well become more frequent and fruitful in the future. Today, at a time of merciless competition among the media and the consequent reduction of expenditure on foreign news (an expensive commodity) in many publications where budgets are tight, there is certainly scope for more of such collective endeavour.

I am certainly proud to have played a small part in revealing the reality of East Timor, and will here relate the often fortuitous circumstances which led me to be among the first Western journalists to visit, and revisit, that territory and to watch the awakening of world opinion to the cruelties of Indonesia's occupation. It is just over nine years since I set foot on the soil of East Timor in the first of four visits, two of which ended in my expulsion by the occupation forces. I went to Dili in 1991 virtually by chance, having devoted most of my career as a journalist to Latin America and the Caribbean, about which I had written for The *Financial Times*, *The Irish Times* and *The Economist* and broadcasted for the BBC among others. I had never been to the Far East; the farthest east I had travelled was to Iran.

My first journey to East Timor owed much to coincidence and little to the limited editorial budget of my employer, *The Observer*, which would scarcely have stretched to sending me to South-East Asia on what many of my colleagues might have considered an ill-defined assignment. In early 1991, I had been invited to one conference in Australia and a second, on a totally different topic, a few days later, across the Pacific Ocean in Santiago de Chile. My fares were paid by two NGOs, the organizers of the conferences. As a journalist who had written for more than 20 years for *The Observer* in London, and who was unlikely to be in South-East Asia again, I wanted to get the best out of a round-the-world trip and do some original reporting. But having made a career writing about Spanish and Portuguese-speaking countries, I felt that there was little I could add to what colleagues with better local knowledge than I had already written about the affairs of the region from Singapore to Sydney. I did not read Chinese or speak any of the various Chinese languages, nor did I know much about Indonesia's history, either as an independent republic or in its earlier incarnation as a part of the Dutch East Indian empire. My views about Australia could hardly add anything to the writings of those who had spent years or a lifetime studying that vast country. At first sight there was little I could offer, as a reporter, that had not been offered before.

What about East Timor, I thought to myself? There seemed to be a nucleus of people in Europe and in the wider world who were always trying to highlight what was happening there, though few others, it seemed, were paying much attention to what they were saying. Having been mesmerized by the history of Portugal since my days at university in Spain and Britain, and having become familiar with Brazil, a Portuguese-speaking country which is the largest and most populous nation in Latin America, I felt that Indonesian-occupied East Timor offered me particular opportunities. Perhaps, in this former Portuguese colony which had been invaded in 1975 by its Indonesian neighbours, the people still spoke a language I was familiar with.

The advantages of compiling a story confined to a small geographical area and my knowledge of Portuguese convinced me to stop off in Dili, the capital of occupied East Timor, on my way from London to Sydney. I set about briefing myself on what I immediately discovered was a major international tragedy. I also learned that a wealth of solid, up-to-date information existed in London among the voluntary agencies, notably the Catholic Association for Overseas Development (CAFOD) and the Catholic Institute for International Relations (CIIR), which had continued to maintain contact with the Catholic Church and the people of the territory from the beginning of the Indonesian occupation. Information on East Timor was distilled in a series of publications, none of which reached the public they merited. Armed with that background knowledge and one or two introductions, I set off for a territory which had only recently been opened up to foreign visitors. The Indonesians, seeking to strengthen the tourist industry, did not demand that visitors obtained visas. I therefore entered their country, and East Timor, without hindrance, taking the precaution of not declaring my journalist credentials, but rather saying that I was a consultant, a fact that was no less true.

As the aircraft came in over the sea to land just outside Dili, I wondered what degree of freedom I would be allowed as I tried to form an accurate picture of what was going on. I passed through the modern and efficient new airport without incident, though the Indonesian officials most probably noted the rare phenomenon of a Western stranger arriving alone and who was not met from the plane. I took a taxi past the market quarter into the city, noticing the military aeroplanes and helicopters which were parked in what I surmised to be a former civilian airport. It was easy to see in the streets who were the natives and who were the occupiers. The indigenous Timorese were considerably darker-skinned than the 'Javanese', as the Indonesians were universally known. The Javanese stood out as having straight, glossy hair, in contrast to the often matted curly hair of the Timorese.

The city proper, hemmed in against the blue waters of a bay by the surrounding mountains, was a sleepy place. The colonial buildings left by the Portuguese regime of António Salazar gave the place some metropolitan pretensions. A monument to Prince Henry the Navigator, whose studies laid the basis of Portugal's foreign expansion, was in the square before the governor's palace, flanked by a pair of old British 25-pounder guns, as used in the Second World War. On the monument stone was set a line from the Lusiads, the long epic poem by Camoens which is the classic hymn to the Portuguese empire, and the ensemble heightened the feeling that this was an antique place, sited in a backwater of history. At the same time, a large number of the East Timorese dwellings were tropical huts, shaded by palm trees, and there was an overwhelming feeling of *rus in urbe*, the countryside invading the city. The street names lingered on in Portuguese, as did the signs over some of the businesses and shops, but all the publicity hoardings and posters were in Bahasa Indonesia, the language of the occupying power.

I settled myself into the Hotel Turismo, near the water's edge, and prepared to seek out and store as many facts as I could in the week I had given myself. As I visited those to whom I had introductions, I soon found that the ability to speak Portuguese was an immediate passport to contact, and indeed intimacy, with those who were opposed to the occupation. They trusted anyone who could speak the tongue of the old colonial power. The older Timorese, who had learned it at school, poured out a flood of Portuguese to a stranger who could understand them; the younger ones, who had been denied an education in Portuguese, wrestled with a language they could not master but which was the key to contact with the outside world.

A reconnaissance during my first few hours in the city was enough to demonstrate the degree of fear of the Indonesian occupiers among the East Timorese community. The searching of the luggage in my hotel room, carried out in my absence and presumably by some police or intelligence agent, made me conscious that a watchful eye was being kept on me. I was nevertheless able to travel at will within East Timor, to Baucau and from there into the mountainous interior and, during the week I spent on this first visit, was able to confirm for myself – from the members of the opposition whom I met – the veracity of the descriptions of the country which I had been given in London.

On my return, I wrote a page-long account for *The Observer*, at the time still the property of the Lonrho company and being edited by Donald Trelford, the witty and mercurial journalist whose career had been bound up with the paper. I presented my work to Martin Huckerby, the foreign news editor. He wisely decided that it should await a Sunday when there was enough space on the foreign pages to allow it to run at full length, free of the cuts which the pressure of other stories and consequent lack of space might have obliged him to make. Huckerby's judgement was in turn supported by his superiors. The reaction to the printed article surprised me greatly. My report, one of the first to have appeared in the Western press on the living conditions of the East Timorese under the Indonesian occupation, created a much more immediate effect than anything I had previously written, including the reports I had filed from Santiago at the time of General Pinochet's military putsch in 1973, from Buenos Aires during the Falklands War in 1982, or from Grenada at the time of the US invasion a year later. In a situation which I had seldom experienced before, all but one of my reporter colleagues in *The Observer* newsroom congratulated me on the piece. I was asked for interviews on radio and television by a succession of stations, from the BBC World Service in London to the Australian Broadcasting Corporation. Interest from inside Portugal was intense and I flew out to Lisbon to take part in a debate on television. The piece was later read into the record of the US Congress in Washington. The process of revealing the modern history of East Timor was well under way. That revelation displeased many. Though I had specifically reported seeing the occupation forces use military equipment supplied by Britain, the British government denied this – even though it was a simple reality that could have been observed by any visitor to Dili.

Nevertheless, the process of revelation continued, receiving a much greater push a few months later in 1991, when I was contacted by Max Stahl, a young British film-maker. He telephoned me to say that he was going to East Timor for a British television company. He had read my piece in *The Observer* and wanted to glean what he could about the working conditions for a journalist in Dili. I was glad to pass on what I knew and to tell him of other possible sources of information available from the British NGOs. The film Stahl shot in November 1991, of one of the many massacres the occupation forces carried out in the former Portuguese territory, had an electrifying effect on public opinion throughout the world. His brave and shrewd action in seizing the tragic opportunity that the Indonesian military had presented him with when they massacred hundreds of peaceful protesters in the Santa Cruz cemetery (and follow-up operation) certainly changed the history of East Timor, revealing as it did the truth that so many had been happy to hide. He not only continued to operate his camera as East Timorese were being cut down around him by the occupation forces, he also had the foresight to bury his film in one of the graves in the cemetery while the firing was going on, lest it be seized by the Indonesian troops. He returned later to unearth it and get it to the outside world.

It understandably caused a sensation, being shown by television stations in many countries, often on several occasions in one day. Whether the Indonesian authorities recognized it at the time or not, Stahl's film was the death knell for the continued dominance of Indonesia in East Timor. It put the territory on the world political agenda in a way that no other document had done, inspiring people around the globe with the desire to help to put an end to the occupation. Stahl's film inspired print, radio and television journalists worldwide to continue the coverage of East Timor. John Pilger and David Munro, for instance, used footage from Max Stahl and others as an indispensable part of a long television documentary, *Death of a Nation* (1994), which was screened widely and updated and re-screened in 1999. As at the beginning, the voluntary agencies continued to provide information which would not have been available to journalists from other sources. CAFOD and the CIIR in Britain took the lead and helped to establish the British Coalition for East Timor (BCET), which has been at the forefront of the campaign in Britain against Indonesia's occupation of East Timor.

As the international interest developed, Tapol, a campaigning agency created and led by Carmel Budiardjo (see Chapter 5), a London-born teacher who had been imprisoned for her beliefs by the Suharto regime, devoted increasing attention to East Timor. The agency's journal, the *Tapol Bulletin*, continues to this day to be a prime and globally respected source of news about the territory. As the solidarity campaign gathered momentum, it attracted the political support of the Campaign Against Arms Trade (CAAT), which had lobbied to reduce the activities of the British arms industry. Of particular importance was the action of a number of dedicated women inspired by the activities of the Ploughshares movement, a group which had its roots among committed Christians in the United States (see Chapter 7). In January 1996, four of them organized a break-in at the British Aerospace factory outside Preston which was manufacturing Hawk warplanes for the Indonesian government. The four women were put on trial in Liverpool but, in a surprising and heartening verdict, the jury acquitted them in July 1996, accepting the rightness of their argument that it was the duty of every citizen to do his or her best to prevent such criminal acts as those committed by the Indonesians against the East Timorese. Though the trial judge appeared to be severely upset by the verdict and spokesmen for the Conservative government of John Major attacked the jury's decision, encouraging the British press to attack it too, it set a valuable precedent in British case law.

During my fourth visit to Dili, in November 1995, I had in fact observed Hawk aircraft flying low over the city as part of a fierce attempt to cow the citizens into silence on the eve of the anniversary of the Santa Cruz massacre. I had reported that fact in *The Independent on Sunday*, only to find myself called a liar by officials of the Foreign and Commonwealth Office (FCO), who were keen that nothing should be done to harm the prospects of further British arms sales to Indonesia. This practice, which might have been expected from a business-friendly Conservative government, has sadly continued under Labour since its election victory in 1997 (see Chapter 8). Journalists accompanying the FCO Minister Robin Cook on his visit to Jakarta shortly after the Labour victory continued to report, doubtlessly with FCO prompting, that there was 'no proof' of British military equipment being used in occupied East Timor. Not until September 1999, at the height of the post-referendum crisis in East Timor (see Chapter 14), did the Foreign Secretary admit to Hawk aircraft being used over the territory.

In Ireland, meanwhile, Tom Hyland, at the time unemployed, was so moved by the East Timor story that he established the East Timor Ireland Solidarity Campaign (ETISC), and quickly transformed it into a lobbying weapon that the occupying forces came to fear. The influence of ETISC on the 1995–97 Fine Gael-Labour-Democratic Left coalition government in Ireland was very appreciable. I well remember going with Tom Hyland to attend a debate on East Timor in the Seanad (Senate) in Dublin. The proceedings did not attract many senators, but those who did take the floor took notice of his presence in the public gallery and felt it incumbent to pay public tribute to his lobbying skills.

The efforts of the ETISC in raising public consciousness of the East Timor situation was very evident when Ireland took its turn at the presidency of the European Union (EU) in the second half of 1996 and Dick Spring, the Minister for Foreign Affairs at the time, managed to put East Timor on the EU agenda (see Chapter 11). That he was not able to achieve more in the EU context was due, to a large extent, to the fierce defence of the Suharto dictatorship by the conservative governments of John Major in the UK and Helmut Kohl in Germany. Nonetheless, Tom Hyland ensured that the cause of East Timor was also taken up by the present Irish adminis-tration (a Fianna Fáil-Progressive Democrats coalition), to the point that in April 1999 David Andrews (Minister for Foreign Affairs) became the first EU foreign minister to visit East Timor since Indonesia's occupation in 1975. Tom Hyland was invited to join the minister's official delegation to East Timor in recognition of his tireless campaigning efforts on behalf of the East Timorese. Moreover, the EU acknowledged Ireland's role in promoting reconciliation in East Timor by appointing David Andrews as a special envoy to the territory.

Among the lobbying tools used by campaigners, the internet was an important factor in the fight to end the unjust and illegal occupation of East Timor. Various internet conferences brought together, promptly and cheaply, those committed to the cause of justice for East Timor and kept them minutely apprised of the latest events. Also, the publication of mate-rial on East Timor realities in the 1990s illustrated the great power of a sensible degree of cooperation between the media and the voluntary agen-cies on issues of importance, which otherwise would scarcely be covered.

As the work of publicizing the truth about East Timor continued, those involved took encouragement from the public acknowledgement that they received from a number of NGOs. Though Bishop Belo remains a shy man who is not at all at home in the world of international lobbying, he realized the worth of the Nobel Peace Prize to the cause for which he was fighting, though he did not use it flamboyantly. More wise to the ways of the world, Ramos-Horta has used his new status as a Nobel Prize winner unashamedly to force open the doors of those who for more than two decades had refused to see him. Carmel Budiardjo received the Right Livelihood Prize in Stockholm in 1996, the Ploughshares Four were awarded the Sean McBride Prize and my reporting helped me to my second British National Press Award in 1992 and, in 1995, to the first Wilberforce Medallion awarded by the City of Hull (to commemorate William Wilberforce, Hull's slavery abolitionist).

As the work of making the conditions in occupied East Timor more familiar in the outside word continued in the 1990s, it would have been easy to think that the process was being automatically assisted by the globalization of information that was supposed to be rapidly making the world more intelligible to its inhabitants. Experience, however, showed that the reality was much more complicated. In Britain, the degree of competition in the media – notably, a drive towards a monopoly position by figures such as Rupert Murdoch – created pressure on budgets and severely limited the foreign coverage of newspapers, radio and television. The same was true of other European countries, while a similar process has gone so far in the USA that many international issues of the greatest importance are routinely ignored. The process has become so marked that *The Financial Times* feels it can increase its American circulation by giving US businessmen the international news that their own media do not supply to them. This increasing degree of competition has gone hand in hand with a push towards trivialization of news presentation.

In 1999, amidst a brutal Indonesian military/militia backlash against the result of the 30 August referendum in East Timor (see Chapter 14), the world's media did indeed give voluminous coverage to a situation that was rapidly spiralling out of control. In this respect, the media played a useful (crisis-driven) role of informing the world of developments. When international peacekeepers entered the territory, though, the world's media suddenly lost interest, failing to engage sufficiently with the real problems still facing East Timor: reconstruction, reconciliation, the safe return of displaced persons, calling the Indonesian human rights violators to account for their actions and so on.

In circumstances of media neglect, the determination of the voluntary agencies that questions of international morality, such as the fate of East Timor, shall not be overlooked or marginalized has become very important. From the standpoint of common sense, the idea of the voluntary agencies and the public which sustains them with donations subsidizing the media seems bizarre. But, in an imperfect world, the role that the NGOs have undertaken in the media, in an effort to prevent people in the richer countries turning their backs on the less affluent and their problems, is a vital one indeed. The rapid and worldwide popularization of the cause of East

Timor has shown that if the private owners of the world's media fight shy of devoting time and money to international affairs, it is right and proper – indeed essential – that their shortcomings should be tackled in new and creative ways.

4

Balibo: The Cover-up that Led to Genocide

Maureen Tolfree

News gathering is costly. In October 1975, it cost the lives of five television newsmen. One of them, Brian Peters, was my brother. Brian's story, and that of East Timor, can be told with the help of two letters to his family in England. One of those letters reached us in September 1975 – the month in which it was written. The other, written the following month, did not reach us until over 20 years later – and then only as a photocopy of the first two pages. This mystery says much about the way East Timor was sentenced to death.

Brian was born in Bristol in February 1949. He was 26 (not, as is often said, 29) when he was killed. After my mother left home, I, at 15 years of age, became the head of the household. I helped my father to bring up the three boys: Gary, then aged 2; David, aged 7; and Brian, aged 11. Brian's passion was photography, and after leaving school he worked in the dark-room of Bristol United Press. In 1968, he emigrated to Australia, where in due course he became a Sydney-based television cameraman for Channel 9 news. In September 1975, Brian wrote to tell us about his 'incredible month'. Part of it had been spent in a place called East Timor. We had never heard of East Timor before. The letter described how Brian and Channel 9 journalist Gerald Stone slipped into East Timor by boat at the end of August 1975. They were there to cover fighting between Fretilin (the Revolutionary Front for an Independent East Timor) and the UDT (Timorese Democratic Union).[1]

Brian's letter described the grim situation at the hospital in Dili (East Timor's capital), a gun battle at the airport, and how Fretilin was 'prepared to let us film anything'. What now seems even more significant, however, is the description that Brian gives of the Australian government's efforts to prevent on-the-spot news coverage of the fighting. Brian's letter mentions that he 'was the only bloke there with a camera', and how he heard later 'that the scene in Darwin was incredible, with well over a hundred pressmen trying to get to Timor, all furious because they knew I was there'.

When Brian and Gerald reached East Timor, the Portuguese governor and his staff had just fled to the small nearby island of Atauro. Gerald was able to get out from Atauro on a Royal Australian Air Force plane after a day or two – probably the one that brought in the Red Cross team. Gerald took with him Brian's initial films.[2] After a week or so, Brian came out on the boat that had brought him in, accompanied by around 140 refugee women and children. With him, Brian carried an appeal to the 'brotherly people of Australia' from Francisco Xavier do Amarol[3] – the then president of Fretilin. Xavier's letter spoke of his people's 'inalienable right' to 'total and complete independence' and, in memory of the sacrifice of the East Timorese on behalf of Australia in the Second World War, requested 'help in order to avoid any foreign intervention'.

Our next news came very late at night, on Saturday 18 October 1975, in a telephone call from Brian's ex-girlfriend in Australia. The date is significant for reasons I did not begin to understand until 20 years later. Genene told me that Brian and four other newsmen had gone missing in East Timor, that four of their bodies had been found, and that one man was still missing. In tears, both of us hoped that the missing man was Brian and that he was in hiding. But Gerald Stone – Channel 9's national news director by then – was in contact several times the following week. He told us that he feared all five were dead.

We were informed officially by telephone on – perhaps – 13 November 1975 that Brian's remains had been taken to Jakarta and that, with the remains of the others, they would be buried there. I protested that we wanted his remains buried in Australia. I was told that all the other families had agreed to a joint burial and that – for health reasons – the remains could not be taken out of Indonesia. Independent advice would have told us that the 'health reasons' were nonsense, but we received no such advice. We gave in.

I felt that I had to do something, so I arranged to fly to Australia to sort out my brother's effects. On arrival, I received a telephone call from Foreign Minister Andrew Peacock of the caretaker government – or from someone in his department – to say how sorry he was about the death of my brother. There was, he said, nothing I could 'do or say that would help in this matter'. I thought, at the time, that he was insinuating that I was looking for compensation. I suspect, now, that he was in a panic.

Within days, I received a telephone call from Bristol. My father was ill; my children missed me. I decided to return early. But how? By then,

Qantas workers were on strike over Governor General Sir John Kerr's sacking of Gough Whitlam's Labour government. A way was found: a seat on a charter flight to Jakarta, so that from there I could pick up a Pan Am flight to England. It was as I prepared to board the charter plane that I realized that there might be some sort of burial service that I could attend.

Once the plane was aloft, I asked the air hostess whether she would be able to arrange for me to remain in Jakarta even though I lacked the right papers. The pilot radioed ahead on my behalf. Soon the air hostess was able to tell me that someone would collect me from my seat after we landed.

Four men collected me. They seemed to be soldiers. They escorted me to a room. One stood guard at the door. We waited in silence. I was not afraid. I had no idea that there was any Indonesian involvement in my brother's death. The telephone rang. The guard soldier indicated that I should take the call. It came from the British or the Australian embassy; I do not recall which. The instructions were quite clear: my security could not be guaranteed so would I, please, join my booked flight? I did so. I assumed this was routine bureaucracy. What I cannot understand, now, is why the diplomat did not offer to collect me in the embassy car so that I could remain in the embassy's care until the burial service. Was it the expense that worried him? Or was he worried that my presence might expose their elaborate preparations – of which I knew nothing – as a charade?

Back in Bristol, I received two letters from my MP – Tony Benn. 'I understand', said his second letter:

> That on 13 November the Australian Embassy in Jakarta received through the Indonesian authorities, who had been investigating the matter, various personal papers and items of television equipment belonging to the five missing journalists. Included among the papers were the passports of your brother and another Briton, Mr Malcolm Rennie. Also handed over were four boxes said to contain the remains of four of the journalists. These were later examined by the Australian Embassy doctor who confirmed that positive identification of the bodies was not possible. At the same time the authorities handed over documents and a camera said to have been found beside the body of a fifth European whose remains had been burned.

The letter ended with Tony Benn's offer of sympathy and further help.[4]

One of the 'personal papers' was later listed as a 'photostatted letter dated 15 October 1975 at Balibo'. Please hold that in your mind. Would Tony Benn have been able to obtain details of those papers had we taken up his offer? All I can say is that we were in no state to ask anything of him. The illness that had struck my father that November was a heart attack; by Christmas 1975 all my hair had fallen out. The list of 'personal papers' (and other items) is in the 18-paragraph document said to be written by David Colin Rutter, consul at the Australian embassy in Jakarta, on 19 December 1975. That 18-paragraph document was in the small batch of papers sent to us in 1976 by the Australian government. Chief among those papers was a long report on an official visit paid to Balibo – the village where my brother and the other TV newsmen died – by Allan Taylor, Rutter and a third diplomat. The official report dismissed any idea of Indonesian involvement in the attack on Balibo, using less than 130 words to do so.[5]

In Australia, dedicated professionals were able to see that the 'investigation' led by Taylor was part of the cover-up. They did not contact us, since they did not know that we existed. We knew nothing of the existence of James Dunn, Jill Jolliffe, Hamish McDonald, or any of the other individuals seeking truth and justice as regards East Timor. Nor did we know about Tapol, the Indonesia Human Rights Campaign, or any other such source of help. We had the 18-paragraph document, Allan Taylor's report, and a few more documents. We could not read them without weeping, let alone analyse them. Nor could we study the small bundle of press cuttings that we received from Australia, some of which contained hints about the truth, as it seems, did an Australian press report that my brother Gary found in Bristol. The report said that the newsmen had been shot – and that the bald one had been shot first. Brian, though only 26, was bald. The Australian government wanted us to believe that Brian and the others had died when a mortar shell hit the building in which they were sheltering – and that this had happened during a civil war. That was what the Bristol papers reported, too, in front-page accounts of Brian's disappearance and death. We did not understand that the Australian government was hiding the truth. Nor did we understand that Indonesian forces had invaded East Timor and begun committing genocide there. The only news report on that invasion that we saw, and were able to absorb, told us that Indonesian forces had gone into East Timor to restore order and that they would leave once that was achieved. And that – until shortly before 22 February 1994 – was what we believed. It was complete fabrication, however, since the Indonesians had not left.

We struggled on with our lives. We brought up children. We coped, somehow, with the loss of Brian. That loss was dreadful. It contributed to the series of heart attacks that turned Dad from a fit man into an invalid. By 1990, he was dead. Meanwhile, despite my very active working life, Brian's loss had destroyed my marriage and begun to make me seriously ill.

Many people in the UK heard about East Timor's Santa Cruz massacre on the news in November 1991, or saw the *Cold Blood* televised documentary about the massacre when it was shown early the following year. We did not – but I saw a short extract from it, somewhere, in the weeks or months before 22 February 1994. When I contacted the TV company concerned, they seemed mildly interested, but did not get back to me. By then, I was too ill to pursue them. At home in Bristol, ill, I turned on BBC Radio 2. It was 22 February 1994. I wanted to listen to the John Dunn show. John Pilger would be a guest, came the announcement. The terrible genocide in East Timor would be the subject, the announcement continued. The room began to spin, it seemed to me. Somehow, I struggled to the telephone. Somehow, I persuaded the BBC to agree to pass a message to John Pilger. The room continued to spin. Later, as the room spun on, I heard John Pilger say that he had had a message from me. I must watch his programme, he said. It was called *Death of a Nation*. It would tell me about my brother's death. He would telephone me. My shock grew. That night, after the film, my telephone line was blocked with weeping friends. They had not known; they would never believe the British government again. For the first time in years, I was almost calm.

Then I learned that John Pilger had had to go abroad. Yet again, the silence was descending. Next, on 16 March 1994, and for the first time in my life, I switched on the HTV news. The scene showed some demonstrators outside the local Rolls-Royce factory. 'No Hawks to Indonesia', said the placards. It was a protest about alleged warplane attacks in East Timor, said the voice-over. The engines that powered the warplanes were made at the Bristol factory. It took me several telephone calls to reach the protest organizer. He was very polite but, I learned months later, he believed very little of what I told him. I am not surprised. How could I, with my broad Bristol accent, be the sister of an Australian newsman of whom he had never heard prior to 1994? I was unhinged, he assumed. Without his efforts since that telephone call, however, the story might have been very different. Working together, we have built up support for a judicial inquiry into what happened at Balibo and into the cover-up. The first MP to support such an inquiry was Dr Roger Berry, the Labour MP for Kingswood (the constituency in which I lived at that time). In the 1994–95 and 1995–96 parliamentary sessions, Dr Berry was the main sponsor of an early-day motion (EDM) with this text:

> That this House notes that the British television newsmen, Malcolm Rennie and Brian Peters, were killed, with three other Australian-based newsmen, at Balibo, East Timor, on 16 October 1975, to prevent them informing the world that Indonesia had begun its invasion of East Timor; notes that Australian Foreign Minister Evans confirmed this when he stated, in the Australian Senate on 7 June 1994, that the five newsmen were executed in a major military invasion; and therefore urges Her Majesty's Government to institute an inquiry into the Balibo killings of 16 October 1975.

Dr Berry created that text from a wide range of sources. The general case put forward is based on years of research carried out by such experts as Jill

Jolliffe and James Dunn, to whose work we were introduced by people like Carmel Budiardjo, Dr John Taylor and Lord Avebury. Just as important, however, are the astonishing admissions made, under pressure in the Australian Senate, by Gareth Evans. We hardly believed our eyes when we read them. The Australian government's Department of Foreign Affairs and Trade (DFAT) had them specially faxed to London, by mistake perhaps, so that they could be presented to us when we visited the Australian High Commission in November 1994.

The 1994–95 EDM was tabled by Dr Berry and Liberal Democrat MP Don Foster on 14 February 1995. It was the first ever EDM on Balibo and it won the support of 162 MPs, the highest total for any EDM on East Timor. The 1995–96 EDM was tabled in December 1995. It had exactly the same text, and was open for signatures by backbench MPs until just before the Queen's Speech of November 1996. This time it won the support of 108 MPs, including 12 Conservatives – the highest number of MPs of that party to support any East Timor EDM. This time Dr Berry's co-sponsors were David Nicholson (Conservative), Don Foster (Liberal Democrat), John Hume (SDLP), the Reverend Martin Smyth (Ulster Unionist), and Dafydd Wigley (Plaid Cymru). Building up such support was wonderfully helpful. But it was not easy. A lot of very hard work was required.

In May 1994, for example, we asked Tony Benn for the help that he had kindly offered me almost 19 years earlier. A letter that he was sent, on 21 June 1994, was signed by the then Foreign Secretary, the Right Honorable Douglas Hurd. Although Evans's revelation had been made several weeks earlier, no hint of was found in Douglas Hurd's letter – which was astoundingly misleading in each one of its five paragraphs.

'Thank you for your letter,' said the text drafted for the Foreign Secretary by his officials, 'about the death in 1975 of Brian Peters and other members of an Australian TV crew in East Timor.' Not true. Brian and Malcolm worked for Channel 9. Gary Cunningham, Greg Shackleton, and Tony Stewart worked for the rival Channel 7. 'Hard facts about the circumstances surrounding Mr Peters' death were difficult to establish in the conflict prevailing in East Timor at that time,' stated the second paragraph, incorrectly. 'However, the enquiries made by the Indonesian authorities (on our and the Australian Government's behalf) concluded that Mr Peters, and other members of the TV film crew, were killed at Balibo on 16 October 1975. Their deaths occurred several weeks before the Indonesian invasion of East Timor in December that year.' The third paragraph stated that:

> Local reports at the time suggested that the house in which the TV crewmen had been sheltering was caught in heavy cross-fire between the forces of the three internal warring parties of East Timor (UDT, Apodeti and Fretilin) and set on fire. There were no survivors.

There were such reports, of course, as part of the cover-up. 'The families of all journalists received copies of a Statutory Declaration made by the Australian Consul in Jakarta detailing the efforts which the Australian authorities had made to establish the facts surrounding the deaths,' began the fourth paragraph. Truth is a difficult concept, a senior British civil servant told Lord Justice Scott's inquiry into arms for Iraq. Douglas Hurd was misinformed: we were not sent that statutory declaration. We were sent the 18-paragraph document said to be written by Consul Rutter. While Rutter's statutory declaration may have told the truth, we have yet to see it. His 18-paragraph document is deeply misleading, though he may have supposed it to be true. Others, very much more senior than Consul Rutter, knew on 16 October 1975 that my brother and the other newsmen had been killed by Indonesia's covert invasion force. Those others included Labour Prime Minister Gough Whitlam, Foreign Minister Don Willesee, and Defence Minister Bill Morrison.

They knew it from Australian secret intelligence monitoring of Indonesian military radio communications – as was revealed in August 1998 – because Allan Taylor and other officials were briefed by Indonesian officials, in advance, that Indonesian troops would attack the Balibo area on 16 October 1975. That is why President Suharto stopped the covert invasion in its tracks after Balibo. Had Whitlam and his colleagues used their knowledge to protest to President Suharto, as Suharto expected them to do, that would have been that. There would have been no full-scale invasion in December 1975, no genocide thereafter.

Paragraph four of the letter signed by Douglas Hurd in June 1994 claimed that: 'We gave Mrs Tolfree whatever information we obtained about the circumstances of her brother's death as it became available.' This was nonsense, as will be obvious from the next section. Douglas Hurd's fifth and last paragraph began:

> I am sorry that recent media speculation about what happened to these journalists has caused further distress to Mrs Tolfree and other surviving relatives. It is difficult to see what benefit those most directly involved could derive from re-opening the issue so long after the event. Facts were difficult to establish in 1975, in what was then a war zone. There seems little prospect of any new evidence emerging twenty years later.

Douglas Hurd's sympathy is welcome, of course, but when in April 1995 I took up the invitation that I eventually won from the Foreign Office to call on its then parliamentary under-secretary, Tony Baldry MP, the latter was somehow able to present me with papers that the Foreign and Commonwealth Office had held for years – but which I had never seen before. One of those papers concerned the high-level diplomats who had been at the

Jakarta burial, an event from which I had been excluded. And then there were the six photographs, newly arrived from the Australian government in March 1995. Two of them were of the headstone that the Australian government claims marks the grave of my brother and the other newsmen; four of them were of the burial service itself. Those were photographs that caused a front-page sensation in the Australian press when two of them were released there in January 1997.

From 1995 on, the cover-up began to unravel. At Lord Avebury's request, James Dunn produced a report – published simultaneously in Australia and Britain on the 20th anniversary of the killings – entitled *Timor: the Balibo Incident in Perspective*.[6] Dunn's press contacts came up with sensational interviews with senior Indonesian military men who – for the first time – admitted that the Channel 7 and Channel 9 news teams had died in an Indonesian attack, but not, of course, that they were murdered. It then became possible for East Timorese participants in the covert Indonesian invasion force to speak publicly about some of what they knew. At that point, Australia's Labour government quickly set up what they saw as a 'damage-limitation' exercise: Tom Sherman's preliminary evaluation of evidence[7] about the deaths of the five newsmen at Balibo and of Roger East[8] in Dili at the time of the full-scale invasion.

On 26 April 1996, I went to London to meet Tom Sherman, the distinguished Australian lawyer. I had no illusions about what he had been asked to do, and insisted on telling him that nothing less than a full judicial inquiry was required. That does not prevent me from praising his kindness. It was from Tom Sherman that I received two photocopied sheets of a letter written by Brian. They were photocopied from his last letter home. It never arrived, but of course I recognized Brian's writing immediately. And only Brian could have begun a letter with these words:

BALIBO   EAST TIMOR   WED 15th Oct.

Hi,

Intended to send you the second half of the story about my trip to Timor this week, but I'm back up here again. Left Sydney a week ago for Dili, now I'm on the border between East Timor and Indonesian Timor. Nine asked me to come up here because fighting has broken out on the border, UDT forces who retreated into Indonesian Timor have been staging counter attacks with the aid of Indonesian forces.

Of the five men killed at Balibo, only Brian was based in Sydney. He had been to East Timor, too, and worked for 'Nine' (Channel 9). Even after months of prodding, the Australian government has declined to tell us whether the above is the letter listed in Rutter's 18-paragraph document. Even if it is not, it came into their hands at some stage. There seem to be three possible reasons why they failed to pass it on to us: culpable negligence, cruelty, or because they were not prepared to let us see a letter that confirms the illegal presence of Indonesian troops in East Timor – and Indonesian warships, in Indonesian waters, signalling to those troops. The Indonesian government's response to Sherman's report was to say that it cleared them completely. The Australian and British governments want that to be the end of the matter. If it is, then the Indonesian government will know that the full story of its former illegal occupation of East Timor will remain untold.

Conclusion: The struggle continues

The families of Brian Peters and Malcolm Rennie continue to campaign, something they were unable to do until the mid-1990s, since they were unaware that there was any issue to do with Balibo – or East Timor – on which to campaign.

In May 1998, the newly installed President Habibie appointed Lieutenant General Yunus Yosfiah as his Information Minister. The New York-based Committee to Protect Journalists (CPJ) protested to President Habibie that same day over the appointment. Yunus Yosfiah, a special forces captain in 1975, had been named, in an article by *Sydney Morning Herald* Asia editor David Jenkins in 1995, as the officer who led the troops at Balibo. The CPJ had gleaned that information from London's *Independent on Sunday* which, as a result of my campaigning, Yunus's London training in 1989, and David Jenkin's article, published a major article on Balibo in its 5 November 1995 editions. It took until October 1998 for Balibo to be seen as a serious news issue in the UK, however. There were three main factors.

- Four-and-a-half years of pressure led the Labour government to see the need to act, or the need to appear to do so: Foreign Office minister (the late) Derek Fatchett obtained President Habibie's 'undertaking' to 'look into' the deaths at Balibo (an undertaking very soon overruled).
- José Ramos-Horta (East Timor's Nobel Peace Prize co-laureate, 1996) agreed to share a press conference on Balibo with myself and Malcolm's cousin – and Ann Clwyd MP agreed to chair that press conference, which called for a judicial inquiry into the Balibo murders.
- A major Australian documentary, for which Jill Jolliffe was associate producer, brought forward witnesses claiming Yunus Yosfiah had supervised the Balibo murders – and includes an interview with Sherman's main witness from the 1996 evaluation, who proceeded to undermine Sherman's report.

On the seventh anniversary of the Santa Cruz massacre – backed by Malcolm's mother and cousin – I sent copies of that documentary to Prime Minister Tony Blair and Foreign Secretary Robin Cook. Next day, I handed a copy to the police.

The families of the five men killed at Balibo – including my own – have endured enormous suffering over the past 25 years because of the duplicitous methods used by the British and Australian governments to prevent the truth surrounding our relatives' deaths becoming public. Neither polite 'undertakings' nor the re-opening of Tom Sherman's evaluation (as happened on 21 October 1998, in response to the Jolliffe documentary) will do. I remain committed to the task of seeking a full judicial inquiry into the events at Balibo and the circumstances in which my brother and his colleagues were killed: East Timor's future deserves nothing less. The lucrative rewards of the arms trade have taken precedence in Britain and Australia's relations with Indonesia at the expense of those who were killed during the conflict in East Timor. We must continue to challenge this morally bankrupt practice in order to stem the flow of weapons to Jakarta, militate against our governments contributing to internal repression, and help in the new millennium to construct a new, peaceful and just East Timor. The new democratic government in Indonesia may provide the necessary impetus to ensure that human rights abuses of the past are properly addressed. Nothing less is required.

References

1   The Indonesian-sponsored civil war lasted from the UDT coup of 11 August 1975 until mid-September 1975. It cost around 1500 East Timorese lives.

2   Those films were shown worldwide, including in the UK. They played a crucially important role in breaking the news blackout on the 'civil war' – and other journalists were able to use their precedent to get into Timor, prior to December 1975.

3   Francisco was subsequently deposed, imprisoned by Fretilin, and then captured by the Indonesians – for whom, tragically, he occasionally appeared in public as a spokesman for 'integration'.

4   At that time, Tony Benn was a Bristol MP – and Secretary of State for Energy. Given what (we know about) the energy potential of the 'Timor Gap', there were serious reasons for others to try to deceive him about Brian's death.

5   Taylor, Alan, et al., Visits to Balibo, April–May 1976 (Australian Department of Foreign Affairs, Canberra, 1976), p. 23. Alan Taylor was a diplomat in the Australian embassy in Jakarta in 1975–76.

6   Dunn, James, East Timor: The Balibo Incident in Perspective (Sydney, 1995, Australian Centre for Independent Journalism).

7   Report on the Deaths of Australian-based Journalists in East Timor in 1975 (the Sherman Report) (Canberra, June 1996).

8   Roger East was a very experienced journalist who went to East Timor, in part, to investigate the deaths of the 'Balibo Five'. It was his report that my brother Gary had read.

5

The Legacy of the Suharto Dictatorship

Carmel Budiardjo

Introduction

In the aftermath of the downfall of President Suharto in May 1998, Indonesia stood on the threshold of a dawning of democracy. However, notwithstanding recent presidential changes, the transition to that status is still fraught with dangers. The economy is in turmoil, with more than 20 per cent of the workforce unemployed or earning a pittance, and poverty staring more than half the population in the face. The armed forces, the ABRI (Armed Forces of the Republic of Indonesia), whose ruthless repression was the hallmark of Suharto's 32-year dictatorship, clung doggedly to its 'special role', and, renamed TNI (Tentara Nasional Indonesia) in April 1999 remains a powerful force, despite recent reforms and setbacks (notably in East Timor). The overall reform programme, which heralded Suharto's political demise – is in its infancy. Many of the state structures set in place by the dictator are still intact. The former president himself is still lurking in the wings, resisting prosecution for past misdemeanours and manipulating 'dark political forces' that have succeeded in instigating racial conflict and enmity between religious communities in Indonesia.

While press freedom has flourished and scores of political parties have sprung to life in the euphoria of the post-Suharto era, the real test of change will be whether the new administration, led by President Abdurrahman Wahid and Vice-President Megawati Sukarnoputri, will be able to achieve a stable democratic system and civil society. Such a system will also have to recognize the rights of outer regions of the archipelago to wide-ranging autonomy in place of the heavily centralized, unitary state which has prevailed for more than half a century. The strains are particularly severe in West Papua and Aceh, where legitimate demands for independence are becoming ever more persistent. Moreover, conditions on the ground in East Timor – after the 30 August 1999 referendum – remain fraught with problems of reconstruction, reconciliation, population displacement and impunity.

Suharto's rise to power

The multiplicity and complexity of Indonesia's current political and social problems can be traced back to the three decades of Suharto's stranglehold on power and the extremely violent way in which he seized control in 1965. On the night of 1 October 1965, a group of army officers claiming to be acting to protect the country's first president, Sukarno, from a coup backed by the US Central Intelligence Agency (CIA), kidnapped six generals (a seventh escaped and an army lieutenant was captured in his stead), who were later put to death. Major-General Suharto, as he was then, had not been a target; indeed, he had been given advance warning of the kidnapping plans, leaving him free to strike back against the plotters, two of whom were his close associates. The Indonesian Communist Party (PKI), which at the time had a following of well over 10 million, was alleged by Suharto to have master-minded the plot and he immediately forced the party underground; it was thus denied the opportunity of defending itself against such an accusation. Suharto took control of the armed forces in defiance of the decision of President Sukarno, the supreme commander, and élite-force troops under his command were sent out to hunt down and slaughter known communists and anyone suspected of communist sympathies. In the six-month 'white terror' which followed, at least half a million people were killed. Hundreds of thousands of communists or communist suspects were thrown into prison and held without trial, in some cases for more than 12 years.

As the Australian scholar Michael van Langenberg has explained:

> The mass violence that occurred in the wake of the [failed coup] was crucial to the consolidation and expansion of state power under the New Order regime. It served three important purposes. First, was the elimination of the leadership of the PKI and the destruction of its mass cadre structure. Second, it issued an unequivocal warning to those who might consider a challenge to the new ruling élite. Third, it created a dramatic historical break, a break since made part of the hegemonic ideology of the state system with the official celebration of 1 October as Hari Peringatan Pancasila Sakti (Day to Commemorate the Sacred Pancasila).[1]

Until 1968, Sukarno remained president, but in name only. He was side-lined and rendered powerless by Suharto, who proceeded to create a system of repression and political control that was to remain intact with minor modifications for the next 32 years. Suharto's blood-soaked seizure of power had the clear backing of Washington and London, where the army's takeover was welcomed as a major victory for the 'free world'; it had rescued Indonesia from a president bent on confrontation with the West and from the threat of communist control. Evidence has come to light on how these two Western powers spurred on the army in its crackdown on the left wing, supplied small-arms to facilitate the massacres, provided hit-lists of PKI activists, and manipulated the news to discredit Sukarno and the PKI and conceal the true character of the massacres as they spread relent-lessly from one part of the country to the next.[2] After six months of slaughter of communists in Indonesia, Washington made no attempt to conceal its delight at what had transpired.[3]

The 'new order' system of repression

Central to the system of repression under Suharto's 'new order' regime were the special powers vested in the armed forces in political affairs as well as in security matters. The ABRI claimed for itself a *dwifungsi* or dual func-tion which incorporated responsibility for defence and security on the one hand and direct involvement in political and social affairs on the other.[4] The latter granted the armed forces the right to occupy positions within the state apparatus, from the lowest to the highest levels. Officers on active service or in retirement still hold key posts in the civil administration, from the village level to provincial governors. The armed forces were allocated seats in parliament and the supreme consultative assembly, and military figures have held key posts in 'new order' cabinets, including the interior ministry on a continual basis, and controlled most government departments by having their men appointed to the top positions in the bureaucracy. All officers holding such posts were under the discipline of the ABRI command through so-called *sos-pol* or social-political chiefs-of-staff, appointed at every level of the army's structure.

The ABRI's security function lay at the heart of its control of Indonesian society. The first measure Suharto took, at the beginning of October 1965, was to set up Kopkamtib, the Operational Command for the Restoration of Security and Order. The special powers of this operational command were held by military commanders from top to bottom. This was the body which rounded up, interrogated and imprisoned hundreds of thousands of people without trial, tens of thousands of whom remained behind bars until the late 1970s. Less than a thousand were brought to trial, the primary purpose of which was not to mete out justice for alleged crimes committed, but to place the blame for the events of 1 October 1965 squarely on the shoulders of the PKI. These were political trials in which the defendants had little chance of mounting a proper defence. There were no acquittals; the sentences passed were all in excess of 12 years and included more than 30 death penalties. Over the years, more than two dozen men on death row have been executed. Even 33 years on, there were still ten of these convicted men languishing in prison, four of whom, already elderly and in some cases very sick, had been under sentence of death for three decades. The Habibie government said on succeeding Suharto in 1998 that these 'PKI prisoners' would not be included in the planned release of political prisoners.

In 1988, Kopkamtib was replaced by Bakorstanas, the Coordinating Body for National Stability, which had more limited powers of arrest but still represented a system of army control that extended down the army command structure to the lowest levels. Although, formally speaking, powers of arrest and detention were vested in the hands of the police (which was not a civilian force, but part of the armed forces), army units frequently take people into custody or interrogate and torture those arrested by the police. In two provinces, West Papua and Aceh – discussed below – the army created 'military operational zones' which gave them unfettered security control with horrific consequences for the local population.

From the 1970s on, the 'new order' regime sought to pursue its security objectives by hounding its opponents through the law courts, to create the appearance that the 'rule of law' was being upheld. It relied primarily on the anti-subversion law and the so-called *haatzai* or 'hate-sowing' articles in the criminal code, which punished acts of rebellion. The anti-subversion law, which sets death as the maximum penalty, was initially enacted as a presidential decree by President Sukarno in 1963 and was incorporated into law in 1969. It defines acts of subversion in such vague terms as to make virtually any political activity punishable as subversion. The first paragraph defines subversion as follows:

Whosoever has carried out an activity with the intention, or evidently with the intention, or which is known, or reasonably considered to be known, as:

a. distorting, stirring up trouble or deflecting the state ideology Pancasila[5] or the course of the state,

b. overthrowing, damaging or undermining state power or the authority of the legal Government or the state apparatus, or

c. spreading feelings of hostility or creating hostility, dissent, conflict, chaos, instability or restlessness within the population or society in general or between the Republic of Indonesia and a friendly state.

The anti-subversion law allows a detainee to be held for up to one year without charge. It is, as one of Indonesia's outstanding human rights lawyers, the late Yap Thiam Hien, once said, 'a peg on which to hang all kinds of charges against a political opponent, even to hang him/her until he/she is dead'.[6] Calls for the repeal of this draconian law have been made since the late 1980s, but it remains on the statute books and prisoners convicted under its provisions are still incarcerated.

The five 'hate-sowing' articles of the criminal code,[7] which are a legacy from the Dutch colonial era, were used extensively during the 'new order' and are still on the statute books. The three most punitive of these laws are Article 134, which allows a maximum sentence of six years for anyone who 'deliberately insults the president or vice-president'; Article 154, which allows a sentence of up to seven years for anyone who 'publicly gives expression to feelings of hostility, hatred or contempt for the Government of the Republic of Indonesia'; and Article 155, which allows a sentence of up to four-and-a-half years for anyone who 'disseminates, displays or hangs out in public words or graphics which express feelings of hostility, hatred or contempt for the Government of Indonesia'. In addition, Articles 106 to 108 of the criminal code, which allow sentences up to life imprisonment for rebellion or taking up arms against the state, have been used on numerous occasions, notably against new order opponents in West Papua, Aceh and East Timor. Prisoners convicted under these articles were also excluded from the releases planned by the Habibie transitional government (1998–99), on the grounds that they had been engaged in acts of violence against the state. Not until Wahid's administration replaced Habibie's, in October 1999, were all political prisoners released. The new Wahid government now also has an opportunity to reform Indonesia's repressive structures and practices.

Political control

Once the PKI and all its associated organizations had been totally destroyed, Sukarno formally removed from power and Suharto appointed president, the 'new order' proceeded to impose control over the remaining political forces. The political parties were required to merge into two officially endorsed parties; one, which became known as the Partai Persatuan Pembangunan (PPP) or United Development Party, was a merger of several Muslim parties while the other, a merger between the nationalist and Christian parties, became known as the Partai Demokratik Indonesia (PDI). Although these two parties had natural constituencies within the population, the electoral system ensured that they never secured more than 30 per cent of the votes between them. Moreover, manipulation of the parties by military intelligence agents always ensured that pliant leaders were chosen at their national conferences. However, state control of the parties was seriously undermined in 1995, when the PDI elected Megawati Sukarnoputri, eldest daughter of the ousted president, Sukarno, as its leader, posing a real threat to Suharto. The regime's operation to remove her led to the first major challenge to the new order's carefully orchestrated political and security structures and led to a clash between the military and Sukarnoputri's supporters on 27 July 1996, over control of the PDI's head office in Jakarta. At least 20 people were killed and scores were arrested during a police assault on the building, as tens of thousands took to the streets in protest.

A third political party, which was never referred to as a 'political party', because politics under the Suharto regime was always seen as 'disreputable', was Golkar or Golongan Karya; this became the state party, whose influence and financial muscle far exceeded those of the emasculated political parties. All government officials and employees automatically became members of Golkar, which also enjoyed the benefit of strong army support during parliamentary elections. Throughout the 'new order', it was the only party permitted, or indeed in a position, to organize the population down to the village level; it achieved this through the presence of local administration officials, on hand to offer inducements and bludgeon villagers into voting correctly. The other two parties were prohibited from establishing branches below the district level, on the grounds that people living in the countryside should be treated as a 'floating mass', undisturbed by political activity, in the interests of promoting the regime's focus on economic development. This three-party system, which was weighted heavily in Golkar's favour, ensured that parliament would always be dominated by the state party, bolstered by representatives of the armed forces in their allocated seats. Parliament was thus little more than a rubber stamp, enacting laws at the government's behest and never initiating legislation of its own. The upper house or MPR consisted of 500 members of parliament plus 500 presidential appointees, charged to elect the president every five years. Suharto claimed that it was never his intention to be appointed president for life, but the system he constructed made certain that he was unfailingly the MPR's unanimous choice – for seven terms, and over 32 years.

In the 1970s, the system came under attack from the student movement. In 1974, thousands of students took to the streets of Jakarta, during a visit by Japanese Prime Minister Tanaka, to protest against the foreign aid programme, rampant corruption and the overall approach to economic development. Dozens of student leaders and human rights activists were arrested and tried, in the first major crackdown of the 'new order'. Four years later, students launched an attack on the regime, in a document known as the *1978 Student White Book*, which was critical of government structures and the concentration of state power in the hands of the president.[8] This time the crackdown was more draconian. Not only were more than 30 student leaders arrested and put on trial, but all student senates were banned, campus organizations were placed under state control, and political activities were outlawed in the universities. With few exceptions, this rendered the students powerless to organize for nearly two decades, until the beginning of 1998, when they emerged to play such a pivotal role in undermining the Suharto dictatorship and forcing him to resign.

In addition to student oppression, a corporatist system was imposed, requiring all sections of society to align themselves in single organizations for students, youth, women, workers and peasants. Freedom of assembly was never given a chance, and all organizations and parties were required to accept the state dogma, Pancasila, as their guiding action principles. The press was subjected to tight state control, and throughout Suharto's tenure in office dozens of media publications and hundreds of books were banned. In 1985, five political laws were enacted which cast in concrete the system of tight political control that had been constructed in the first two decades of the 'new order'. Political activity was limited to the three parties nurtured and endorsed by the state. Legislation was tightly controlled by the state, and all parties and organizations were required to adhere to the Pancasila as their 'sole ideology'. In the run-up to the adoption of these laws, there were rumblings among Muslim preachers, who saw the 'sole ideology' principle as an infringement of their religious freedom. Following an army provocation in a mosque on the outskirts of Jakarta in September 1984, thousands of Muslims – protesting against the arrest of mosque officials – were shot at close range. Hundreds of people were killed in a massacre which, to this day, has not been investigated.[9] Other, smaller massacres of 'aberrant' Muslim communities occurred during the 1980s.

Indonesian expansionism: Military operations in West Papua

West Papua, the western half of the island of New Guinea, was incorporated into the Republic of Indonesia following a 1962 deal, the New York Agreement, which was brokered by a US official acting in the guise of a United Nations diplomat, the Netherlands and Sukarno's Indonesia. After seven months under a UN executive authority, the territory was placed under the administration of Jakarta. Six years later, with the army now in control, an 'act of free choice' on the future of West Papua was staged, but this was not enacted by universal suffrage as provided for in the New York Agreement, but by a council of 1026 hand-picked tribal leaders who were forced virtually at gunpoint to vote unanimously to remain in the republic.

The UN General Assembly gave tacit consent to this flagrant violation of West Papua's right to self-determination, even though the UN mission which had monitored, but not supervised, the event warned that serious human rights violations had surrounded this 'act of free choice'. Since then, indigenous opposition to illegal annexation has smouldered in West Papua, with guerrillas fighting in the bush and numerous attempts at open defiance in the cities, usually by means of unfurling the West Papuan flag. Tens of thousands of West Papuans have been killed in military operations over the years. Untold numbers were killed in operations in the central highlands in 1977–78, when villagers openly defied efforts by local administrators to force them to participate in Indonesia's general elections of 1977. Helicopter gunships were used to strafe villages from the air.[10]

West Papua, known in pre-Wahid Indonesia as its 26th province, Irian Jaya, is hugely valuable to Indonesia as a source of abundant natural resources. The first foreign investment contract concluded by Indonesia following Suharto's rise to power was with the US mining company Freeport-McMoRan, signed in 1967 to exploit the world's richest copper and gold deposits on the southern slopes of the central mountain range in West Papua. The unlawful seizure of tribal lands and the degradation of the environment, so damaging to the local tribes who were driven from their ancestral homes, have been a constant focus of protest by West Papuans and human rights groups, culminating in a New Orleans lawsuit against the company, which is still under consideration. Two reports on human rights violations in the vicinity of the mining company were made public in 1995, documenting the killing of more than three dozen people and drawing attention to the use of Freeport patrol posts, guards and equipment in perpetrating human rights abuses. Following the release of British and Indonesian hostages taken captive by a guerrilla force, the Organization for a Free Papua (OPM), in May 1996, a broad swathe of territory close to the mine was placed under heavy military occupation, forcing villagers to flee their homes. Church investigations, which were not made public until immediately after Suharto's resignation in May 1998, identified yet more killings by troops, whose presence in the area was justified on the grounds of hunting down guerrillas. Following Suharto's resignation, West Papuans have taken to the streets in several cities, affirming their support for an independent country by unfurling the West Papuan flag. Indonesian troops opened fire on flag raisers in Biak on 6 July 1998, killing and injuring several people. The precise number of dead is still under investigation, amid reports of bodies being washed ashore which are believed to be those of people who were removed by force on a naval vessel. Trials of flag raisers are either under way or pending in three cities. The army has condemned all expressions of support for independence as acts of treachery, but this has failed to halt the pressure for the status of West Papua to be fully discussed, and for the circumstances in which West Papua was integrated in 1969 to be investigated as a violation of international law.

Atrocities in Aceh, North Sumatra

Aceh, whose population is devoutly Muslim with a long history of resistance to colonization by the Dutch and opposition to rule from Jakarta, is now emerging from nearly a decade of atrocities. Like West Papua, Aceh is blessed – or cursed – by abundant natural resources, in particular the world's richest onshore reserves of natural gas, making it the most important source of revenue for the central government.[11] The gas is exploited by US-based Mobil Oil and turned into liquefied natural gas for export by PT Arun, a state company in which Mobil Oil holds a significant share. Only a small percentage of the oil revenues is ploughed back into the region, and poverty has persisted for the Acehnese people, living as they do cheek by jowl with a foreign investment enclave which, like Freeport in West Papua, has always enjoyed special protection by the armed forces.

During the 1970s, the Aceh-Sumatra National Liberation Front launched guerrilla activities to assert the region's independence. The movement was largely crushed and scores of activists took refuge in nearby Malaysia, where many of them still live precariously as refugees. The movement re-emerged in the late 1980s, enjoying substantial support from the local population and forcing the army on to the defensive. In May 1990, Aceh's district military commander was quoted as saying that security was vital because there were five major industries in the region. 'We don't want to take any risks since there are many vital projects and many foreign nationals work here,' he said.[12]

In 1991, Suharto gave orders for Aceh to be designated a military operations zone or DOM, and sent in special troops to quell the unrest. Human rights organizations, including Amnesty International, Human Rights Watch and Tapol (the Indonesia Human Rights Campaign), had already reported widespread abuses taking place in Aceh before this new deployment. In December 1990, Tapol called for an international tribunal on crimes against humanity to be convened to investigate the abuses in Aceh. A 1993 (July) Amnesty International report estimated that 2000 civilians, including children and the very elderly, had been killed by the military.[13] However, it was not until after the downfall of Suharto that the true extent of the tragedy came to light. The first to speak out about human rights abuses in Aceh were widows whose husbands had been murdered or disappeared. They also spoke of being raped in front of their children. Local human rights organizations began the gruesome task of collecting data, exhuming bodies and investigating at least a dozen known mass graves. According to one local newspaper, NGOs visiting villages compiled information about 1679 abuses, including rape, torture and disappearances.[14] Confronted by such exposure, the Indonesian armed forces commander-in-chief was forced to make a public apology and declare the end of the DOM, but no military personnel have been charged and army chiefs have caused deep offence by claiming that reports of the scale of the abuses were exaggerated. The legacy of the Suharto regime in Aceh is fierce animosity towards the army, and thus clashes remain likely to erupt at the slightest provocation. One sign of hope for the future, though, was the surprise statement from the new Indonesian president, Abdurrahman Wahid, in October 1999 that Aceh – like East Timor – would be allowed to determine its future through a referendum process.

More bloodshed before Suharto's downfall

The economic crisis which engulfed Indonesia in July 1997 sounded the death knell of the Suharto regime. By that time, pro-democracy forces had already been making their mark on the political scene. In *1992*, the first durable independent trade union, the Indonesian Prosperity Trade Union (SBSI) was set up. In *1994*, shortly after three major publications were banned, journalists established the Independent Alliance of Journalists (AJI). The birth of the People's Democratic Party (PRD), also in 1994, injected an element of radical militancy into the campaign against the Suharto dictatorship, with the party leading a number of mass strikes and helping to mobilize students to support worker and peasant campaigns outside their campuses. The bloody events of 27 July 1996 at the PDI head office, described above, led to a crackdown on the pro-democracy forces, which had been campaigning not only against the regime's attempts to remove Megawati as leader of the PDI, but also for the repeal of the authoritarian political laws of 1985. The economic crisis exposed the Suharto regime to charges of cronyism, collusion and nepotism, practices which had enabled the dictator to build up a huge business empire run by his sons, daughters, grandchildren and others closely associated with the 'first family'. Yet, with public opprobrium becoming more tumultuous and students beginning for the first time in two decades to campaign vigorously against the regime, Suharto nevertheless insisted on having himself re-appointed president by the MPR for a seventh term in March 1998. His decision to appoint a new cabinet which included his eldest daughter, a notorious businesswoman, and other cronies, was met with universal outrage. Students on campuses throughout the country staged daily protests, and were confronted by troops ordered to prevent these disturbances from spilling on to the streets at all costs.

On 12 May 1998, troops opened fire on students as they were returning to their campus at Trisakti University, on the outskirts of Jakarta. Four students were shot dead, bringing the crisis to a head. The next day, riots broke out in the heartland of the capital's Chinese commercial centre and raged for three days. Thousands of business premises were burnt down or looted and around 1200 people died during the unrest. By contrast with their very public actions to suppress demonstrating students, the troops of the Jakarta military command were conspicuous by their absence as the riots gathered pace. It soon became clear that an organized mass rape had occurred and scores of ethnic-Chinese women had been raped by men, many of whom were identified, by their build, tattoo marks or hairstyles as being soldiers. The initial investigation of these events was conducted by Tim Relawan (Team of Volunteers), which concluded that 168 women had been sexually assaulted and raped and in some cases killed. A later investigation undertaken by a joint fact-finding team headed by a leading member of the National Human Rights Commission, which had more limited access to the victims, documented a smaller number of rapes while confirming that gang rapes had occurred. Moreover, it pointed the finger at elements within the armed forces based in Kostrad, the army's strategic command, under the command of Suharto's son-in-law, Major-General Prabowo Subianto. These bloody riots injected an element of racism into the crisis, as thousands of Chinese families fled the country in fear of their safety. There had been a number of earlier incidents on a smaller scale, involving well-organized Muslim crowds, during which Chinese had been targeted and churches burnt down. These incidents, which have continued in the post-Suharto era, are a foretaste of potential future ethnic and religious strife which could seriously undermine the country's infant democracy.

Other killings which have cast a deep shadow over the transition are the unexplained assassinations of more than 200 men who were hunted down and killed by hooded gangs. The targets were traditional healers, some of whom practised black magic, known as *dukun santet*, or traditional Muslim leaders, known as *kyais*, who were mostly members of Indonesia's largest Muslim organization, the Nahdatul Ulama (NU). Most of the murders were committed in East Java and Madura, where the NU is acknowledged as being by far the most influential organization. The murders appear to have been systematic and targeted against people who had been identified in advance, rather than random or spontaneous crimes. The failure of the security forces to halt the killings, which at their height were occurring almost daily, has reinforced the widely held view that military forces were behind the campaign, and that it was probably the brain-child of Suharto loyalists intent on destabilizing the fragile political and economic situation in a region of the country where the economic crisis had hit particularly hard. As with so many such deadly incidents, the *ninja* killings, as they came to be known, have remained unsolved.

The objective of those who instigated the May riots was to create social and ethnic friction, enabling forces close to Suharto to take control of the armed forces in the interests of 'safeguarding stability' and protect the dictator against the groundswell of opposition. These same elements are also believed to have been responsible for the killings of the four Trisakti students a few days earlier, which had triggered the riots. Others within the regime, including the Commander-in-Chief General Wiranto, who had long regarded Prabowo as a rival scheming to take over as commander-in-chief, realized that it was no longer possible to safeguard Suharto's position. As protests mounted relentlessly, Wiranto acted decisively. He issued a threat that he would create a 'Tienanmen' tragedy if plans to hold a 1-million-strong mass meeting in Jakarta on 20 May were not abandoned. The meeting did not take place, but the centre of the capital was placed under siege by heavily armed troops. Later that night, Wiranto took over proceedings at the presidential palace and brokered a transfer of power from Suharto to his Vice-President, B. J. Habibie, on the morning of 21 May, bringing to an end the Suharto new order after more than 32 years. In instigating the transfer of power, Wiranto certainly had his sights on retaining the armed forces' role at the heart of government.

Reformasi under the transitional government

The transitional government of Habibie had little legitimacy outside the circles of those still loyal to the former dictator and the coterie of ministers and bureaucrats who were themselves a hangover from the Suharto period. It fell to the Habibie administration to prepare the way for general elections in June 1999, following which a new MPR would elect a new president before the end of the year. The state organs responsible for the new laws and decrees were the unreconstructed parliament and MPR, in which Golkar held a huge majority. The immediate aftermath of Suharto's downfall was marked by widely reported accounts of atrocities perpetrated by troops under his authority in Aceh and West Papua. Victims and human rights groups have called for the many massacres that occurred during his three decades of rule to be thoroughly investigated and the perpetrators punished. Today the Indonesian press can devote many column inches to the brutal activities of the army unlike when limitations were imposed on their reporting under the 'new order' regime. The military's reputation is now in tatters, forcing it to define a new role for itself, and even accept a gradual and eventual diminution of its *dwifungsi*, albeit of course on its own terms.

One case of abuse that did become the subject of investigation was the abduction of 23 pro-democracy activists during the final months before Suharto's downfall. These disappearances were widely reported, especially following the re-emergence in April 1998 of one of the abductees who publicly denounced his torturers and took his complaint to Washington for a congressional hearing. Altogether, nine of the abductees have re-emerged and a tenth was found dead, but the 13 others remain unaccounted for. Persistent pressure from the families of the victims compelled the army to conduct an investigation which led to the *honourable* dismissal from the army of Major-General Prabowo who, as commander of the élite corps Kopassus and later of Kostrad, under whose command the élite corps mostly operated, accepted responsibility for the abductions without admitting authorization. In December 1998, 11 lower- and middle-ranking Kopassus officers went on trial for the abductions before a military court – accused not of torture and the violation of people's personal freedom, but of committing 'procedural errors'. The indictment asserted that they had acted on their own initiative and as 'a matter of conscience' to protect the state from elements whom they regarded as a threat to the regime. Human rights lawyers have condemned the trial as a sham, effectively closing the door to the indictment of the responsible senior officers, first and foremost Prabowo. It also means that, as with all atrocities throughout the Suharto dictatorship, top-ranking army officers are likely to continue to enjoy impunity. Meanwhile Prabowo, who was not charged, fled the country several months before the trial opened. He took refuge in Jordan under the protection of the late King Hussein, out of the reach of justice in his own country or the accountability of international law.[15]

Another legacy inherited by the Wahid government from the 'new order' was the continued incarceration of hundreds of political prisoners, convicted under Suharto for subversion, spreading hatred or rebellion. Releases were sporadic under Habibie and designed to impress the international community of the *reformasi* credentials of the new administration. The release programme was vetted by a special cabinet committee, headed by a representative of ABRI, and the justice minister announced that the programme would exclude the ten 1965 'PKI' prisoners and those who have acted to undermine the state ideology and committed acts of violence. Some prisoners, like the woman trade union activist Dita Indah Sari (a *cause célèbre* internationally), were offered release on condition that they give a pledge not to get involved in political activity, which she refused to do. In order for there to be a complete break from the past, the release programme needed to be non-discriminatory and unconditional, allowing all the incarcerated victims of the Suharto regime to go free. The continued incarceration of the ten elderly 'PKI' prisoners could only be explained in terms of keeping alive the communist bogey, whose violent destruction provided Suharto's 'new order' with its claim to 'legitimacy'. Over the years, hundreds of those convicted for alleged involvement in the events of 1 October 1965 have been released, while some who were given death sentences had them commuted to life and were eventually released. Ideally, if *reformasi* was indeed genuine, the Habibie administration should have moved to free these ten remaining prisoners as a long-overdue humanitarian gesture, but the armed forces were determined not to allow this to happen, as their own legitimacy is too intricately bound up with the lengths to which they went, under Suharto's instructions, to destroy the PKI.

Preparing for new elections

When the MPR held its first post-Suharto session in November 1998, tens of thousands of students went on the streets in Jakarta and other cities, condemning the session as a charade and calling for an end to the armed forces' *dwifungsi*, and for Suharto to be tried for corruption and his many political crimes. In preparation for the demonstrations, General Wiranto announced that, in addition to his 40,000 troops, he would recruit 125,000 civilian vigilantes, armed with sharpened bamboo spears, to protect the session against disruption. This did little to cool the students' militancy. During the four days of the meeting, students were repeatedly blocked in their attempts to get near the MPR building. On the final day, thousands were pushed back to the clover-leaf bridge overlooking Atma Jaya University, where they were attacked by water cannon and tear gas. When the students refused to disperse, troops launched a ferocious attack; the sound of gunfire rang out and continued intermittently for seven hours, during which live ammunition was used as well as rubber bullets. By the end of the day, which has since become known as Black Friday, seven students had been shot dead and hundreds wounded. Some of the vigilantes were also killed during scuffles with local residents in several parts of the city. The demonstrations helped to expose the illegitimacy of the MPR, which had spent four days – at huge government expense – producing virtually nothing of any note. In the first six months of the Habibie government, it became clear that the banner of *reformasi* had been kept alive by the student movement. The studented believe they had initiated the process of political reform, so it was also their movement which should complete it.

The task of drafting new laws on political parties and the elections was in the hands of a parliament which was itself elected under laws enacted in

1985, which did not augur well for the conduct of free and fair elections. The legislation on political parties made it impossible for parties representing special-interest groups, such as the ethnic Chinese, to obtain official recognition. Parties whose constituency of support exists only in certain parts of the country, such as West Papua, fell foul of a rule requiring all parties to have branches in at least one-third of the 27 provinces and half of the administrative districts. Leaders of most of the emerging political parties suspected that parliament would succeed in concocting a law benefiting Golkar, the party whose chairman, Akbar Tandjung, was state secretary and a close associate of President Habibie. The leading opposition parties, which were contenders for substantial electoral support, had no say in the law-making process and were naturally mistrustful of the outcome, but they were unable to secure a more representative governing body to take Indonesia through the transitional stage to elections in its advance towards democracy.

Meanwhile, the economic crisis has continued to worsen. At the end of 1998, experts were predicting that 140 million Indonesians would be destitute by the millennium. The Indonesian economy contracted by 15 per cent during 1998 and by a further 5 per cent in 1999. Indonesia already ranks as the world's most indebted country. On top of the $55 billion public debt and the $80 billion private debt has come credit under the International Monetary Fund's (IMF) 'rescue' package of $43 billion and, at the end of 1998, government sources announced that they would be seeking financial assistance of $10 billion from Indonesia's Western creditors in 1999. Inflation reached a crippling 80 per cent by the end of 1998.

In all parts of the country there have been rice riots, protests by farmers against the exorbitant price of fertilizers, by truck drivers unable to purchase essential spare parts, and by people driven by desperation to feed their families. Making capital out of this desperate poverty, forces believed to be close to or financed by the ousted dictator and his family provoked inter-religious and inter-ethnic conflict. An incident in Jakarta on 22 November 1998, during which Muslim mobs attacked Ambonese simply because they were Christian, and then went on the rampage, burning down two dozen churches, provoked Christians in West Timor into attacking mosques. Local disputes erupting into violence are happening on an almost daily basis. A continuation of this state of unrest will undoubtedly threaten the fledgling democracy throughout the archipelago.

Building democracy in Indonesia

There is a deep sense of anger throughout Indonesia at the brutalities and venality of the Suharto dictatorship, and the period since his downfall has seen an outpouring of this anger as reports of the years of widespread injustices and corruption have filled the pages of newspapers. Demands for the dictator to be tried for his many crimes have been overwhelming, but the transitional government included many of his loyal cronies and business associates, not least his successor, Habibie. They knew very well that putting Suharto on trial for corruption could also drag them into the morass, as prime beneficiaries of the deals that were concluded by presidential approval. The students, who pressed on with their demonstrations against the Habibie government following the disastrous MPR session, also placed great emphasis on the demand for the former dictator to go on trial. Efforts to take their demonstrations to the ex-dictator's residence were held back by units of combat troops. But such has been the public outcry that Habibie's attorney-general, himself a Suharto loyalist, was forced to initiate proceedings, though refrained from laying formal charges or even summoning Suharto for questioning as a possible suspect. But punishing Suharto for his crimes against humanity is even more important for the Indonesian nation and for the people of East Timor. Pressure for this will need to come from the international community, as well as from the people of Indonesia and East Timor. One of the tests for the new democratic Indonesia will be its ability to try the man who has done so much harm to the country and its people.

The Habibie transitional administration agreed – under intense international diplomatic pressure – to hold free elections in Indonesia which would inexorably lead to its own dissolution. In October 1999, the MPR elected the Muslim leader Abdurrahman Wahid as the new president of Indonesia and he selected as his vice-president, Megawati Sukarnoputri, the defeated leader of the PDI (See Chapter 14). This infant democracy has much to contend with given the social and economic turmoil which was Sahurto's legacy to his nation. The military remains a potent and dangerous player in the political scene although Wahid impressed many with his dismissal of the discredited General Wiranto from his cabinet following revelations of human rights abuses perpetrared by troops commanded by Wiranto in East Timor.

Without doubt, the military itself is now low on morale and has faced ever growing demands on reform and an end to impunity. Nevertheless, the new democratic movements which emerged in Indonesia from the shadow of Suharto's dictatorship will be conscious of the threat of a resort to military rule. For more than three decades, Indonesia has been one of the most militarized countries in the world and now requires the full support of regional allies and the international community to ensure that its first tentative steps to democracy can be sustained and herald a new beginning for a troubled country.

References

1 van Langenberg, Michael, 'Gestapo and state power' in Cribb, Robert (ed.), *The Indonesian Killings 1965–1966*, Monash Papers on Southeast Asia, No. 21, 1990.

2 Kolko, Gabriel, *Confronting the Third World, United States Foreign Policy 1945–1980* (New York, 1994, Pantheon Books), Chapter 14; Curtis, Mark, 'Democratic genocide', *The Ecologist*, September/October 1996; Lashmar, Paul and Oliver, James, 'Indonesia: Prelude to the slaughter' in *Britain's Secret Propaganda War* (Stroud, 1998, Sutton).

3 Reston, James, 'A gleam of light in Asia', *New York Times*, 19 June 1966. In an article entitled 'Elated US officials looking to new aid to Indonesian economy' in the *New York Times*, 12 March 1966, Max Frankel writes: 'The Johnson Administration found it difficult to hide its delight with the news from Indonesia, pointing to the demise of President Sukarno and the Communist Party.'

4 The ABRI (Angkatan Bersenjata Republik Indonesia – the Armed Forces of Indonesia) were separated from Polri (the Indonesian police force) on 1 April 1999 and subsequently renamed Tentara Nasional Indonesia (TNI). Despite this restructuring within the Indonesian security forces, Polri remains under the control of the commander-in-chief of the TNI. For further details on the new military structures, see *Tapol Bulletin*, No. 154/155, November 1999.

5 Pancasila embodies five principles: belief in one God, humanitarianism, national unity, democracy and social justice. Under Suharto's rule criticism of or deviation from the ideology of Pancasila was punishable by law. For further information, see *Power and Impunity: Human Rights Under the New Order* (London, 1994, Amnesty International), pp. 20–21.

6 TEMPO, 12 August 1978, quoted in *Tapol Bulletin*, No. 30, October 1978, p. 5.

7 For more on the hate-sowing articles and the Indonesian legal system, see Chapter 3, 'Law and impunity', in Amnesty International, *Power and Impunity*, pp. 36–48.

8 See supplement to *Tapol Bulletin*, No. 30, October 1978.

9 See Tapol, 'Indonesia, Muslims on trial' (London, April 1987) for an analysis of this event and the hundreds of trials that occurred at the time.

10 See Tapol, 'West Papua, the obliteration of a people' (London, 1988).

11 *Business Week*, 28 December 1998.

12 *Jakarta Post*, 14 May 1990.

13 See Amnesty International, *Indonesia: 'Shock Therapy', Restoring Order in Aceh, 1989–1993* (London, 1993, Amnesty International).

14 *Searmbi Indonesia*, 29 July 1998.

15 *Tapol Bulletin*, No. 151, March 1999.

6

The Indonesian Propaganda War against East Timor[1]

Estêvão Cabral

There is not a shred of truth in the Indonesian version of events... East Timor was an undefended sitting duck for the expansionist Indonesian generals. A slaughter of tens of thousands followed, but little factual reporting on the bloodiest atrocities left the island; the Indonesians made sure of that, effectively blockading East Timor, cutting off communications, turning back journalists and Western observers, terrorizing the population and lying to the world about it, as now.[2]

Introduction

From 1975–99, the Indonesian regime made massive use of propaganda in the war against East Timor. The early propaganda campaigns have been well documented.[3] Solidarity groups working with the East Timorese resistance movement in different parts of the world have built up substantial records of Indonesian propaganda activities and have provided detailed accounts of these in publications such as the *Tapol Bulletin*, *Timor Link*, *Timor Leste*, *A Paz é Possível em Timor Leste*, *Network News* and *East Timor Estafeta*. In addition, we have penetrating analyses of the collusion and cover-up in the North American and Australian media.[4] There is also some relatively recent writing on the themes which recur in reports by the official Indonesian news and press agency, Antara, and in official government documents.[5]

My aim in this chapter is to add to this growing body of knowledge about Indonesian propaganda. In the first section, I will briefly survey the channels of communication that the Indonesian government and its secret service have used since 1975 to disseminate their version of political and military events. In the second section, I will look at the themes which recurred in official Indonesian discourse about East Timor, building on the work by Matsuno.[6] In the third section, I will examine specific tactics employed by the Indonesian regime in their propaganda up to the overthrow of Suharto in May 1998. Then, in the last section, I will present a detailed analysis of one piece of Indonesian propaganda, arguing that close textual analysis can provide particularly revealing insights into Indonesian propaganda strategies.

Indonesian propaganda: Past and present

Inside East Timor before the Indonesian invasion

The first extensive use of propaganda in the war against East Timor by the Indonesian government and its secret service was through an operation code-named Operasi Komodo.[7] The aim was to destabilize East Timor in the lead up to the first elections to be held in the territory. The Indonesian secret service began by using radio broadcasts. A radio station was set up in West Timor called Radio Ramelau;[8] the broadcasters were East Timorese supporters of Indonesian expansionist ambitions. Taylor reports that Bakin, the Indonesian intelligence service, had already begun training East Timorese radio broadcasters even before the 1974 events in Lisbon.[9] These broadcasts were dominated by grossly misleading propaganda about the political goals of Frente Revolucionária do Timor-Leste Independente (Fretilin),[10] and by threats directed at Fretilin leaders and their supporters.

By using radio broadcasts, the Indonesians wanted to reach as wide an audience as possible. However, this kind of propaganda had little or no impact at all. There were two main reasons for this. Firstly, only about 10 per cent of the East Timorese population had a radio at the time, and those who did have access to a radio were already supporters of União Democrática Timorense (UDT)[11] or Fretilin and other small political parties. Secondly, the languages spoken during the broadcasts were Tetum and Portuguese. Tetum is a lingua franca which is now widely used among the East Timorese, but the proportion of the East Timorese population who spoke Tetum at that time was under 50 per cent, while only 15 to 20 per cent (including pupils at primary school) spoke Portuguese. Moreover, political terminology had still not been developed in Tetum, so Portuguese terms had to be used to express certain meanings such as 'independence', 'democracy' and 'liberty'. This meant there was limited understanding by the majority of East Timorese targeted by the propaganda.

The Indonesian secret service also distributed leaflets; again, the main target was Fretilin. Some leaflets represented the Fretilin 'threat' in a dramatic image of a hand with long nails alongside a hammer and sickle. The purpose was to evoke an image which would be disturbing to the small but powerful Catholic minority in East Timor, portraying Fretilin as a communist 'devil'. However, again the propaganda strategy misfired. The Indonesian agents seemed to have forgotten two things: firstly, the image of a hand with long nails, the image of a devil, did not affect many ordinary East Timorese, because in the mid-1970s most East Timorese were still animists. Those who were Catholic were already members of Fretilin or one of the other political parties. The main reason why people supported Fretilin was because it was fighting for independence: this was the main objective, not the spread of communism. Secondly, the hammer and sickle would have no meaning at all to the vast majority of East Timorese, who did not know what this symbol represented and knew nothing about communism.

Before and after the invasion in Indonesia: misinformation and censorship

Bakin and certain elements within the Indonesian military were also planting articles in the Indonesian press in the lead-up to the invasion of East Timor. Their aim was to impose a definition of events in East Timor which would eventually justify a full-scale invasion. One newspaper in particular, *Berita Yudha*, served as a mouthpiece for the military. According to Taylor, an article published in this newspaper in August 1975 made a deliberately false claim about ASDT[12]/Fretilin 'seeking Communist support'.[13]

Conflict generated as a result of the covert cross-border incursions by the Indonesian military and the activities of the Operasi Komodo were represented in the Indonesian press as evidence of increasing political turmoil and upheaval in East Timor. False reports were also made about Fretilin. Taylor points out that Antara reported in September 1975 that Fretilin forces had killed seven villagers in West Timor in a cross-border attack.[14] No such cross-border incursion had in fact taken place. However, this report caused considerable anger and apprehension in West Timor and Indonesia, and contributed to the image of Fretilin as a threat to the security of the Indonesian nation. Antara and some daily newspapers, such as *Sinar Harapan*, also made regular reports about 'military successes' by the UDT and Associação Popular Democrática Timorense (Apodeti),[15] with the help of some 'volunteers'.[16]

The Indonesian media was heavily censored before, during and after the invasion. It was therefore very difficult for ordinary Indonesians to receive any accurate information about the situation in East Timor, and this remained a problem until the fall of Suharto in May 1998. There were occasional attempts to address the East Timor issue in the Indonesian media, but the government reaction to this was very heavy-handed. There are more Indonesians speaking out critically, and able to do so, in the post-Suharto era.

Over 23 years later: Indonesian propaganda and censorship in the 1990s

The Indonesian propaganda machine has operated in different ways during the 24 year illegal occupation of East Timor. This section describes some of the ways in which the Indonesian regime has disseminated its version of events and identifies some of the channels used. The focus is on the period from 1975 to May 1998.

The Indonesian government line on East Timor was most obviously reported through official sources such as Antara, foreign ministry pamphlets and official newsletters disseminated through local embassies (see Table 6.1 for details).

In addition, articles were regularly planted in the South-East Asian and Western press by Indonesian government officials or embassy staff. For example, one former member of the London embassy staff, Dino Patti Djalal, often sent in pieces to the *Jakarta Post*, an English-language daily produced in Jakarta. However, when these pieces were published no reference was made to the fact that he was an Indonesian government representative. In contrast, the former Director of Foreign Information at the Indonesian Department of Foreign Affairs, Irawan Abidin, placed his own signed articles in the press. Take, for instance, the article from the '5th Column' of the *Far Eastern Economic Review* (*FEER*), which is analysed later in this chapter. This was written by Irawan Abidin. Before this, Abidin had also written an article accusing Amnesty International of 'waging a political campaign' against Indonesia.[17]

Another approach the Indonesians adopted over the years was to encourage journalists, former diplomats, politicians and members of the clergy to write articles for newspapers and magazines presenting an Indonesian point of view. The encouragement offered by Indonesian officials to such apologists for the regime sometimes took the form of an invitation to visit Indonesia (and usually East Timor), with all expenses paid. People who have received this kind of encouragement include Patrick Nicholls, the British Conservative MP,[18] two Ulster Unionist MPs, Roy Beggs and Cecil Walker, and Thomas Michel, a prominent Jesuit and secretary to the Conference of Asian Bishops in Thailand. Former diplomats and academics have also written articles in the press which clearly echoed the usual Indonesian account of the situation in East Timor. These include Gough Whitlam, the former Australian Prime Minister,[19] Edward Masters, former US ambassador to Indonesia,[20] and Billveer Singh, a Singaporean academic.[21]

The Indonesian authorities also staged media events, using television as a medium. The most striking example of this kind of orchestration of the media came with the arrest of Xanana Gusmão on 20 November 1992. A week after his arrest, an 'interview' with him was staged on Indonesian television (with Abílio Osório, the Indonesian-appointed governor of East Timor, as interpreter) in which Xanana appeared to be 'renouncing' the struggle. The Indonesian government also tried to make a lot of mileage out of the coverage of Gusmão's 'trial'.

Another strategy was the use of a small number of East Timorese people to make public statements sympathetic to the Indonesian position on East Timor. One example of this was the statement made by Paulino Gama at the UN Sub-Commission on Human Rights in Vienna in June 1993.[22] Since then, the Indonesian regime has been represented at the Geneva meeting every year to counter statements made by members of the East Timorese resistance.

For many years, few people in Indonesia were willing to speak out about the situation in East Timor, since there were huge risks involved. Those who did speak out were often threatened. Some Indonesian academics, like George Aditjondro, consistently contested the official Indonesian government line on East Timor.[23] Indonesian journalists have had few opportunities to report accurately on the situation in East Timor because of the heavy censorship. The press has often been under strong attack in Indonesia: two major main newspapers and a news magazine, *Tempo*, *De Tik* and *Editor*, were closed down in mid-1994.

Recurring themes in Indonesian propaganda

Matsuno has provided a penetrating analysis of Indonesian propaganda about East Timor. He identified four recurring themes in this propaganda:

* communist phobia
* paternalism and an attitude of 'they don't know what they are doing'
* insistence on 'development' rather than self-determination
* preoccupation with the 'disintegration' of Indonesia.

Matsuno has shown how these themes have been articulated in different types of political texts in Indonesia. He has noted, too, that they were also taken up in the Western press.[24] One other common theme of the Indonesian propaganda needs to be added to those already identified by Matsuno: obsession with 'foreign' intervention. All five of these themes are discussed below.

Communist phobia

Communist phobia was a central theme in the Bakin-organized propaganda inside East Timor in the 1974–75 period, particularly in radio broadcasts and leaflets. This phobia featured prominently in the Indonesian media and in official government discourse: all those who were opposed to the Indonesian presence in East Timor were regarded as supporters of Fretilin, and therefore 'communist revolutionaries' and a threat to the existing political order. Xanana Gusmão was still identified with Fretilin even after he left it in 1986. He was referred to by the Indonesians, and by many foreign journalists, as the Fretilin leader and not as the leader of the Conselho Nacional da Resistência Maubere (CNRM).[25] Linking Gusmão with Fretilin served as a powerful propaganda tactic because, as Matsuno points out, in this way the Indonesian government was trying 'to conceal the development of East Timorese nationalism, and the fact that the leadership of the Resistance is no longer a political party but an umbrella organization'.[26]

Paternalism

Matsuno points out that in Indonesian media reports East Timor was often referred to as the 'youngest-child' province (*propinsi bungsu*) or the 'youngest' province (*propinsi termuda*) of Indonesia. The implication of this family metaphor was that the government in Jakarta was the adult or parent, with the main responsibility for the territory. This paternalistic discourse has been particularly evident in media treatment of the young people involved in the resistance inside East Timor. Take, for example, an article cited by Matsuno which appeared in the Indonesian news magazine *Tempo* on 30 November 1991. In this article, the young people who risked their lives in a peaceful demonstration against Indonesian rule just before the Santa Cruz massacre of November 1991 are described as 'easily mobilized' and as 'bravely expressing what has become troubles in their thoughts'. The journalist then claimed that the troubled 'thoughts' of the young people were due to the influence of 'former activists' and 'foreign radio broadcasts which tend to be anti-integration'.[27]

'Development' rather than self-determination

In the discourse of the Indonesian regime, at least until recently, the idea of self-determination was out of the question. Officials of the Suharto regime repeatedly argued that the East Timorese were at last enjoying some 'development', and claimed that East Timor was underdeveloped under Portuguese colonial rule. They appealed to the international community, using 'statistics' and pointing to the 'development' undertaken by the Indonesian government. This is a common theme in pieces written by outside 'observers' such as Thomas Michel and Edward Masters (see Table 6.1).

The 'disintegration' of Indonesia

Another recurring theme in Indonesian nationalist discourse is that the invasion of East Timor involved the 'return' of the territory to a wider community with shared cultural and linguistic identity. In official government discourse, there were references to myths about a pre-colonial empire which united all the islands in the so-called Nusantara archipelago. The great 'project' of the Indonesian republic was seen as the 'reunification' of the archipelago, and thus any opposition to 'integration' was seen as a direct threat to the Indonesian nation.

As Matsuno notes:

> The 'integration' rhetoric is produced and consumed, consciously or unconsciously, through government documents and mass media, by Indonesians and non-Indonesians. At the bottom of the rhetoric lies a grammar which enables those who share it to understand what is meant and implied. Ultimately this amounts to a shared illusion. But this illusion is powerful and indeed had become an obsession in Indonesian élite thought.[28]

With the Indonesian military and administration withdrawing from East Timor following the August 1999 referendum (see Chapter 14), the threat and fear of Indonesian national disintegration are all the more potent.

Obsession with 'foreign propaganda' and 'interference'

The word 'foreign' in Indonesian official discourse means anyone who is not Indonesian or East Timorese. This included the Portuguese government (recognized by the United Nations as the administering power). It also included other governments and international bodies such as the UN. But the main preoccupation in Indonesian political discourse has been with 'interference' in the affairs of East Timor by non-governmental organizations (NGOs) and solidarity groups working with the East Timorese resistance front. Some of these groups, and even associated individuals, have been singled out for repeated propaganda attacks (see list of articles in Table 6.1).

Propaganda tactics used by the Indonesian regime

A common propaganda strategy was to launch attacks against individual leaders, such as Xanana Gusmão and José Ramos-Horta, the deputy president of the CNRT, to undermine their authority and credibility. I will mention just two examples of this. First, a few weeks after Xanana Gusmão's capture on 20 November 1992, the Indonesian newspaper controlled by the military ran an article on him which was a poorly disguised attempt at character assassination. In the article, Gusmão was accused of raping a young woman and killing innocent people. The article went on to say that he was threatening the family hiding him before he was arrested. However, some months later, a letter from East Timorese women, dated 10 January 1993 and entitled 'The Timorese women scream out to the world for help',[29] provided evidence that the newspaper's allegations were pure fabrication and that the young woman named in the article was raped by Indonesian soldiers. The second example arose with the award of the Nobel Peace Prize to Bishop Belo and José Ramos-Horta. Very soon after the announcement of the award, Ramos-Horta was described by Ali Alatas, the Indonesian Foreign Minister, as a 'political adventurist'. This remark was followed by a number of other slurs on his character and his political work.

In addition to these attacks on the character and reputation of East Timorese leaders, the Indonesian regime also tried to undermine their authority by misrepresenting what they said or wrote. The propagandist article examined next goes even further and refutes the authenticity of letters and audio-tapes sent out of prison by Xanana Gusmão.

After 1975, the Indonesian propaganda machine continued to produce distorted versions of political and military events in East Timor. It is instructive to see the lengths the Indonesian state was prepared to go in constructing a propaganda line. The tactics varied from the complete omission and recasting of terms used by the East Timorese resistance to total misrepresentation. The Suharto regime was also preoccupied with numbers games. It refuted and/or distorted the numbers of people killed during and after the invasion of 1975 – this distortion recurs in several of the sources listed in Table 6.1. As already intimated, official Indonesian publications also produced statistics about the 'facts' of 'development' in East Timor since the Indonesian takeover: the most common statistics were about how many roads were built, how many schools and hospitals and so on. These statistics were then reproduced by external supporters of the regime (see articles by Thomas Michel and Edward Masters in Table 6.1).

An analysis of a sample of Indonesian propaganda

The text selected for analysis[30]

Ideally, a study of the Indonesian use of propaganda in the war against East Timor should be based on a comprehensive series of texts from different moments since the invasion in 1975. However, this is beyond the scope of this chapter. Here, I will examine one text in detail: an article about Xanana Gusmão which appeared in the '5th Column' of the *FEER* in August 1995. As indicated earlier, it was written by Irawan Abidin of the

Indonesian Department of Foreign Affairs. This article has been chosen because it refers to historical events and assumes a lot of (readership) knowledge about the history of the East Timorese struggle.

Based in Hong Kong, the *FEER* is a news magazine which is widely circulated in East Asia, South-East Asia and elsewhere in the world. The readership is mostly the business and political élite in the region. The '5th Column' of the *FEER* is designed as a forum for debate and it is common for people who are prominent in politics in South-East Asia to write pieces for this column. In July 1995, the *FEER* published an article by José Ramos-Horta which was critical of Ali Alatas, the Indonesian Minister for Foreign Affairs. The Indonesian government's response to Ramos-Horta's article was published on 3 August 1995. This article was not a direct reply to Ramos-Horta, but instead the Indonesians used the facility to launch an attack on Xanana Gusmão.

The article focused on foreign media reports about messages, letters and answers to interview questions sent out of Cipinang prison, Jakarta, by Gusmão. As a piece of propaganda, the article did two things: firstly, it claimed that the media reports about Xanana Gusmão's messages from his prison cell were 'fabrications'; and secondly, it constructed particular images of him as a previously dangerous revolutionary, someone who had renounced violence and 'fiery' political statements (see line 134) and who was serving a sentence for 'common crimes'. As illustrated earlier, this was not the first time that the Indonesian government had launched attacks on Gusmão through the media.

The attack on the foreign media for their reports of Gusmão's messages and letters from Cipinang coincided with the cancellation of a three-month reduction in his prison sentence of 20 years. In fact, the imprisoned leader had been so successful in sending letters, messages and statements to the UN out of prison, in his own handwriting, that this had become an acute embarrassment to the Indonesian regime. There is ample evidence available to demonstrate that the article by Abidin was itself a complete fabrication. It is nevertheless an intriguing example of Indonesian shadow puppetry.

The 5th Column article: a critical analysis

This article provides a good illustration of two of the five themes which have recurred in Indonesian propaganda: obsession with 'foreign propaganda' and 'interference'; and preoccupation with the Fretilin 'threat' (and, by implication, the 'communist threat' and the threat of 'rebellion' against the existing political order). The article is organized into three simple narratives, which are described below. Narrative serves as a powerful genre in propaganda for presenting selected versions of events. The first theme is most prominent in the first narrative. The anti-Fretilin rhetoric is more prominent in the second narrative.

Abidin's article also provided evidence of two propaganda tactics adopted by the Indonesian government and its secret services: launching attacks on individual East Timorese to undermine their authority; and misrepresentation and distortion.

As indicated earlier, one of the main aims of this piece of propaganda was to cast doubt on the authenticity of the letters and taped messages sent out of prison by Gusmão. This is the first propaganda line pursued in the article. The foreign media reports based on Gusmão's messages are described as 'falsifications' (following the sub-heading which appears in the middle of the page).

The first narrative is developed by means of a blow-by-blow account of different media uses of Gusmão's texts and tapes. The Portuguese media is singled out for particular attention here. The narrative is presented, in simple declarative form, as a set of 'facts' about a series of media events (and what Abidin claims to be the strategic timing of these events). The use of the narrative genre is actually brought to the foreground when Abidin says (line 48) 'The story does not end here.'.

Interspersed in this narrative are wordings which echo, over and over again, the notion of 'fabrication'. The idea of misreporting or making false claims is repeated in different ways to build a chain of related meanings from line 9 onwards: 'supposed to have asked' (line 9); 'propaganda capital' (line 18); 'foisted upon the world as having been written' (lines 19–20); 'purported' (line 29); 'surface' (line 33); 'supposed' (line 43); 'claimed to have obtained' (line 52); 'again we hear' (line 59); 'if you believe the propaganda' (lines 102–103); 'single-handed political propaganda campaign' (lines 109–110); 'unmask the most clever mimic' (line 130); and 'exposed as a fabrication' (lines 136–137). Particularly striking is the insistence on the description of foreign media accounts as 'propaganda', with the implication that this article is an honest account, an exposé: another layer of misrepresentation, given that this article is actually a piece of planned propaganda.

The attack on Gusmão takes several forms throughout the article; it is most prominent in the second and third narratives. In the second narrative, the attack on him is tied up with a distorted account of the East Timorese struggle against the Indonesian occupation. In addition to these two narratives, there is an attempt to undermine the captured leader's authority by distorting his words.

The second narrative firstly gives a brief and slanted account of Gusmão's life in narrative form in response to the question in the title of the article: 'Who is Xanana Gusmão?'. This question is reiterated in the text at line 65 just before the narrative begins.

There are several distortions in the second narrative, of which four are worthy of mention. Firstly, the so-called 'integration' with Indonesia is represented as a peaceful political process; there is no reference to the fact that East Timor was invaded and occupied by Indonesian troops in 1975. This occupation was repeatedly condemned by the UN. Secondly, no mention is made of the massive violence which has perpetrated by the Indonesian army in East Timor. However, Fretilin is represented as a dangerous group of people 'with violent ways' (line 89). Thirdly, Abidin is keen to mention that 'Xanana Gusmão assumed leadership of the rebellion' (line 93), but does not mention what he was 'rebelling' against. This has the effect of suggesting that Gusmão and Forças Armadas da Libertação Nacional de Timor-Leste (Falintil)[31] attempted to disrupt an established political order rather than resisting the occupation of their country. Fourthly, Abidin fails to mention anywhere that Gusmão left Fretilin in 1986 to become the chair of the CNRM while continuing as commander of Falintil. The absence of this point is very significant. The Indonesian regime continually refused to accept that a broad resistance front had emerged, showing that this was a national struggle for self-determination and not a Fretilin-led 'rebellion'. Matsuno showed this to be a common ploy in Indonesian propaganda.[32]

In addition to the glaring absences in this narrative account of Gusmão's life, there are major distortions in the account of specific events. Take, for example, the phrase: 'Even after the political exercise which saw the overwhelming majority of the East Timorese people choose independence through integration with Indonesia' (line 85). This statement is a crude distortion of East Timorese history. In fact, until August 1999 the East Timorese had no opportunity to engage in any democratic process of this kind. The event referred to here is the so-called Balibo Declaration. A secret document was prepared by the Indonesian intelligence service in a hotel in Bali, Indonesia. They obliged the leadership of the UDT, Apodeti, Klíbur Oan Timur Assuaín (KOTA)[33] and Trabalhista[34] to sign this at gunpoint. The fake declaration was coined the 'Balibohong Declaration' by Gusmão, using the Indonesian words for 'Bali lie declaration'.[35]

Here and elsewhere in the text, there are phrases which clearly articulated the Indonesian political stance on East Timor, such as 'independence through integration'. Indonesian communist phobia is also evident in the references to the Mozambican and Angolan independence struggles in the words 'copied the agenda' (lines 16 and 76–77). In fact, the concepts of 'rebellion' (line 94) or 'revolution' (lines 122 and 124) occur with particular frequency in this text. The terms 'rebel' (line 141) and 'rebel leader' (line 55) are also used. Note also the reference to the Portuguese 'Flower Revolution' (actually Carnation Revolution) and the use of the full name of Fretilin, highlighting the word 'revolutionary' in the name of the party.

Another way in which Abidin distorts the account of the East Timorese resistance to the Indonesian occupation and Gusmão's role in this is by obscuring the people who were responsible for particular actions. To draw attention to two places in the text where there is no clear reference to the perpetrator of an action, take, for example, the words 'Lobato, chairman of the armed wing of Fretilin, was killed back in December 1978...'. There is no mention here of who killed Lobato. In fact, Indonesian troops killed him on 31 December 1978. Secondly, Abidin says (in lines 94–97) that '...he [Gusmão] was arrested in 1992. He has since been tried... sentenced to life imprisonment'. Again, there is no mention of who sentenced Gusmão and under which laws he was tried and by whom.

A third and rather brief narrative appears towards the end of the article. It also revolves around Gusmão, but this time (in answer to the question in the title, 'Who is Xanana Gusmão?') he is portrayed as 'an inmate in Cipinang Prison' who has been 'convicted of common crimes'. There is also a rather sinister account of an 'interview with prison authorities', where Gusmão is purported to have denied that he had written letters attributed to him in recent media reports. The way this incident is described suggests that it was likely to have been an interrogation rather than an 'interview'. The aim of the writer in this final narrative is clearly to undermine Gusmão's status as a symbol of the East Timorese resistance to Indonesian rule.

The article also targets the voice of Gusmão, both his spoken and written words, as part of the broader project of undermining his authority. In the first part of the article (the first narrative), when Abidin is referring to media reports about messages produced by Gusmão, he represents the latter's voice in those messages. The wording of the indirect speech here portrays Gusmão as a hard hitting resistance leader. Take, for example, lines 44–45, where Gusmão is described as 'lashing out against Indonesia's military presence' or line 46, where he is portrayed as 'predicting the ultimate triumph of the ... resistance'.

The representation of Gusmão's voice here contrasts sharply with the way it is represented in the third and final narrative. As indicated above, in this narrative Gusmão, the prisoner, is alleged to have made a statement to the prison authorities denying he sent out any messages from Cipinang. No mention is made of the language that Gusmão used to make these statements, but it is likely to have been Portuguese, the language he writes in most often. (He only began learning Bahasa Indonesia during his imprisonment.) Since it is unlikely that Gusmão made written statements voluntarily saying that others were writing on his behalf, the only possible interpretation here is that the 'interview with the prison authorities' – the context in which Gusmão's statements were made – was less an 'interview' than a forcibly extracted statement.

In the penultimate paragraph, Abidin makes the contrast between the two representations of Gusmão's voice quite explicit. He says 'the real Xanana Gusmão has spoken and his message is not a political exhortation but a denial that he ever made any of the fiery statements attributed to him' (lines 131–135). For 'the real Xanana Gusmão' here, read 'the identity imposed on Xanana Gusmão by the Indonesian regime'.

The writer, the text and the readers

A salient characteristic of propaganda is the way in which it conditions the reader's thinking: readers are imagined as receivers of information or indisputable 'facts'. This article certainly constitutes an example of this propagandist approach. Most of the points are put forward in a simple declarative form, which makes the text seem more 'authoritative', like statements of 'facts'. In this way, Abidin (or his ghost writer) asserted the Indonesian propaganda line on the media reports, along with their version of Gusmão's life and their line on his identity. There is actually very little overt argument – the information is just presented in narrative form to the reader. The author of this text also assumes the power to formulate the question to which these 'authoritative' answers are given. The interrogative form is used three times with maximum effect: firstly, in the headline; secondly in line 65; and thirdly, in line 138. Each time the same bald question is asked: 'Who is Xanana Gusmão?'. The article is thus framed as being all about the construction of an identity.

So, who were the readers being addressed? They were most likely to be members of élite political and economic groupings in South-East Asia, people likely to be concerned about issues of security and political stability. So, in characterizing Fretilin and the East Timorese resistance movement as a threat to that order, Abidin was using a familiar propaganda ploy. The readers were directly addressed just once in the article. In lines 102–103, Abidin threw out a challenge: 'if *you* believe the propaganda…' (my emphasis). First, the media reports about Gusmão's messages from prison are constructed as 'fabrications' and 'propaganda capital', and then, the reader is warned against being a sop to this propaganda!

It is difficult to assess what impact articles like this actually had. The Indonesians clearly believed they had some value as they invested so much effort in producing them. However, such texts were likely to be interpreted in different ways. It depended on who the readers were and how aware they were of the political situation in East Timor. People who were not familiar with the details of the history of East Timor would not be aware of what was absent from this text nor equipped to discern the distorted wording employed.

Strategies of resistance: Present and future

In building strategies of resistance to the Indonesian propaganda war against East Timor, one needed to develop a firm understanding of where and how it operated. This chapter focused first on the channels that were used by the Indonesian regime for disseminating its version of political and military events in East Timor. It then looked at the themes which emerged in this propaganda and the tactics that were used, in pre-referendum propaganda material. The last section drew attention to the manner in which one piece of propaganda was written: the ways in which distorted meanings were encoded in it and the ways in which the readers were positioned.

Those of us who have campaigned for an independent East Timor have needed to access flows of information to disseminate our version of events and express our political goals, whilst being aware of the propagandist methods and the channels of communication used by the Indonesians authorities. As we have seen, over the years, the Indonesian regime has used its propaganda machine to undermine political parties, solidarity groups, media and individuals sympathetic to the cause of East Timor. Despite the recent changes to East Timor's status, we must continue to monitor the discourse and campaigns of post-Suharto political leaders and governments. As they have done in the past, the Indonesian intelligence services are still capable of infiltrating East Timor to stir up or manufacture problems within our country and to create tension and unrest. We must therefore be on our guard and also be prepared to counter such insidious and unsettling practices at a particularly critical stage of development in East Timor.

References

1   I would like to thank the following people for their invaluable help in writing this paper. Firstly, my thanks go to Carmel Budiardjo and the Reverend Patrick Smythe for giving me copies of newspaper articles and Indonesian government publications which were excellent examples of Indonesian propaganda. Secondly, I am grateful to Greg Myers, Marilyn Martin-Jones, Norman Fairclough, Romy Clark, Paul Hainsworth and Stephen McCloskey for the challenging comments they gave me on earlier drafts.

2   An article by C. Philip Liechty in *The Washington Post*, cited in Pilger, John, *Distant Voices* (London, 1994, Vintage Books), p. 297.

3   Taylor, John G., *Indonesia's Forgotten War: The Hidden History of East Timor* (London, 1991, Zed Books); Aarons, M. and Domm, R., *East Timor: A Western Made Tragedy* (Sydney, 1992, Left Book Club); Barbedo Magalhães, A., *East Timor: Indonesian Occupation and Genocide* (Oporto, 1992, Oporto University Press); and Pilger, *Distant Voices*.

4   Chomsky, N. and Herman, E. S., *The Washington Connection and Third World Fascism* (Boston, 1979, South End Press); Roff, Rabbitt, *Timor's Anschluss: Indonesia and Australian Policy in East Timor 1974–1976* (Australia, 1992, Edwin Mellen Press); Herman, E. S. and Chomsky, N.,

Manufacturing Consent: The Political Economy of the Mass Media (London, 1994, Vintage Books); Gunn, C. G., *A Critical View of Western Journalism and Scholarship on East Timor* (Manila, 1994, Journal of Contemporary Asian Publishers).

5 Matsuno, A., 'Reading the unwritten: An anatomy of Indonesian discourse on East Timor', unpublished paper presented at a symposium on East Timor at Oporto University, June 1993.

6 *Ibid.*

7 Operation Giant Lizard.

8 Named after the highest mountain in East Timor.

9 Taylor, John G., 'Decolonization, independence and invasion' in *International Law and the Question of East Timor* (London, 1995, CIIR/IPJET), p. 24.

10 The Revolutionary Front for an Independent East Timor (Fretilin), the party that defended, from its foundation, the total independence of East Timor from Portugal.

11 Timorese Democratic Union (UDT). This was the political party which initially defended the idea of progressive autonomy from Portugal while remaining under the Portuguese flag. The party now stands for independence.

12 Associação Social Democrata Timorense (ASDT) was the original name of the party when it was founded on 20 May 1975, before it changed to Fretilin on 11 September 1975.

13 Taylor, 'Decolonization, independence and invasion', p. 26.

14 Taylor, *Indonesia's Forgotten War*, p. 59.

15 Timorese Popular Democratic Association (Apodeti), the party which defended the integration of East Timor into Indonesia.

16 Taylor, *Indonesia's Forgotten War*, p. 59.

17 Abidin, Irawan, *Indonesian News*, November 1994, p. 2.

18 Nicholls chaired the All-Party Indonesian Parliamentary Committee in the House of Commons.

19 Article by Whitlam for the *Sydney Morning Herald*, see Pilger, *Distant Voices*, p. 249.

20 Masters has written in the *Asian Wall Street Journal* (see Table 6.1).

21 Singh has written a book entitled *East Timor, Indonesia and the World: Myths and Realities* (Singapore, 1995, Singaporean Institute of International Affairs).

22 See my response to this statement in Cabral, Estêvão, 'Indonesian propaganda and Timorese puppets', unpublished paper, July 1993.

23 Aditjondro has written several papers on East Timor challenging the Indonesian government's claim over the territory. See, for example, Aditjondro, G., 'Prospects for development in East Timor after the capture of Xanana' in *International Law and the Question of East Timor* (London, 1995, CIIR/IPJET).

24 Matsuno, 'Reading the unwritten'.

25 The National Council of Maubere Resistance (CNRM): the umbrella organization for all East Timorese opposing the Indonesian occupation. This was superseded by a new resistance front entitled Conselho Nacional da Resistência Timorense (CNRT), founded in April 1998.

26 Matsuno, 'Reading the unwritten', p. 4.

27 *Ibid.*, p. 5.

28 *Ibid.*, p. 1.

29 See *FITUN Bulletin*, No. 9 (London, February 1993, Praxis).

30 Abidin, Irawan, 'Who is Xanana Gusmão?' (5th Column), *Far Eastern Economic Review*, Hong Kong, 3 August 1995.

31 The Armed Forces for the National Liberation of East Timor (Falintil), was created on 20 August 1975 as the armed wing of Fretilin. Today, this is the National Army of the Resistance as a result of changes in the structures of the resistance under the CNRM.

32 Matsuno, 'Reading the unwritten', p. 4 .

33 United Timorese Heroes (KOTA) is a monarchist party, Trabalhista is the Labour party.

34 The four East Timorese political parties opposed to Fretilin. For further details on political parties in East Timor, see Barbedo Magalhães, A., *East Timor: Land of Hope* (Oporto, 1990, Oporto University Press).

35 Cabral, Estêvão, 'Whose case for integration? A response to Thomas Michel S.J.' (Kuala Lumpur, 1997), paper circulated by Just World Trust, pp. 4–5.

Table 6.1:   Examples of Indonesian propaganda on East Timor

I. Abidin, 'Letter to Amnesty International', reprinted in *Indonesian News*, London, November 1994.

I. Abidin, 'Review of Indonesia's human rights record', *News and Views Indonesia*, London, January 1995.

I. Abidin, 'Review of Indonesia's human rights record', *News and Views Indonesia*, London, February 1995.

I. Abidin, 'Who is Xanana Gusmão?' (5th Column), *Far Eastern Economic Review*, Hong Kong, 3 August 1995.

Department of Foreign Affairs of Republic of Indonesia, *East Timor: Building for the Future*, Jakarta, July 1992.

D. Djalal, 'Pilger's films smack of opportunism', *Jakarta Post*, Jakarta, 1 August 1994.

P. Gama, 'Oral statement to the World Conference on Human Rights, on behalf of International Justice and Peace Commission', United Nations conference, Vienna, June 1993.

E. Masters, 'East Timor record is not all bad', reprinted in *Indonesian News*, London, August 1994.

T. Michel, 'East Timor: The case for integration', *The Month* (Jesuit bulletin), Bangkok, May 1995.

P. Nicholls, 'Response to John Pilger's film, *Death of a Nation: The Timor Conspiracy*', letter to the editor, *The Guardian*, London, 4 March 1994.

'Response to Amnesty International's advertisement published in several British and Irish newspapers', anonymous article, *Indonesian News*, London, April 1994.

7

Seeds of Hope – East Timor Ploughshares Disarming the Hawks

Andrea Needham, Jen Parker and Jo Wilson

In January 1996, we were making the final preparations for an action which we knew might lead to our being imprisoned for several years. We were busy tying up the loose ends of our lives, putting our affairs in order, in preparation for a long absence. We went round visiting old friends; it felt rather like having a terminal illness and wanting to leave relationships in good order before one departed. Andrea was having panic attacks and often would be walking down the street when her legs would turn to jelly at the thought of what was to come. What would be the consequences and effects of our principled and purposeful disarming of a Hawk aircraft?

The British government first sold Hawk ground-attack aircraft to Indonesia in 1978, when the Labour Party was in power. David Owen, the Foreign Secretary at the time, justified these sales by stating that the estimates of the killings had been 'exaggerated' and, anyway, 'the scale of the fighting had been reduced'. In fact the genocide in East Timor was at its height when the arms deal was agreed.[1] Almost as soon as the planes were delivered, reports started coming out of East Timor that they were being used there to bomb civilians in the mountains. Undeterred, the subsequent Conservative government allowed British Aerospace (BAe) to strike a further deal in 1983, followed by yet another in 1993, this time for 24 Hawk aircraft.

The campaign against the 1993 deal began a year earlier, in 1992, when the transaction was still under negotiation. Over the next few years, thousands of people were involved in every imaginable method of campaigning. We wrote hundreds of letters to the government, to our MPs and to BAe.

We wrote to newspapers, alerted the local media, and even occasionally reached the national media. MPs signed up to early-day motions condemning the sale. The government and BAe, however, refused to respond to our correspondence and continued to support the sale of Hawks to Indonesia. By early 1995, we started thinking about whether there was something further we could do to stop this dreadful sale if all else failed. We were faced with a choice. We could say: 'Well, we did everything we could and ultimately we were unsuccessful.' Or alternatively, we could say: 'There is one more thing we could do.' We chose the latter.

A group of ten – all women – met regularly from April 1995 to plan a Ploughshares action on the Hawks. We decided early on that four of us – Jo, Angie, Lotta and Andrea – would carry out the disarmament whilst the others would act as the support group, helping with the planning of the action, publicizing it afterwards, and supporting us through the court process and prison. We saw ourselves as a team of ten, playing different roles but all equally important to the process of disarmament, and the practical and emotional support of the rest of the group was absolutely vital to the four activists whilst we were in prison.

Ploughshares takes its inspiration from Isaiah: 'They shall beat their swords into ploughshares and their spears into pruning hooks.' The first such Ploughshares action was in 1980, when a group of eight people entered a General Electric plant in Pennsylvania, USA, and hammered on the nose cone of a nuclear missile. Since then, there have been over 60 actions around the world – and ours was number 56. Although inspired by a verse from the Bible, activists have come from many different spiritual backgrounds. The two things which all actions have in common are non-violence and the desire to take personal responsibility for disarmament. Nobody carries out a Ploughshares action and then runs away: it is about staying with, and claiming responsibility for, actions. Consequently, almost all activists have been convicted of property damage and most have been sentenced to prison, for periods ranging from a few months to 18 years.

Over the ten months that we were planning the action, we covered a huge range of topics. We talked at length about prison – how we would cope, what we would do while we were in prison, what kind of support we would like while inside. We talked about our fears – of the action itself, of imprisonment, of being separated from loved ones, and about deportation (Lotta is Swedish). We spent many months putting together a video and a report to leave at the BAe site. These contained our personal statements of intent, as well as the background to the Hawk deal and the situation in East Timor. We hoped that they would be used in court as evidence against us, thus bringing in all the important issues which we feared we would be prohibited from talking about during our trial. Jo and Andrea lived in Warton, Lancashire, near the BAe site where the Hawks are manufactured, and we spent many days and nights lying in icy ditches watching the site through binoculars. We wanted to know all we could about security measures – where the cameras were, whether the fences were alarmed, the frequency of the security patrols, and if there were people in the hangars at night. More importantly, we wanted to know where the Hawks were stored. Afterwards, there was official suspicion that we might have had inside knowledge about the Hawks and the site but, in fact, the information was all in the public domain and one just had to be prepared to spend time looking for it.

By the end of January 1996, it was clear that the delivery of Hawks was going to go ahead as planned, and we decided that we had to act at once. At that point, we decided that three of us – Jo, Lotta and Andrea – would go into the site and disarm the planes, whilst Angie would remain on the outside and continue the work she was doing (including trying to get her local magistrates' court to accept that BAe was breaking the law by selling weapons to Indonesia, and that the company should thus be prosecuted), which involved mobilizing support for our action. On 28 January, we packed our bags and headed for Warton. We got there by public transport – three buses and a train. Given that it was a Sunday night, when public transport is notoriously unreliable, it was something of a miracle that we got there at all. There was an hour to wait in Preston before we got the last bus and we went into Pizza Hut for a cup of tea. We were each carrying huge bags packed with a variety of tools, including hammers, crowbars, bolt cutters and wire cutters. They clanked against the doors as we struggled in, and many people looked up from their meals, curious at what we might be up to. It felt almost surreal sitting there amongst people going about their everyday lives, whilst we were drinking what would probably be our last cup of tea on the 'outside' for some time.

After getting off the last bus at about midnight, we had a further three kilometres to walk across frozen fields before we reached the site. Jo and Andrea had walked the route many times, planning down to the minutest degree so that we would avoid roads and houses: we could have got there blindfolded by that point. We stopped near the perimeter fence and put on the clothes we had brought for the action – blue boiler suits like the ones BAe mechanics wear, and black woolly hats which we hoped might disguise our gender from a distance (female mechanics not being too common at BAe). Then we sat in a ditch and watched and waited.

Finally, after two security patrols had passed, it was time to go. We held hands and had a few minutes silence, thinking about what we were about to do, and why. Then, we walked up to the fence, cut it, hung some peace

cranes, and headed for the hangar. It was totally lit up and there were security cameras on each corner so, when we could not open the first door we
tried, we started to panic, thinking that we must surely have been spotted by
then. However, we gathered ourselves together and headed for another
door, which opened very easily with crowbars, much to our amazement.
None of us had ever used a crowbar before and we were not too confident
about our ability to break into what appeared to be a high-security site.

And then we were in. Right in front of us was a Hawk bearing what we
knew to be the serial number of the Indonesian batch. Pulling out our
hammers we got to work at once. We hammered on the cockpit controls
which were used for targeting and bomb release, and on the nose, which
contains the radar. Then, since nobody had arrived to stop us, we
continued hammering all over the plane. The media later misreported our
action as a 'frenzied attack' on the plane. In fact, it was nothing of the kind:
it was very calm and controlled, and it just felt like a job we had to do. The
four of us had spent many months making a banner, which we hung on the
plane, and we scattered seeds over the wings as symbols of life and new
growth. We had called our action 'Seeds of Hope Ploughshares' for that
reason. Andrea stuck photographs of children she knew on the wings, to
symbolize the ordinary children who would be killed by this plane if it were
delivered to Indonesia.

All the time whilst we were hammering we were fully expecting to be
discovered, but nobody came. There was only one Indonesian-bound
Hawk in the hangar – had there been others, we would have disarmed
them too – and when we felt we had sufficiently put it out of action, we
thought it was time to let BAe know we were there. There were regular
security patrols driving around the site, so we went outside and waved as
they drove by – but there was no response. We danced in front of the security cameras – but still there was no reaction. Finally, in desperation, we
tried an internal phone but there were no phone numbers displayed. Eventually, we found an external phone. First, we rang Angie and told her what
we had done and then we rang journalists at the Press Association,
explained the situation and asked them to ring BAe for a comment.

Fifteen minutes later, two rather sheepish-looking security guards
arrived. We had role-played this encounter many times, expecting that they
might be angry at us but, in fact, they seemed emotionless. A few minutes
later the police arrived and we were arrested for criminal damage. The next
four days were spent in police custody, a strangely calm and quite happy
interlude before the rigours of prison. The police were pleasant enough, but
quite patronizing, suggesting that we did not know what we had got
ourselves into. At the time, they were estimating the damage at between £1
million and £3 million, which seemed incredible: how could our little

hammers have done that? But we felt the amount of damage was, in any case, irrelevant: BAe could pluck any figure they liked out of the air, but can a monetary value be put on human life?

We were taken to court twice at that time. The prosecutor claimed that we had been 'caught' at the site, rather than saying that we had in fact informed BAe of our presence. She opposed bail on the grounds that the offence was very serious and that, if released, we were likely to re-offend. We pointed out that, since we had not committed an offence in the first place, we could not really re-offend, but this argument made no impression on the magistrates, who ordered that we be remanded in custody. A few hours later, we were in handcuffs and on our way to Her Majesty's Prison (HMP) Risley.

Meanwhile, Angie was busy encouraging others to join with her in continuing the work of disarming the Hawks. She presented evidence of British Aerospace's weapons production and the British government's complicity in genocide to Norwich magistrates court, and appealed to the courts, politicians and the public to take urgent action. She gave several media interviews, openly describing her role in the Seeds of Hope Ploughshares action and her intention to go back to BAe to carry on the disarmament. A week after the action, Angie was arrested, on her way into a public meeting, and charged with conspiracy to cause criminal damage. The four of us were then held together at HMP Risley for six months, awaiting trial.

Imprisonment is never a pleasant experience, but our spirits were kept up by the support of the hundreds of people around the world who wrote to us, as well as by the unstinting efforts of our support group on the outside. They worked around the clock to make sure that our needs were met, as well as to raise awareness of the issue, nationally and internationally. The prison classified us as a 'security risk' because of the political nature of our 'offence', and we were thereby denied privileges accorded to all other women. But we were kept together and were able to support each other throughout our time in prison, which made life much easier for us.

On 23 July 1996, we finally came to trial at Liverpool Crown Court. A group in Liverpool had been organizing tirelessly for weeks and, by the time the trial started, there can have been few people in the city who did not know what it was about. Along with our support group, they organized vigils and daily processions to court, ceremonies outside the court to remember those killed in East Timor, prayer services, street stalls, and several events to celebrate our act of disarmament. Each day, the courtroom was packed with supporters, and it boosted our spirits enormously to come up from the cells each morning to be greeted be a sea of beaming faces.

Ideally, we would have represented ourselves in court, but we were aware that some difficult legal issues might arise, so we compromised and had one of us formally represented whilst the other three represented themselves. The trial lasted six days – a rather gruelling time, as we had to return to prison each evening and had little time together to work on our case. The essence of our case was that in British law (Criminal Law Act 1967, Section 5), one is allowed to use 'reasonable force to prevent crime': we said that we were using reasonable force to prevent the crime of genocide in East Timor. We considered that what we did was reasonable because we had spent three years using every other method we could think of to stop the Hawk deal. In addition, Angie presented a defence based on international law. To back up our defence we used several witnesses, including José Ramos-Horta, the East Timor special representative in the UN and now Nobel Peace Prize laureate, who gave evidence about human rights abuses in East Timor. We also called the renowned investigative journalist John Pilger, to talk about his experience of East Timor, Carmel Budiardjo of Tapol, a former political prisoner in Indonesia, and Dr Paul Rogers, a professor of peace studies at Bradford University, who nailed the lie that the Hawk is a training aircraft. We each gave evidence in our own defence and were able to talk at length about our motivation for taking this action. In addition, we were able to show the video we had made and had taken to the scene of the action to use as our statement, and also able to give each member of the jury a copy of our report.

The prosecutor's case argued that our action had nothing to do with prevention of crime, but was merely a publicity stunt. He also suggested that the action did not have the capacity to prevent crime – despite evidence that the Hawk we disarmed had still not been sent to Indonesia, six months after it was due for delivery. Several British Aerospace employees were called to give evidence of the 'damage' we had caused to the Hawk. One of them admitted in the witness box that, whilst he was very concerned about the damage we had done to the Hawk, he had no concern at all for the damage or loss of life which might have resulted from the delivery and use of the aircraft in East Timor.

The judge allowed our defence, and presented it to the jury in his summing up on the final day of the trial, along with the prosecution's case. Then the jury retired and we were taken back to the cells to await the verdict. Four hours later, the jurors came back to report that they could not reach a unanimous verdict, and they were sent back by the judge with a direction to reach a majority verdict. Just one hour later, the gaolers came to our cell. We went back into the court, this time with four guards instead of the usual two. There was a deadly hush in the court, and the usual smiling faces were tense. As the foreman of the jury stood up to deliver the verdicts (on conspiracy charges against all four of us, and criminal damage charges against three of us), we grasped hands and hardly dared breathe.

Suddenly the words 'not guilty' rang around the court. There was a collective gasp from the public gallery, the judge called for silence, and then one after another the rest of the verdicts came. Not guilty on all charges!

Supporting the action[2]

The role of the support group was very important to the success of the East Timor Ploughshares action. Once Andrea, Lotta, Jo and Angie had disarmed the Hawk and were in custody, the support group was responsible for publicizing the action and making sure that the women in Risley had practical and emotional support. Since we came from different parts of the country, we could only meet monthly to update each other on developments and take responsibility for different tasks. We also needed to support each other, since often the role of a support group was stressful and demanded a lot of time. Within the group, we took on different roles, such as organizing the prison visits, managing the press work, ensuring publicity (in the form of a newsletter), dealing with requests from prison, and liaising with the lawyers in the run-up to the court case.

Although the press were not immediately responsive to the Seeds of Hope action (only brief reports appeared in the national press describing the Hawk disarmament immediately after the event), we were soon aware of the amazing effect the action had had on ordinary people in Britain and abroad. Information requests and donations landed on the doormat of the Seeds of Hope office (the home of one of the support group), as well as moving letters of support from all over the world. We heard from the women inside prison that they were inundated with letters expressing the inspiration that many people had drawn from their act of disarmament.

The trial

In the run-up to the court case, the work of the support group became even more frenzied, as an immense amount of last-minute research and liaison needed to be done in preparation for the trial – and sometimes redone when Risley prison mysteriously 'lost' parcels of vital information! We also had to negotiate moving the Seeds of Hope office up to Liverpool – the venue of the trial – so that we could continue to carry out press and publicity work throughout the court case.

Anyone who was involved in the Seeds of Hope group's July 1996 trial will recall how incredible the atmosphere was. Prior to the trial, hundreds of local people joined in marches from the old cathedral (bombed in the

Second World War) down to the court-house, where there were daily prayers, rituals and remembrances for East Timor. When the trial had begun properly (after a few days' delay), we received reports of solidarity actions, vigils and marches from all over the world. For instance, in Portugal, the home of many East Timorese who had fled the Indonesian occupation, East Timorese people occupied the British embassy in Lisbon.

The trial lasted just over a week. For those in the courtroom there were many moments of sadness, anger and even a little humour as the trial unfolded. Mostly, though, there was a background of tension and worry as we constantly tried to gauge the response of the jury – were the jurors understanding the issues which were being presented? Did they believe the women had acted lawfully? During the trial, two of us from the support group acted as 'McKenzie Friends'. This is the name given to someone who is not legally trained, but assists a person who is defending themselves in court. I am not sure how helpful we actually were with the technicalities of the court case, but being regarded as part of the legal team by the court officials was a definite bonus when it came to communicating with Andrea, Lotta, Angie and Jo in court. We were able to sit with them in court, go down and talk with them in the holding cells during breaks in court proceedings, and also pass on messages of support from family and friends.

After a week of testimonies, legal arguments, cross-examination and experts' reports, the day of the final verdict came. When the jury went out to consider their verdict many people gathered outside the crown court buildings to sit and think and wait. In the hours that passed, there were singing, prayers, drumming, meditation, and also the planning of responses to the verdict. We were finally called back into the court to hear the jury announce a majority verdict of 'not guilty' on all counts, and the courtroom erupted in a happy chaos of tears, singing and bewildered relief. The presiding judge, realizing that there was no way to keep this courtroom in order, quickly left! British Aerospace, realizing that the women's action had been vindicated, promptly attempted to serve injunctions on all four. These were disposed of by supporters (though – see below – proper injunctions were issued sometime later).

Evaluation

Once the celebrations of success in both the action and trial were over, the group (the support group and those who had hammered on the Hawk) got down to the serious business of evaluating the action. We questioned what we could have done better, what we had learned for the future, and where next to take the campaign. Despite the fact the one of the 24 BAe Hawks was successfully disarmed and delayed for a least a year, BAe has continued sending the aircraft to Indonesia, with the consent of the British government (see Chapter 8). It became clear to us as a group that the support for the people of East Timor and opposition to Britain's arms supply to Indonesia needed to expand into a larger campaign before the government and arms companies would change their policies and practices. Jo, Andrea, Lotta and Angie have now been injuncted by BAe to prevent them from taking further action against the company. Included in the list of things that amount to breaking the injunction (which could result in a prison sentence) is the 'incitement' of others to take action against BAe. However, there are many of us who have not been injuncted against speaking out. I, for one, would urge those concerned about human rights and justice issues to campaign against arms sales to repressive regimes. The ploughshare action showed that public opinion can be influenced on this important issue. Non-vioelnt direct actions can be affective and persuasive methods of maintaining public pressure on governments and private companies alike. Whilst there have been positive developments in the case of East Timor it is important to ensure that similar situations are not repeated elsewhere.

References

1   Letter from David Owen to Lord Avebury, 19 June 1978, quoted in John Pilger, *Hidden Agendas* (London, 1998, Vintage).
2   Jen Parker takes up the writing here.

8

New Labour, New Codes of Conduct? British Government Policy towards Indonesia and East Timor after the 1997 Election

Paul Hainsworth

Introduction

This chapter will examine the consequences of the change of government in the United Kingdom as a result of the Labour Party's landslide victory in the general election of May 1997. It will focus on key foreign policy, arms and aid questions opened up by New Labour's accession to power, with specific emphasis on Indonesia and East Timor. (New Labour is the political label increasingly used by the British Labour Party since the mid-1990s. It is particularly bound up with the leadership of Tony Blair and serves to distinguish the contemporary and modernized party – in policy and presentation – from its historic predecessor, whilst still nevertheless claiming lineage with the latter.) There have been some significant markers put down by the Blair government: crucial here are foreign policy ethics and arms sales criteria. The decisions taken in these policy arenas have been seized upon by critics to illustrate the unfortunate dichotomy between stated intent and actual practice. To what extent has the Labour government been able to realize objectives set out in primary documents such as the 1997 Labour Party election manifesto and the July 1997 mission statement for the Foreign and Commonwealth Office (FCO)? Broad human rights and ethical themes formulated by New Labour will be identified. In particular, an assessment will be made of the government's record in these spheres, using Indonesia and East Timor as a test case. The chapter will seek to highlight what needs to be done to ensure that practice measures up to policy aims.

From Conservative to Labour

For human rights activists and monitors, the previous Conservative governments' policy and practice in foreign affairs, arms sales and development aid
matters left much to be desired. For instance, in 1996–97, export licences
were granted for the sale of weaponry and equipment to Indonesia – in
particular, armoured personnel carriers (APCs), Tactica water cannons and
Hawk aircraft – which have been used for purposes of internal repression.[1]
The Conservatives were of the opinion that an arms embargo would not
improve human rights in Indonesia or East Timor. At the same time, the
Conservative government denied that their export licences allowed equip-
ment likely to be used internally for repressive purposes to reach Indonesia.
The fact that licences were authorized precisely for such ends prompted
condemnation from a number of UK-based organizations, including
Amnesty International (AI), Tapol (the Indonesia Human Rights
Campaign), the British Coalition for East Timor (BCET) and the Campaign
Against Arms Trade (CAAT). Other criticisms focused on the training of
Indonesian military officers in the UK and/or the use of British-made
equipment. The latter practice was graphically exposed in a *World in Action*
(1997) British television documentary, made by Martyn Gregory.

Alongside condemnations of Britain's arms trade policy, serious questions
were asked about the circumstances under which development aid had been
allocated to Jakarta by the Conservative regime (1979–97). This issue has
been well documented, notably in a 1996 report by the National Audit
Office.[2] In essence, the Conservatives stood accused of providing aid not on
the basis of need, but in order to attract and protect trade and arms orders.
Of special concern, for instance, was the aforementioned provision of
training by British forces for the Indonesian national police, which was an
integral part of the military establishment. As Paul Barber pointed out: 'The
Indonesian police force is part of the armed forces (ABRI) and cannot,
therefore, be dissociated from the widespread repression and human rights
violations perpetrated by the military.'[3] These violations have often been
criticized by United Nations (UN) agencies and respected non-governmental organizations (NGOs).[4] A study of British aid to Indonesia compiled
by Ann Clwyd MP (at that time chair of the Parliamentary Human Rights
Group) also concluded that through the police training programme: 'It is
likely ... that the Government is looking to foster its influence over senior
officers ... who are potential buyers of British arms/security equipment. In
any event, there is ... absolutely no consideration for human rights and
poverty reduction.'[5] The same study questioned British government support
via development funding for internal monitoring and surveillance work by
the Indonesian authorities. It also raised the issue of the legitimization of

Indonesia's occupation and annexation of East Timor through the funding of a highly controversial transmigration policy and related operations which served to resettle over 40,000 Indonesians in the occupied territory.

The revelations of the 1996 National Audit Office report provoked strong criticisms from Labour's opposition front bench, and led to a call for an urgent inquiry into the link between government aid to Indonesia and arms sales.[6] Thus, according to the Shadow Minister for Overseas Development, Clare Short (appointed Secretary of State for International Development in May 1997):

> There is evidence in this report of a possible link between aid and arms... It is imperative that we have a full inquiry with access to all evidence, in order to investigate whether there was a link between aid to Indonesia and arms sales ... Indonesia has violated human rights. Yet government aid to state projects in Indonesia has increased by 50% in recent years, whilst the overall aid budget has been slashed.[7]

It is clear that successive Conservative administrations placed insufficient emphasis on human rights criteria in formulating their arms, aid and foreign policy with regard to Indonesia and East Timor. It was not that Conservative spokespersons did not recognize that human rights violations had taken place in East Timor. Rather, they favoured a quiescent, mildly disapproving and ultimately ineffective diplomacy in human rights terms. A token exception was the signing up to the European Union's 1996 Common Position on East Timor (see Chapter 9 and Table 8.1). The landslide Labour victory in the 1997 general election raised speculation as to whether the new government might adopt a different approach towards Indonesia, given the party's strong criticism of the policies of Conservative administrations from the opposition benches.

New Labour, new perspectives?

Labour's 1997 election manifesto emphasised the importance of 'telling the truth' and 'being prepared to give a moral lead'.[8] The choice of language was clearly intended as a criticism of the Conservatives' political style and record in office. Moreover, in the foreign policy section of the manifesto, Labour promised to be 'an advocate of human rights and democracy the world over'.[9] In the sub-section on arms control, the party made the following commitment:

> Labour will not permit the sale of arms to regimes that might use them for internal repression or external aggression. We will increase the transparency

and accountability of decisions on export licences for arms. And we will
support an EU code of conduct governing arms sales.[10]

The wording of the manifesto at this point certainly offered some encouragement to campaigners against arms sales to Indonesia. As one interested
source suggested, the first commitment – with its stress upon 'might' – was a
'potentially significant' shift from the Conservatives' policy of claiming to
deny export licences for equipment that was 'likely' to be used for internal
repression.[11] A similar assessment was made by Malcolm Chalmers in a
report for Saferworld, an independent research group working on international conflict resolution issues. According to Chalmers, the wording 'may,
or may not' represent 'a significant difference from the policy of the last
government'.[12] Unsurprisingly, the two 1996 East Timorese Nobel Peace
Prize laureates, José Ramos-Horta and Bishop Carlos Filipe Ximenes Belo,
and Indonesia's foremost trade union leader, Muchtar Pakpahan, were at
the forefront of those calling upon the Labour government to cut back on
arms sales to Indonesia. It was clear that Labour's record in office would be
closely monitored to assess whether front-bench politicians would translate
laudable manifesto promises into good practice.

In opposition, Labour had been critical of the Conservatives' policy
concerning the 'arms-to-Iraq' scandal, in which British arms suppliers had
circuitously avoided sanctions restrictions on Iraq even after the August
1990 invasion of Kuwait. The resulting furore over this revelation had
forced the Conservative government of John Major to set up a public
inquiry, which produced the Scott report (1996). Prior to the general election, therefore, Labour had made known both its criticisms and intentions
on arms sales. These were elaborated upon in *Labour's Policy Pledges for a
Responsible Arms Trade: Eight Steps to Stop the Arms-to-Iraq Scandal Happening
Again*. Some of the wording in this document was to find its way into the
Labour manifesto. Step one, for instance, declared that:

> A Labour Government will not issue export licences for the sale of arms to
> regimes who might use them for internal repression or external aggression,
> nor will we permit the sale of weapons in circumstances where this might
> intensify or prolong existing armed conflicts or where these weapons might
> be used to abuse human rights.[13]

Noteworthy here, then, was the Labour Party's restated commitment on
export licensing, which was linked to a critique of the Conservative government's record – with the clear implication that 'Britain deserves better'.
There was also a clear intention to link foreign policy to human rights standards. Again, this found an echo in the Labour manifesto, with the promise

to use Britain's permanent seat on the United Nations Security Council to press for the protection of human rights. Furthermore, in a specific sub-section on human rights, the manifesto contended that:

> Labour wants Britain to be respected in the world for the integrity with which it conducts its foreign relations. We will make the protection and promotion of human rights a central part of our foreign policy. We will work for the creation of a permanent international criminal court to investigate genocide, war crimes and crimes against humanity.[14]

All these aspirations again offered some hope for those campaigning for human rights and justice for East Timor and beyond. An international criminal court (ICC), if it came into being, would provide a forum in which human rights violations might be properly assessed. A further positive step was the publication of a mission statement by the newly appointed Foreign Secretary, Robin Cook, which was launched at a high-profile press conference at the Foreign and Commonwealth Office (FCO) on 12 May 1997, only a few days after Labour came to power. Cook's statement proclaimed that the Labour government would 'give a new momentum to arms control and disarmament'. Especially commented upon by the media and other interested observers was the Foreign Secretary's pledge to bring an 'ethical dimension' to British foreign policy:

> The Labour Government does not accept that political values can be left behind when we check in our passports to travel on diplomatic business. Our foreign policy must have an ethical dimension and must support the demands of other people for the democratic rights on which we insist for ourselves. The Labour Government will put human rights at the heart of our foreign policy and will publish an annual report on our work in promoting human rights abroad.[15]

Significantly, the Foreign Secretary presented the mission statement as evidence of 'new directions in foreign policy': 'It supplies an ethical content to foreign policy and recognises that the national interest cannot be defined only by narrow *realpolitik*.'[16] Furthermore, Cook projected the statement as a blueprint for overseas diplomatic staff, whose skills would be important in helping government ministers to 'achieve our aims and measure up to our benchmarks'. In fact, he explained that he would personally communicate the new line to senior FCO staff, with the assistance of a specially commissioned video programme made with the help of the prominent film producer, Labour supporter and peer, Sir David Puttnam.

Other government ministers confirmed the new approach to British foreign policy, at the same time strengthening and extending it. For example,

the (then) Minister of State at the FCO, Tony Lloyd, promptly promised that
Britain would now be a 'responsible player' in the international arms market,
contributing to human rights and displaying a 'responsible attitude'.[17]
Addressing a Saferworld seminar on 9 June 1997, Lloyd made or confirmed a
number of promises, including the non-issue of export licences where arms
might be used for internal repression or international aggression, increased
transparency and accountability of decisions on export licences, and stronger
monitoring of end use. The minister promised tougher monitoring standards
at a national level, but also planned to work with partners in Europe (and
beyond) to establish an EU code of conduct on arms exports.[18] Several prominent NGOs (Oxfam, Saferworld, the British American Security Information
Council (BASIC) and Amnesty International) had collectively sponsored an
EU code of conduct on the arms trade, stressing that whilst certain standards
should be adopted at EU level to prevent human rights abuses, they would
not be enough in themselves: 'An effective Code will also require *inter alia* the
implementation of clear provisions for consultation, for end-use certification
and monitoring, and for parliamentary scrutiny.'[19]

Lloyd refused to be drawn into naming any specific country in terms of
applying any of the above criteria, not wishing to prejudge the outcome of the
inter-departmental review of British arms sales. However, the Foreign Secretary was reported as being alarmed at the particular media focus on arms
sales to Indonesia, following his FCO mission statement.[20] This only
confirmed the increasingly widespread view that Indonesia had now emerged
as a *de facto* litmus test of the Labour government's policy resolve. A decision
was reported to be imminent on the export licences for 16 remaining Hawk
fighter aircraft to Indonesia (part of an earlier deal), but there were suggestions too that the previous government had misled parliament on past sales
and licensing. Thus, according to Fran Abrams: 'The disclosure means that a
decision on whether to allow new exports, expected to test Robin Cook's new
ethical foreign policy, may not have to be made in the near future.'[21] Nevertheless, the Liberal Democrat spokesperson on defence, Menzies Campbell
MP, suggested that a cancellation of the former government's export licences
for the Hawks would show that the Labour government was 'serious' about
an ethical policy, while Barry Coates, director of the World Development
Movement (WDM), called for a 'clear statement to say [that], in future,
orders like this would not be permitted'.[22] In the event, the Foreign Secretary
approved the export licences for aircraft, water cannons and armoured truck
sales and justified the decision in the following terms:

> The present Government were not responsible for the decisions on export
> licences made by the previous Administration. We do not, however, consider
> that it would be realistic or practical to revoke licences that were valid and in
> force at the time of our election.[23]

This decision understandably angered and outraged human rights activists and anti-arms campaigners. First, it rested on a curious interpretation of the British constitution, which implied that a government was bound by the policies and decisions of its predecessor. Second, it seemed to contradict the very notion of an ethical foreign policy and sent out mixed signals as to the government's resolve in implementing the strict criteria it had so recently announced for arms sales. The Foreign Secretary moved swiftly to consolidate the FCO mission statement, by reiterating some positive-looking guidelines on human rights and arms sales. On 22 July 1997, in a major speech on 'Human Rights into a New Century', Cook announced 12 policy initiatives designed to underscore the government's commitment on human rights. These included condemnation of human rights violations, the potential resort to sanctions, support for the work of NGOs such as Amnesty International, backing for pertinent resolutions at international fora, a review of military training assistance, and the publication of an annual report on the government's human rights promotional work. On arms sales, he said specifically: 'Britain will refuse to supply the equipment and weapons with which regimes deny the demands of their people for human rights.'[24]

The following month (August 1997), the Foreign Secretary embarked on a major tour of South-East Asia. In Indonesia, following meetings with President Suharto and Foreign Minister Ali Alatas, he announced a six-point plan for improving human rights in Indonesia. The plan included meetings with human rights leaders during the visit, funding equipment for human rights activists, scholarships and places at British universities, and a lecture series by British senior police officers on non-confrontational crowd control. Cook also proposed a top-level EU delegation to East Timor and reminded his hosts of the British government's new criteria for arms sales. The intention was to 'combine ethical foreign policy with "positive partnership" – practical steps to help moderate harsh regimes around the world'.[25] The UK's forthcoming presidency of the European Union was seen widely as a useful vehicle for pursuing these human rights safeguards.

Labour government presidency of the European Union (January–June 1998)

Having assumed the EU presidency in early 1998, the new Labour government was seemingly well placed to influence the international human rights debate. The presidency provided an ideal platform to broaden Britain's ethical foreign policy remit. The government was also responsible for coordinating the EU's resolution on East Timor for the United Nations Human Rights Commission (UNHRC) in Geneva (March) and chairing the Asia-Europe Meeting (ASEM II) in London (April). In fact, the FCO mission statement had proclaimed that the 'next twelve months provide the greatest opportunities in a generation for Britain to take a leading part on the world stage'. Robin Cook also stressed the 'cluster of opportunities' for British leadership in this period.[26]

As regards East Timor, the British Euro-presidency will be best remembered for the three-day visit (27–30 June 1998) to the territory by the EU ambassadors' troika (the Dutch, British and Austrian ambassadors in Jakarta). According to Milena Pires, of the Catholic Institute for International Relations (CIIR), the conclusions of the ensuing ambassadorial report contained 'the strongest position' ever taken formally by the EU on East Timor.[27] The report also called for a withdrawal of Indonesian troops from East Timor, an immediate cease-fire, further releases of political prisoners, including Xanana Gusmão, military accountability for human rights violations, impartial investigation procedures, direct East Timorese participation in the peace process, and a more proactive and supportive role from the international community (meaning the deployment of peace monitors). The troika visit was marked by a strong-arm intervention by the security forces in the town of Baucau, which left one person dead and five wounded, causing the ambassadors, in protest, to cut short their stay and cancel their scheduled meeting with the governor of East Timor. Derek Fatchett, then Minister of State at the FCO, welcomed the ambassadors' report and stressed the urgency of finding a solution to the problem of East Timor, whilst Foreign Secretary Cook explained that the purpose of the visit 'was to mark the EU's continuing concern about the situation ... and to support the UN search for a fair, comprehensive and internationally acceptable solution to the problem'.[28] However, as Pires again suggests, both the report and the British government response needed improving on:

> In CIIR's view, the British government needs to press the European Union to go further than the action recommended in the report, by supporting a referendum, as called for by the East Timorese pro-independence movement. This should give options on independence, integration and association with another state and would provide a means for the East Timorese to exercise their right to self-determination.[29]

Notwithstanding these reservations, the troika visit could still be seen as a worthwhile and positive contribution of the British presidency of the EU. However, the British presidency was also notable for a weaker-than-expected UNCHR resolution on Timor. In fact, the British role here prompted Ramos-Horta to revise his hitherto optimistic assessment of the Labour government. Both publicly and privately,[30] the Nobel laureate had expressed optimism about the change of government in the UK. For instance, in a 1997 interview, he stated:

There seems to be a real commitment to be more positive, and genuine interest on the part of Robin Cook to support the efforts of Portugal and the United Nations. The UK is, as we know, a major player in the European Union. In the past Britain has been the major stumbling block to any initiative on East Timor in the European Union and in the UN Commission on Human Rights in Geneva; and it is the biggest arms supplier today to Indonesia. So the change of government must be welcomed.[31]

At Geneva, though, the British government spearheaded a last-minute, somewhat diluted, EU-sponsored consensus statement on East Timor. This was in line with the FCO's philosophy of 'constructive engagement' with Indonesia, but it prompted Ramos-Horta to air his doubts about the Foreign Secretary's 'public promises and pronouncements'.[32] In addition, the British hosting of the ASEM II summit in April 1998 yielded little tangible evidence of offending participants being called to account for human rights abuses. However, the occasion did provide an opportunity for a broad range of rights, development and solidarity organizations to come together for an alternative programme of criticism and protest in which Indonesian and East Timorese matters loomed large.

The British EU presidency was also noteworthy for the adoption of a common code of conduct on arms exports. The declared intention was to take into account respect for human rights and freedoms in recipient countries. The government aspired to circumvent a situation whereby EU partners undermined each other's arms embargoes on countries using arms imports for internal repression. As the government's first annual report on human rights put it: 'We are ... pressing for early EU agreement on a Code of Conduct setting high common standards, based on the UK measures, for arms exports from all member states.'[33] The EU code of conduct was widely welcomed; indeed, as already pointed out, various NGOs had lobbied for it. Yet doubts remained over the efficacy of this pan-European development. The NGO lobby, for example, never envisaged that the code would be sufficient in itself to achieve the desired ends: 'An effective Code will also require *inter alia* the implementation of clear provisions for consultation, for end-use certification and monitoring, and for parliamentary scrutiny.'[34]

An ethical dimension to foreign policy?

Much critical attention has focused on New Labour's ethical foreign policy dimension. Speculating on what this might mean for East Timor, Stephen Baranyi – then CIIR policy officer for human rights in Asia – confessed to be heartened by Robin Cook's 'commitment to enhancing the ethical dimensions of British foreign policy and particularly his promise to tighten the application of arms export control criteria'.[35] Certainly, the effect of the high-profile mission statement (see above) was to place the government's ethical foreign policy commitment on a pedestal, as a signal of positive change and practice. An interesting evaluation of this initiative was provided by David Goodall, an ex-British high commissioner to India:

> It is a declaration of intent by the new British Government to make concern for human rights a central factor in its dealings with foreign governments and an invitation to judge the success of British foreign policy by the extent to which it helps to improve the lot of people in countries where human rights are being violated. No previous government has nailed its colours to the mast of universal human rights with this degree of ostentatious determination.[36]

However, from the beginning, the ethical foreign policy got off to an ambivalent start. The Foreign Secretary's simultaneous announcement of new arms-sales criteria and his attempt to justify the decision to proceed with the previous government's arms export licences for Indonesian-bound weaponry opened up New Labour to immediate charges of double standards. Significantly, lawyers representing the World Development Movement were told by Whitehall civil servants that the confirmation of the previous government's licensing arrangements was essentially now a matter of 'political judgement' rather than a constitutional or legal imperative.[37]

Critical observers were not convinced that trade interests (as reflected in the £438 million in British arms sales to Indonesia in 1996) and human rights could be so neatly balanced. Certainly, just prior to the annual Labour Party conference in October 1997, the government did announce a freeze on the sale of sniper rifles and armoured vehicles to Indonesia. However, whilst welcome, the cancellations could with hindsight be seen as pre-conference sweeteners, aimed to deflect criticism. Significantly, other licences for strategic weapons to Indonesia had been approved, with decisions on further applications still pending.

The extent of British arms trading to Indonesia throughout the first year of Labour government can be seen in Table 8.1, taken from Amnesty International's *Human Rights Audit* (1998) of the UK's foreign and asylum policy.[38] Amnesty's audit was a direct response to the government's own annual human rights report.[39] Whilst recognizing FCO/Department for International Development (DFID) human rights policy as 'an important step forward from the policy of previous governments', Amnesty expressed concern *inter alia* about the centrality, effectiveness and consistency of that policy. These aspects are discussed further below. As regards Indonesia, Amnesty was critical of deficiencies in the Labour government's human rights report and policy:

No mention is made in the report of the export of arms to Indonesia, despite the considerable public interest and concern expressed on this in the previous year, and the fact that the UK was now the largest exporter of arms to Indonesia. Given the controversy over such actions, the report should make some reference to the human rights criteria applied when making these decisions, any guarantees sought from Indonesia on end-use of arms exports and the efforts of UK officials based in Indonesia to monitor the use of such equipment.[40]

Amnesty was also regretful that the government had honoured its predecessor's arms export licences to Indonesia, in the face of 'widespread public, parliamentary and NGO concerns that this equipment would be used to commit human rights violations'.[41] Indeed, during the last days of the Suharto regime, in April and May 1998, global television pictures showed the use in Indonesia of British-made tanks and water cannons against pro-democracy demonstrators. Whilst government sources claimed that the sale of such equipment was authorized by previous governments operating under less stringent criteria, it was clear that at least 64 arms export licences for Indonesia had been granted by New Labour in its first year in office. As already intimated, Indonesia emerged as a veritable test case for Labour. In December 1998, there was strong criticism from members of the Labour-controlled House of Commons Foreign Affairs Committee (FAC) – reporting at length on the ethical foreign policy – against the official record of arms sales to Indonesia. Moreover, committee members were particularly scathing about the photograph in the FCO/DFID *Human Rights Annual Report*, which depicted a smiling Foreign Secretary shaking hands with President Suharto in Jakarta. Again, it could be argued that, under a policy of so-called 'constructive engagement', the Labour government was sending out confusing or wrong signals. According to Labour MP and FAC member Diane Abbott, the photograph was 'a standing indictment of the Foreign Secretary'.[42]

Despite these criticisms, the select committee was willing to give Robin Cook credit for what it perceived to be positive aspects of the ethical foreign policy (see below). At the same time, it recognized that the good intentions of some government departments could be diluted by the practices of others. This raises the crucial question of how far the ethical policy dimension was the adopted child of the government as a whole. It was highly significant, for instance, that when the Foreign Secretary did freeze sales of armoured vehicles to Indonesia, using his newly adopted arms-sales criteria, the (then) Minister of Defence, George Robertson, intervened to warn about loss of business, suggesting that the vehicles were simply for defensive purposes. In the same inter-ministerial communication, the Defence Minister even referred glowingly to a renowned human rights abuser: 'The head of Kopassus (i.e. Indonesian Special Forces) is General

Prabowo, the son-in-law of President Suharto. The general is recognised as an enlightened officer, keen to increase professionalism within the armed forces and to educate them in areas such as human rights.'[43] In fact, nothing could have been further from the truth since, as *The Independent*'s correspondent in Indonesia, Richard Lloyd Parry, explained, Prabowo was widely regarded as 'one of the most brutal and dangerous men in Indonesia'.[44] Obliged to retract, Robertson alluded to 'defence intelligence' and information that had changed since autumn 1997. However, this was still very insensitively wide of the mark for, as Lloyd Parry continued, evidence of Prabowo's brutal activities had 'been around for years'.[45] Undoubtedly, it was badly managed incidents like this, the failure to revoke predecessors' arms export licences and the continued issuance of licences that helped to drive a coach and horses through New Labour's ethical foreign policy. As Oxfam rightly pointed out, if the policy was to succeed it needed the support of the whole government.[46]

It is not just the Ministry of Defence that is less than wholeheartedly supportive of the ethical foreign policy. The Department of Trade and Industry (DTI) is at the heart of the export licensing process. Here, there are a number of problems. First, the Scott report on the arms-to-Iraq affair pinpointed the conflict of interests inherent in the DTI's multipurpose role as licenser, promoter and controller of arms sales. Thus Oxfam has called for a 'single arms control agency whose primary function is to ensure that the rules of export policy are effectively implemented'.[47] Second, the system of export licensing lacks effective parliamentary or public scrutiny. Whilst questions are certainly asked in parliament, all too often the ministerial answers are incomplete, evasive or hedged by resort to unhelpful concepts such as 'commercial confidentiality'. The Campaign Against Arms Trade (CAAT), for instance, has argued for details of individual export licence applications to be made public. Assessing the 64 UK export licences granted for Indonesian-bound arms sales in the first year of the new Labour government, Amnesty International's considered view was that some of the categories (see Table 8.2) were 'so broad as to be almost meaningless': 'the data currently available on arms exports from parliamentary questions does not provide sufficient detail to confirm that licences have not been granted for equipment which may lead to human rights violations'.[48] Amnesty is also concerned that some government departments may be working against others in the implementation of an ethical foreign policy, a charge rejected by the DTI, which argued that: 'Every export licence is issued on a case-by-case basis. We don't issue a licence without consulting the Foreign Office or the Minister of Defence or any other relevant Government department.'[49]

However, some of the practices referred to in a critical report by Oxfam – *Out of Control* (1998) – still need attending to if countries such as Indonesia are not to benefit almost at will from British-originating arms sales.[50] Oxfam highlighted three main loopholes in small-arms sales to destinations where human rights abuses and internal repression were prevalent: brokering by UK companies, without a statutory requirement for weaponry to actually pass through the UK; overseas production under licence from UK companies; and the failure to achieve end-use monitoring and control. To take one pertinent example, in July 1998, Heckler and Koch (a British Aerospace/Royal Ordnance affiliate enterprise) sold 500 high-powered sub-machine guns to the Indonesian police force via an intermediary company based in Turkey.[51]

Admittedly, the EU code of conduct and the DTI's white paper on strategic export controls (July 1998) may be seen as steps in the right direction of tightening up criteria for arms sales but, unless rigorously implemented and strengthened, the aspirations within these documents will not in themselves suffice. Thus the EU code looks to be ineffective against evasive brokering practices whilst the white paper fails to detail how end-use monitoring will be realized.[52]

Undeniably, then, there are continuing concerns that New Labour's arms policy is not qualitatively – nor possibly even quantitatively – different from what it was under the Conservatives. This was certainly the view of Indonesian trade unionist, Muchtar Pakpahan, when he addressed a conference at the London School of Economics in October 1998.[53] As already suggested, Nobel laureates Bishop Belo and José Ramos-Horta have also pleaded on several occasions with New Labour to reverse their predecessors' policy. In the opinion of veteran Indonesia human rights campaigner and chair of Tapol, Carmel Budiardjo: 'Their record is exactly the same as the Conservatives.'[54] The view of Oxfam, too, was that there has been 'little change' from the 'business-as-usual' approach of the Conservatives. Arms are still being sold to countries involved in difficult situations of internal conflict, even though 'licence applications are indeed taking longer to process, which implies they are being more thoroughly scrutinised'.[55]

One of the key problems here is the very basis of the ethical foreign and arms policy. Whilst the rhetoric of human rights has inevitably captured the imagination of a discerning and critical public, it should be noted that this is only one of four elements in the FCO's mission statement – the other variables being security, economic prosperity and quality of life. As the FCO/DFID 1998 *Annual Human Rights Report* points out, 'we have given human rights concerns a higher profile, but choices still have to be made in uncertain circumstances'.[56] In response to a parliamentary question in July 1997, the Foreign Secretary (announcing the non-cancellation of the Conservatives' export licences for arms to Indonesia) elaborated upon the new arms-licensing criteria: 'The criteria will constitute broad guidance. They will not be applied mechanistically and judgement will always be required.'[57] Herein lies the dilemma then: there is no guarantee that human rights criteria will prevail. An ethical dimension to foreign policy has been formulated but the devil is in the implementation. Human rights considerations will be weighed against other variables. Again, as Robin Cook explained, it is important to strike a balance, bearing in mind that Britain – with over 20 per cent of world arms sales[58] – is one of the world's largest arms exporters.[59]

In 1999, many of the familiar criticisms of the government's ethical foreign policy and arms sales practices were voiced again. For example, Amnesty International's 1999 (September) *UK Foreign and Asylum Policy: Human Rights Audit* pointed to some of the continuing problems, such as a DTI out of step with other government departments in delivering an ethical foreign policy; failure to provide essential details on weapons and equipment transfers; end-use verification difficulties; and the ongoing reluctance to close damaging loopholes – including brokering and licensed production agreements (see above) – in the strategic export control system.[60] Also, the Campaign Against Arms Trade has questioned the secrecy surrounding the Export Credits Guarantee Department's workings, as well as the principle of aiding arms exports to countries – like Indonesia – with appalling human rights records. The CAAT was mindful that the delivery of 16 Hawk aircraft to Indonesia, approved in 1996, had recommenced in April 1999 – with half the contract fulfilled by October 1999.[61]

The issue of the Hawk sales was given additional publicity when Foreign Secretary Cook admitted, in September 1999, that the aircraft had in fact been used over East Timor in July, despite end-use assurances from the Indonesian authorities. Cook therefore, following two weeks of post-referendum violence in East Timor (see Chapter 14), suspended the licences for the Hawks. Whilst this official admission and belated step were most welcome to human rights campaigners, it illustrated the weakness of end-use guarantee promises and underlined the need for tougher monitoring procedures.

The latest Hawk controversy coincided with the escalation of the human rights crisis in East Timor, following the 30 August referendum on the territory's future. The UK government, at the height of the crisis, took a number of positive steps, including lobbying the Indonesian government to accept international peacekeepers and put a stop to the killing and destruction in the territory. The UK government also authorized sanctuary in the British embassy in Jakarta for the recently released East Timorese resistance leader Xanana Gusmão, and agreed to a four-month EU moratorium on arms sales to Indonesia. In addition, Sir Jeremy Greenstock, the UK ambassador to the UN, visited Dili (as part of a small UN Security Council mission) to assess the crisis situation on the ground in East Timor.

The UK also provided some (Gurkha) troops for the peace-making force, Interfet. However, there was great reluctance, even at the peak of the storm in East Timor, to cancel invitations to Indonesian military élites to attend a major arms bazaar in the UK in 1999, with FCO Minister Baroness Symons stubbornly insisting that the Indonesians had a right to purchase weapons for self-defence. Ultimately, the Indonesian military representatives themselves opted not to attend the event.

In the year 2000, it was virtually business as usual. Despite a European Parliament resolution to the contrary, the British government opted not to support the position of some other EU member states to renew the arms embargo on Indonesia. A few months later, generous invitations were provided by the British government to attract Indonesian top brass to the latest UK arms show-case in Farnborough. In contrast, the Clinton administration had extended its own arms moratorium, pointing to unresolved questions over East Timor. These included the continuing impunity for the Indonesian military, notwithstanding the considerable evidence of human rights violations, and the non-return of tens of thousands of East Timorese refugees (in effect, hostages), who had been herded out of the territory in a military/militia attempt to sabotage the result of the August 30 referendum in East Timor. The British government view, as expressed by Prime Minister Blair, was that it was important not to destabilize the new (October 1999), democratically elected regime in Jakarta. For the same reason, the Labour government seemed content, in early 2000, to leave Indonesia to conduct an internal (rather than an international) investigation into the mayhem and human rights abuses that had preceded and followed the referendum (see Chapter 14).

The lifting of the UK and EU embargo meant, of course, that the sale of the Hawks and other military equipment could be recommenced. Unsurprisingly, government critics argued that the wrong signals were being sent out to the military in Indonesia, for commercial reasons. The rapid turn of events (not least, the economic crisis and the massive depreciation of the rupiah currency) in Indonesia and East Timor, since the fall of Suharto, in fact, had contributed to a fall in UK arms exports to the country. The British government's 1999 arms sales report (covering the preview year) actually had recorded a drop in the overall value of arms exports from £3.3 billion to £1.986 billion, but there was still evidence that the UK had continued to sell arms to countries with repressive regimes, despite the formulation of an ethical foreign policy. Defending the report before a grouping of House of Commons scrutiny committees, the foreign secretary maintained, for instance, that the government could do nothing about licensed production agreements which enabled the sale of Heckler and Koch weapons via Turkey to Indonesia – again illustrating the need to close loopholes in arms sales licensing, policy and codes of conduct.[62]

The report put sales of arms to Indonesia at a value of £72.65 million, a considerable reduction when compared to the figures (see above) under the under the Conservative government. However, again, there were wide-spread complaints that the categorization of weapons under individual export licences was so broad that it was impossible to know the precise nature and purpose of the equipment. All in all, 68 licenses had been granted for sales to Indonesia, including open-ended licenses and others covering items such as military utility vehicles and combat aircraft compo-nents. Assessing Labour's record, a recent Campaign Against Arms Trade report accused the government of failing to deliver on ethical foreign policy pledges, supporting the upgrade of the Indonesian military in personnel and material terms and not being sufficiently open on arms sales. [63]

One of the key problems here, of course, is that New Labour is attempting to reconcile two impossible opposites: retention of the UK's status as a top-flight arms merchant and espousal of a policy and criteria that simultaneously militate against this position. Moreover, the sale of arms is inherently an unethical business since, in practice, it involves selling to (often poor, Third World) countries that are involved in internal repression (like Indonesia), external aggression and the short-changing of their popula-tions on socio-economic needs. Indeed, most arms sales are to Third World countries and serve to fuel conflicts, human rights violation and poverty. A more genuinely ethical policy points in the direction of defence industry diversification and conversion, and the suspension of heavily protectionist export credit guarantees and financial services.[64]

Conclusion

The change of government in the UK in 1997 resulted in considerable interest in Labour's ethical foreign policy dimension. As illustrated above, certain key policy statements and declarations served to focus much attention on Labour government aspirations and practice. Undoubtedly, there have been some positive developments, including the incorporation of the Euro-pean Convention on Human Rights into domestic law; inauguration of an EU code of conduct and stricter national criteria for arms exporting; an annual human rights report; a ban on anti-personnel landmines; moves to set up an international criminal court; prohibition on the export of electro-shock torture equipment; a more open dialogue with human rights NGOs; tighter monitoring of development aid; and even a greater sense of urgency in confronting human rights and problems. Indonesia and East Timor, too, have preoccupied the New Labour government, with ministers (including the prime minister) raising human rights issues with the Indonesian authorities, pushing for the EU troika mission to East Timor, engaging with prominent Timorese interlocutors, promising to target development aid to East Timor through NGOs (not through the Indonesian government) and contributing to pressures for change through bilateral, European and multilateral channels. In February 1999, Ramos-Horta praised the efforts of UK government ministers – Robin Cook, Clare Short and Derek Fatchett – noting the latter's close involvement in the Timor issue, including his three visits to the imprisoned Timorese leader Xanana Gusmão. Indeed, just prior to his death in May 1999, Fatchett again visited Gusmão and also became the first UK government minister to visit East Timor. Moreover, the UK offered to send troops and funds to East Timor in the context of an UN-sponsored peacekeeping mission. As East Timor's constitutional status became the subject of intense speculation in early 1999 (see Chapter 14), Ramos-Horta expressed the view that 'the United Kingdom would be a major contributor to Timor'.[65] In the event, the UK played a role in the post-referendum situation in East Timor, working to promote the acceptance and intervention of external peacekeepers, and subsequently making a contribution of troops to Interfet (see above). Ramos-Horta was later to praise Tony Blair for helping to get President Clinton moving on East Timor.

Nevertheless, and as argued above, the signals have been mixed and ambiguous with, *inter alia*, questionable arms sales continuing to take place, signs of an apparent inter-departmental disharmony on ethical foreign policy and serious doubts about the strategy of constructive engagement. As regards the last point, for instance, Amnesty International's evidence to the Westminster Foreign Affairs Committee investigation into 'Foreign Policy and Human Rights' (1998) stressed: 'It is important that political dialogue does not become an end in itself.'[66] Moreover, the FAC – alluding to 'sustained criticism' of government policy in Indonesia – reached the following telling conclusions:

> If the policy of constructive engagement is to be meaningful, we recommend that the Government conducts a rigorous examination of the failures of assessment and judgement in the case of Indonesia ... we recommend that the Government establishes and maintains clear and consistent principles for the implementation of constructive engagement policies, and that such policies should be kept under regular review.[67]

At the same time, it should be noted critically that the government remains resistant to prior notification procedures for arms sales (therefore falling behind best practice elsewhere), reticent on extending parliamentary scrutiny of such transactions (to cover individual licence applications) and even tetchy towards the FAC for simply doing its monitoring job.

Nevertheless, the post-Suharto era and the pressures for change in Indonesia and East Timor continue to represent a window of opportunity, and it is crucial that New Labour endeavours genuinely to assist the forces for progress and democratization therein. Thus, initially, arms codes and export licensing criteria need tightening up to ensure that British-originating weapons do not contribute towards human rights abuses and internal repression. After Labour came to power, a total of 92 licences were granted to Indonesian-bound arms exports in their initial 20 months in office, including 25 between May and December 1998. Only seven applications were rejected.[68] Second, the UK Labour government must continue to press relentlessly for full and unfettered access to West Timor and other parts of Indonesia (where East Timorese displaced persons have been held) for universally recognized human rights monitors. Months after the 30 August referendum, the safe return of East Timorese refugees remains at the top of the international agenda. Third, the human rights element of the ethical foreign policy should be prioritized, if it is not to be superseded by the other elements in the equation. Fourth, there ought to be greater consistency across government departments to ensure an integrated approach – through which the totality of the Labour administration is 'singing from the same hymn sheet' in these matters. Fifth, the government should utilize bilateral, European and other international avenues to proactively support reconstruction in and justice for East Timor. With East Timor now at a critical phase in its history (see Chapter 14), the international community (including New Labour) needs to be vigilant and engaged in ensuring developmental progress in the territory.

In conclusion, New Labour in office has taken some positive steps towards supporting progressive change in Indonesia and East Timor, but the rhetoric of an ethical dimension to foreign policy has not always been translated into coherent and effective government action.

References

1   European Network Against Arms Trade (ENAAT), *Indonesia: Arms Trade to a Military Regime* (Amsterdam, 1997, ENAAT).

2   *Ibid.*; Clwyd, Ann, 'British aid to Indonesia: The continuing scandal', unpublished report (1995); National Audit Office (NAO), *Aid to Indonesia*, report by the comptroller and auditor general (London, 1997, The Stationery Office, HC 101 Session 1996–97).

3   Barber, Paul, *Partners in Repression: The Reality of British Aid to Indonesia* (London, 1995, Tapol), p. 13.

4   See, for instance, Amnesty International, *Indonesia and East Timor: Power and Impunity: Human Rights under the New Order* (London, 1994, Amnesty International).

5   Clwyd, *British Aid to Indonesia*, p. 28.

6   NAO, *Aid to Indonesia*.

7 'Labour calls for inquiry into aid for Indonesia', Labour Party press release (London, 29 November 1996, Labour Party).

8 *Because Britain Deserves Better*, Labour Party general election manifesto (London, 1997, Labour Party).

9 *Ibid.*, p. 37.

10 *Ibid.*, pp. 38–39.

11 *Tapol Bulletin*, No. 141, July 1997.

12 Chalmers, Malcolm, *British Arms Export Policy and Indonesia* (London, 1997, Saferworld), p. 7.

13 *Labour's Policy Pledges for a Responsible Arms Trade: Eight Steps to Stop the Arms-to-Iraq Scandal Happening Again* (London, no date, circa 1997, Labour Party).

14 *Because Britain Deserves Better*, p. 39.

15 Cook, Robin, 'Mission statement', opening statement by the Foreign Secretary, press release of the Foreign and Commonwealth Office (FCO), (London, 12 May 1997, FCO).

16 *Ibid.*

17 Lloyd, Tony, 'Speech by Mr Lloyd: Saferworld Seminar' (London, 9 June 1997, Saferworld).

18 *Ibid.*

19 Amnesty International, British American Security Information Council (BASIC), Oxfam and Saferworld, *An EU Code of Conduct on the Arms Trade: Essential Standards*, 1997.

20 See, for instance, *The Guardian*, 12 June 1997.

21 *The Independent*, 14 July 1997.

22 *Ibid.*

23 House of Commons (Hansard), 'Parliamentary Questions', 28 July 1997.

24 Cook, Robin, *Human Rights Into a New Century* (London, 22 July 1997, Human Rights Policy Department, FCO), p. 6.

25 *The Guardian*, 29 August 1997.

26 Cook, FCO mission statement.

27 Pires, Milena, 'Britain's EU presidency', *Timor Link*, No. 45, October 1998.

28 See House of Commons (Hansard), 'Parliamentary Questions', 14 July 1998. For the troika report, see House of Lords (Hansard), 'Written Answers', 23 July 1998.

29 Pires, 'Britain's EU presidency', p. 1.

30 Author's interview with José Ramos-Horta, One World Centre (OWC), Belfast, April 1997. See *One World Centre for Northern Ireland Annual Report 1996/7* (Belfast, 1996–97, OWC).

31 Interview with José Ramos-Horta, 'The final miles', in *CIIR News*, December 1997, p. 2.

32 As quoted by John Pilger in *The New Statesman*, 15 May 1998.

33 FCO/Department for International Development (DFID), *Annual Report on Human Rights 1998* (London, April 1998, FCO/DFID), p. 35.

34 Amnesty International *et al.*, *An EU Code on the Arms Trade*, p. 1. For a comprehensive critique of the EU code of conduct, see the UK Working Group on Arms' memorandum to the Trade and Industry Committee in 1998, Appendix 7, 'The EU Code of Conduct on Arms Export', Trade and Industry Committee (second report), *Strategic Export Controls* (House of Commons, HC 65, Session 1998–99, December 1998). The working group comprises Amnesty International (UK), BASIC, Christian Aid, International Alert, Oxfam (GB), Saferworld and Save the Children Fund.

35 Baranyi, Stephen, 'Will Labour seize the moment?', *Timor Link*, No. 45, July 1997, p. 1.

36 *The Tablet*, 18 October 1997.

37 *The Independent*, 22 December 1998.

38 Amnesty International UK, *UK Foreign and Asylum Policy: Human Rights Audit 1998* (London, 1998, Amnesty International UK).

39 FCO/DFID, *Annual Report on Human Rights 1998*.

40 Amnesty International UK, *UK Foreign and Asylum Policy*, p. 57.

41 *Ibid.*

42 *The Independent*, 22 December 1998.

43 *The Observer*, 26 July 1998.

44 *Ibid.*

45 *Ibid.*

46 Oxfam, *Small Arms, Wrong Hands: A Case for Government Control of the Small Arms Trade* (Oxford, April 1998, Oxfam).

47 *Ibid.*, p. 3.

48 Amnesty International UK, *UK Foreign and Asylum Policy*, p. 59. Lack of parliamentary scrutiny (and absence of updated legislation) on strategic export controls was also at the heart of the criticisms of and NGOs' evidence to the House of Commons Trade and Industry Committee. One of the main points to emerge was concern at the government's failure to produce an annual report on strategic export controls, despite promises. Many of the familiar criticisms on brokering, licensed production and end-use control were also central to the committee's deliberations. See Department of Trade and Industry (DTI), *Strategic Export Controls* (white paper), Cmnd 3989, July 1998.

49 *The Times*, 23 September 1998.

50 Eavis, P. and Sprague, O., 'Does Britain need to sell weapons?' in Davies, Ian (ed.), *Britain in the 21st Century: Rethinking Defence and Foreign Policy* (London, 1997, Spokesman), cited in Cooper, N., *How the UK Government Subsidises the Business of Death* (London, June 1997, Campaign Against Arms Trade).

51 Oxfam, *Out of Control* (Oxford, 1998, Oxfam), pp. 14–17.

52 For a fuller discussion of these themes see *ibid.* See also DTI, *Strategic Export Controls*.

53 Muchtar Pakpahan is president of SBSI (the main independent trade union in Indonesia), which has an estimated 40,000 members. Recently released from imprisonment for peaceful trade union activity, he was participating in the Amnesty International (UK) Human Rights Festival, October 1998, organized as part of Amnesty's programme to commemorate the 50th anniversary of the universal declaration of human rights.

54 *The Observer*, 3 May 1998.

55 Oxfam, *Small Arms, Wrong Hands*, p. 3.

56 FCO/DFID, *Annual Report on Human Rights 1998*, p. 10.

57 House of Commons Debates (Hansard), 28 July 1997.

58 *The Guardian*, 27 July 1997

59 *Ibid.*

60 Campaign Against Arms Trade, submission to Export Credits Guarantee Department review, October 1999, pp. 11–16.

61 *The Guardian*, 4 November 1999. See also Ministry of Defence/FCO/DFID, *Strategic Export Controls: Annual Report*, October 1999.

62 Amnesty International, *UK Foreign and Asylum Policy: Annual Report 1999* (London, 1999, Amnesty International).

63 Campaign Against Arms Trade, *Arms Exports to Indonesia* (London, October 1999, CAAT).

64 For a fuller discussion of these themes, see Cooper, *How the Government Subsidies the Business of Death*.

65 *The Independent*, 20 February 1999.

66 'Supplementary memorandum submitted by Amnesty International', House of Commons Foreign Affairs Committee (1998) first report, *Foreign Policy and Human Rights*, Vol. 3, Appendices to the Minutes of Evidence, Appendix 23, p. 295.

67 'Summary of conclusions and recommendations', House of Commons Foreign Affairs Committee (1998) *Foreign Policy and Human Rights* , Vol. 1, Report and Proceedings of the Committee, p. lxi. It should be noted that whilst this chapter has focused on East Timor and Indonesia, a number of other country-specific and broad concerns were voiced about the government's ethical foreign policy and human rights stance. For further elaboration, see the full report of the Foreign Affairs Committee (cited here) and Amnesty International UK, *Foreign and Asylum Policy.*

68 *Tapol Bulletin*, No. 151, March 1999.

Table 8.1:   The European Union's Common Position on East Timor

In its 'Common Position Concerning East Timor' (cleared for publication on 25 June 1996) the Council of the European Union says it intends to pursue the following aims:

- to contribute to the achievement of fair dialogue, comprehensive and internationally acceptable solution to the question of East Timor, which fully respects the interests and legitimate aspirations of the Timorese people, in accordance with international law;

- to improve the situation in East Timor regarding respect for human rights in the territory.

To further these aims, the document says, the European Union:

- supports the initiatives undertaken in the United Nations framework which may contribute to resolving this question;

- supports the current talks under the aegis of the UN Secretary-General with the aim of achieving effective progress;

- encourages the continuation of intra-Timorese meetings under the auspices of the United Nations;

- calls on the Indonesian government to adopt effective measures leading to a significant improvement in the human rights situation in East Timor, in particular by implementing fully the relevant decisions adopted by the United Nations Commission on Human Rights;

- supports all appropriate action with the objective of generally strengthening respect for human rights in East Timor and substantially improving the situation of its people, by means of the resources available to the European Union and aid for action by NGOs.

Source: CIIR Comment, *East Timor: The Continuing Betrayal* (1996).

Table 8.2:   Licences granted for export of equipment to Indonesia by military list category, 2 May 1997–10 May 1998

Military list category	Military list definition as set out in UK Export of Goods (Control) Order	Number of licences granted
ML1	Small arms, machine guns and accessories	3
ML2	Large-calibre weapons and accessories, including howitzers, mortars and flame-throwers	4
ML3	Ammunition for ML1, ML2 and ML26	1
ML4	Bombs, torpedoes, rockets, missiles, mines, charges, and specially designed components therefor	3
ML5	Fire control and warning equipment, including weapon sights, targeting computers, surveillance and tracking systems	1
ML6	Vehicles designed or modified for military use, including tanks, self-propelled guns, armoured vehicles and components therefor	1
ML7	Toxological agents, riot control agents, and related equipments, including tear gas and specially designed components therefor	1
ML10	Aircraft, and aircraft equipment, including combat aircraft, engines, parachutes and crash helmets	16
ML11	Electronic equipment not specified elsewhere, specially designed for military use	21
ML13	Armoured or protective goods, such as armoured plating, military helmets and body armour	5
ML14	Specialized equipment for military training or for simulating military scenarios, and accessories therefor	4
ML15	Imaging equipment specially designed for military use, including cameras, image-intensifier equipment, infrared or thermal-imaging equipment, and radar sensor equipment	2
PL5006	Apparatus or devices for military use used for the handling, control, discharging, decoying, detonation, disruption, or detection of explosive devices (including mines, rockets, bombs and explosives)	2
Total		64

Source: Amnesty International, *Human Rights Audit 1998*.

9

The United States: From Complicity to Ambiguity

Charles Scheiner

Introduction

More than any other country, the United States (USA) has dominated world events over the last half century. In its desire to maintain safe access to markets, labour and resources for multinational corporations, the USA has favoured 'stability' and opposed manifestations of socialism. In Indonesia, this was accomplished by facilitating a military takeover of the archipelago and, in 1975, East Timor. However, especially after the 1991 Dili massacre, several new factors developed which caused Washington to re-examine that position. This chapter explores the nature of those factors and the policy changes they have produced, which have contributed to the Indonesian withdrawal from East Timor.

Before the Dili massacre

Since well before the 1965 Suharto coup and subsequent bloodbath in Indonesia, the US government had supported the Indonesian military. From massive covert campaigns to overthrow President Sukarno in the 1950s[1] and CIA (Central Intelligence Agency) collaboration in the assassination of alleged communists in 1965 and 1966,[2] through to President Suharto's overthrow in 1998, Washington consistently supported repression in Indonesia. East Timor was no exception. In fact, the US support for the invasion and occupation is a prime example of the Washington cliché that 'politics stops at the water's edge'. For 23 years, through six Republican and Democratic presidents, the US government steadfastly provided weapons, military training and diplomatic support for the Indonesian invasion and occupation of East Timor. This position finally began to change after the 1991 Santa Cruz massacre, as a result of focused pressure by the public and Congress, but the US government was reluctant to embrace self-determination for East Timor.

A few months prior to the 1975 invasion, the US ambassador to Indonesia was quoted as saying that, if Indonesia were to invade East Timor, he hoped they would do so 'effectively, quickly, and not use our equipment'.[3] But Suharto wanted more official assurance, so he waited until President Gerald Ford and Secretary of State Henry Kissinger visited him in Jakarta. Hours after getting the American green light, the massive invasion of East Timor began. Weapons supplied from the USA were used in the invasion and subsequent occupation, and arms shipments multiplied as Indonesian forces needed more armaments. This was in direct violation of a 1958 treaty between the USA and Indonesia which limits the use of US-supplied weapons to 'legitimate self-defence' and strictly forbids their use for 'an act of aggression'.[4]

When a US diplomat mentioned that inconvenient fact in a secret cable to Washington, Secretary Kissinger was outraged. He berated his top advisers:

> I want to raise a little bit of hell about the Department's conduct in my absence. Until last week I thought we had a disciplined group; now we've gone to pieces completely. Take this cable on [East] Timor. You know my attitude and anyone who knows my position as you do must know that I would not have approved it. The only consequence is to put yourself on record. It is a disgrace to the Secretary of State this way... What possible explanation is there for it?... You had to know what my view on this was. No one who has worked with me in the last two years could not know what would be my view on Timor.[5]

Although Kissinger and his subordinates were well aware that Congress and the American people would not see the invasion of East Timor as within the scope of the treaty, he blustered: 'And we can't construe a Communist government in the middle of Indonesia as self-defence?' The irate Kissinger continued: 'I know what the law is but how can it be in the US national interest for us to ... kick the Indonesians in the teeth?'

War criminals and apologists often have faulty memories. In 1995, Henry Kissinger was asked about his endorsement of the invasion by the East Timorese activist Constâncio Pinto. Dr Kissinger replied:

At the airport as we were leaving, the Indonesians told us that they were going to occupy the Portuguese colony of Timor. To us that did not seem like a very significant event... Nobody had the foggiest idea of what would happen afterwards, and nobody asked our opinion, and I don't know what we could have said if someone had asked. Now there's been a terrible human tragedy in Timor afterwards. [The] population of East Timor has resisted and I don't know whether the casualty figures are correct, but they're certainly significant. All I'm telling you is what we knew in 1975. Timor, it's a little speck of an island in a huge archipelago, half of which was Portuguese. We had no reason to say the Portuguese should stay there. And so when the Indonesians informed us, we neither said yes or no.[6]

But the reality was that the USA actually saw Suharto's stable anti-communist regime as a key Cold War ally. Six months after being defeated in Vietnam, Washington was grateful for political support and corporate access to what President Nixon called 'by far the greatest prize in the South-East Asian area'[7] and was glad to do a painless (at least for Americans) favour for a loyal friend. Thus, after the invasion, the USA doubled military aid and quadrupled the sale of weapons, particularly helicopters. Over the next two decades, the USA sold or gave Indonesia more than $1.1 billion worth of weaponry, including OV-10 Bronco counterinsurgency aircraft that devastated East Timorese villages. Until 1994, the USA continued to deliver $30 million or more in killing tools every year.[8]

The East Timorese people took their case to the United Nations (UN). Two weeks after the invasion, the UN Security Council unanimously supported their 'inalienable right to self-determination and independence' and called 'upon the Government of Indonesia to withdraw without delay all its forces from the Territory'.[9] Similar resolutions were passed by the Security Council the following year (although the USA and Japan abstained this time), and by the General Assembly (by decreasing margins) every year from 1975 through to 1982. In the UN General Assembly, the USA abstained in 1975 and voted against every East Timor resolution for the next seven years. The votes illustrate a policy recorded in the memoirs of Daniel Patrick Moynihan, US Ambassador to the UN in 1975–76:

The United States wished things to turn out as they did [in East Timor], and worked to bring this about. The Department of State desired that the United Nations prove utterly ineffective in whatever measures it undertook. This task was given to me, and I carried it forward with no inconsiderable success.[10]

Now a senator, Moynihan has rethought his actions about a place he considered to be 'of no great importance'.[11] In a 1996 talk in New York, the ex-ambassador was clear: 'I was instructed not to object [to the invasion]. And I did not. Arrest me if you will.'[12] But, in letters to constituents, he now called the Indonesian occupation of East Timor a 'long-standing violation of international law'[13] and supported congressional efforts to end it.

Throughout the 1970s and 1980s, the US media and Congress continued to ignore East Timor. Between the day after the 1975 invasion and the 1991 Dili massacre, East Timor was covered precisely once among 100,000 US network television news pieces. East Timor rarely made the newspapers, and was almost totally absent from public view. In spite of repeated efforts to bring it to congressional awareness, including devastating eyewitness testimony from refugees, policy remained as first expressed in 1976: that the USA accepts the *de facto* incorporation of East Timor into Indonesia without maintaining that a valid act of self-determination had taken place. A few dedicated educators, notably Arnold Kohen and Noam Chomsky, made it possible for interested American officials and journalists to learn the truth about East Timor, and Catholic Church networks passed on the information. In Congress, Representative Tony Hall (Democrat, Ohio) almost singlehandedly kept the issue alive, and by the late 1980s nearly half of the members of Congress and the Senate had signed letters decrying human rights abuses in East Timor. But little could be done in the midst of Cold War mentalities and a media near-blackout.

Throughout the Cold War, anti-communism was the overriding concern of US foreign policy. As a result, American support for authoritarian Third World regimes was unhesitating so long as they were dependably anti-Soviet. When the Soviet Union collapsed at the end of the 1980s, the Cold War perspective was no longer sufficient to determine or justify US foreign policy. Together with events that occurred in East Timor and Indonesia, this change in East-West relations forced the USA, for the first time, to look at the unique characteristics of the struggle between Indonesia and East Timor.

The 12 November 1991 Dili massacre was carried out by Indonesian troops firing American-made M-16 rifles. Two American journalists, Amy Goodman and Allan Nairn, were beaten while US-supplied bullets killed more than 270 unarmed Timorese civilian protesters all around them. Their testimony, together with photographs and videotapes of the massacre, sparked some coverage in the US press and initiated the formation of the East Timor *Action* Network (ETAN), the first US grassroots movement on East Timor in more than a decade. After the massacre, a majority of the Senate wrote to President Bush calling for active US support for the implementation of the UN resolutions on East Timor, 'with an eye toward a political solution that might end the needless suffering in East Timor and bring about true self-determination for the territory'.[14] It was the first of many bipartisan House and Senate letters affirming support for East Timor's self-determination.

Military training

Friday 13 March 1992 marked the beginning of Congressional restraint on US support of the Indonesian regime. In front of an audience of 1000 people at Brown University, Congressman Ronald Machtley (Republican, Rhode Island) railed against the occupation of East Timor. His passion was answered by Dili massacre survivor Allan Nairn, who asked the representative if he would introduce legislation barring US military training aid to Indonesia. Machtley took up the challenge and, with Representative Tony Hall, introduced the Machtley-Hall amendment to end the international military education and training (IMET) programme for Indonesia's army. Under IMET, the only overt US military aid programme to Indonesia at the time, about 150 Indonesian soldiers were guests of US taxpayers each year, receiving training in a wide range of military and strategic subjects.

The battle to pass the amendment was hard fought, and came down to intensive lobbying of a House-Senate conference committee in September 1992. Although Indonesia and its corporate allies (notably General Electric, McDonnell-Douglas, Freeport-MacMoRan and AT&T) leaned heavily on their congressional allies, the new grassroots campaign managed to overcome their vested interests. Informed by a national ETAN phone-banking effort, conducted mostly by Brown University students, peace-minded people in key states across the nation called their senators and congressmen and, at least in this case, democracy prevailed. On 2 October, Congress barred IMET training for Indonesia for the fiscal year (FY) 1993.[15] Subcommittee chairmen Representative David Obey (Democrat, Wisconsin) and Senator Patrick Leahy (Democrat, Vermont) were key to this victory, which was opposed by the Bush administration's State Department, the Pentagon and lobbyists for the Indonesian military.

One of IMET's strongest advocates was Wisconsin Republican Senator Robert Kasten, who was in the midst of a hotly contested election. His young Democratic opponent, Russell Feingold, understood the public appeal of this issue and raised it in his campaign, challenging Kasten's support of Indonesian repression in East Timor. Feingold was elected with 53 per cent of the vote, and has been a Senate leader for East Timorese rights ever since. When the Indonesian regime failed to improve the situation in East Timor or to account for the dead and missing from the Santa Cruz massacre, Congress re-enacted the IMET cut-off in 1993 and 1994. By 1994, Congress had become aware that the Clinton administration was violating the spirit of the law by allowing Indonesia to buy as aid the same training that was banned. The House committee report accompanying the bill expressed 'outrage' that the administration, 'despite its vocal embrace of human rights', allowed the purchase of training.[16]

At the end of 1994, the Republican Party (often more pro-military than the Democrats) took control of Congress. The following year, Congress continued to ban IMET on military subjects, making it clear that they do not accept the human rights conduct of Indonesia's military. However, some IMET – the 'expanded' variation (E-IMET), which purports to focus on human rights and civilian control of the military – was allowed. From each fiscal year from 1996 through to 1999, Congress barred IMET for Indonesia while permitting E-IMET. In June 1997, Indonesian president General Suharto wrote to President Clinton rejecting E-IMET and a proposed US$250 million F-16 warplane sale. Suharto stated that he would not accept the conditioning of military transfers on human rights considerations. Nevertheless, Congress continued to bar IMET and permit E-IMET.

In March 1998, Representative Lane Evans (Democrat, Illinois), along with *The Nation* magazine[17] and ETAN, released Pentagon documents showing that US Green Berets and Marines had conducted, without interruption since 1992, 36 training sessions in Indonesia under the JCET (joint combined exchange training) programme. In violation of the intent of the law banning IMET, US soldiers were training Indonesian Kopassus (special forces) and other units in sniper tactics, urban terrain combat, demolitions, psychological operations and other repressive techniques. Kopassus troops have been implicated in some of the worst atrocities in East Timor, Aceh, and other parts of Indonesia. The training revelation sparked a congressional and public outcry, and the Pentagon reluctantly suspended planned JCET exercises a month later.

In September 1998, Congress enacted legislation barring the Pentagon from training units of foreign militaries if 'a member of such unit has committed a gross violation of human rights, unless all necessary corrective steps have been undertaken'.[18] This law, which applies to all countries but contains loopholes, was motivated by the case of East Timor and Kopassus. Congress also insisted on in-depth reporting of past and future international military training, so that they will be better informed about what the Pentagon is doing with their funding. US military training for soldiers from Latin America is also a topic of public controversy, sparked by grassroots protests over the 'School of the Americas'.[19] Such training, which is increasingly important as the USA uses other countries' soldiers to enforce its policies, will continue to be controversial for the foreseeable future.

Arms sales

The USA has been Indonesia's principal overall weapons supplier since the 1960s, and greatly increased its arms shipments after 1975, supplying 90 per cent of the weapons during the period in which the most excessive human rights abuses were perpetrated in East Timor. In the years immediately following the Dili massacre, the State Department licensed more than 300 military sales to Indonesia. The items sold ranged from machine guns and M-16s to electronic components, from communications gear to spare parts for attack planes. Every shipment sent the political message that the Indonesian armed forces still enjoyed US government support for their illegal occupation of East Timor. But grassroots pressure, transmitted through Congress, helped to reverse that pattern, forcing Indonesia to diversify its weapons sources. By 1995, Indonesia was receiving less than a quarter of its weapons imports from the USA, with Germany and the UK picking up most of the rest.[20]

In 1993, under congressional pressure, the State Department blocked a transfer of US-made F-5 fighter planes from Jordan to Indonesia, citing human rights as one of the reasons. The *Jakarta Post* editorialized that the blockage of the deal 'resounded like [a] sonic boom' in Indonesia.[21] Three months later, the Senate Foreign Relations Committee unanimously adopted Senator Feingold's compromise amendment to condition major arms sales to Indonesia on human rights improvements in East Timor. Although it never reached the Senate floor, the Feingold amendment sent political shockwaves through Jakarta. Early in 1994, the State Department prohibited the export of small and light arms and riot control equipment to the Indonesian regime – the first time an across-the-board prohibition had been imposed on any type of weapons sale to Indonesia.

With the small-arms ban, the State Department tacitly admitted that withholding weapons sales could advance human rights in East Timor, although administration officials told Indonesia's supporters that they adopted the ban to avert more stringent congressional restrictions. In June 1994, however, the Senate defeated legislation to prohibit the use of US-supplied weapons in East Timor. Indonesia's supporters, reneging on a negotiated arrangement, successfully argued that Jakarta would never accept such a limitation, and that the measure amounted to a total cut-off on US military sales to Indonesia. Nevertheless, Congress legislated for a prohibition on the sale of small arms to Indonesia a month later, translating State Department policy into law and restating the intent of the aforementioned 1958 treaty. Congressional pressure has caused the Clinton administration to restate the small-arms ban policy every year since then, and it has been steadily expanded to include helicopter-mounted equipment and armoured personnel carriers.

In 1997 and again in 1998, Congress enacted laws requiring the US government to state in arms sales contracts with Indonesia that the US 'expects' that any lethal weapons or helicopters will not be used in East Timor.

These measures were significant not only because they could prevent weapons deals, but also because they stated that East Timor was distinct from Indonesia.

The Clinton administration

During the 1992 presidential election, candidate Bill Clinton depicted past US policy on East Timor as 'unconscionable'. But after he defeated George Bush, the same State Department bureaucrats and the same policies on Indonesia and East Timor remained in place. At the UN Human Rights Commission (UNHRC) in Geneva in March 1993, however, the State Department reversed its pro-Jakarta stand under pressure from Congress, co-sponsoring a successful resolution criticizing Indonesian abuses in East Timor. Since then, the USA has been less obstructionist relative to East Timor at the UN, supporting other actions by the Human Rights Commission and allowing the UN Secretary-General to pursue efforts to resolve the situation. The USA even sponsored a successful UNHRC resolution in 1997, passed after Indonesia refused to honour commitments made to the commission in previous years. In 1998, the USA supported another such resolution, but it was replaced by a chairman's statement (a negotiated consensus between Indonesia and its critics) in which Indonesia agreed to allow UN investigators to visit East Timor, and to allow access to the disputed territory by Jakarta-based UN personnel. In the past, Indonesia had failed to keep similar commitments.

When President Clinton journeyed to Jakarta for the 1994 Asia-Pacific Economic Cooperation (APEC) summit, two dozen East Timorese students climbed the fence of the US embassy and asked to meet with him. Although they were not pushed out into the hands of waiting Indonesian police, the students were forced to occupy a parking lot for two weeks, on rice and water, before being allowed to leave for Portugal. President Clinton and other high-ranking US officials refused to see them, although Clinton did say that 'the people of East Timor should have more say over their own local affairs'.[22]

Clinton met with Suharto nearly every year from 1992 to 1998, and he almost always raised the issue of human rights in East Timor. But the sincerity of the US president (already questioned because of his continued arms-sales policy, military training and other forms of support for Suharto) was further undermined by the 'Lippogate' campaign finance scandal of 1996. Indonesian-born James Riady, son of a billionaire banker, funnelled millions of dollars of illegal campaign contributions to Clinton and other Democrats during the 1992 and 1996 presidential elections. Although it was never clear what Riady received in exchange for this money, the scandal brought Indonesia to the attention of the US media and raised public awareness as never before. When the Nobel Peace Prize was awarded to José Ramos-Horta and Bishop Carlos Ximenes Belo at the height of the scandal, many Americans became aware of the Clinton-Suharto-East Timor connection, which increased pressure on Clinton. Seven months after his re-election, President Clinton dropped in on a Washington meeting with Bishop Belo, although co-laureate Ramos-Horta has thus far been refused presidential or cabinet-level meetings. Long before Monica Lewinsky caught the world's attention, President Clinton's financial misconduct had already forced him to be circumspect with regard to the Indonesian dictator; Clinton could not provide economic, military or political support to help Suharto remain in office. Even on Suharto's last day in power, State Department and White House officials promulgated deliberately mixed messages about whether the USA wanted him to resign.

Self-determination for East Timor

In recent decades, the US government verbally supported human rights in East Timor many times, but no administration was forthcoming on the legal and moral right of the people of East Timor to determine their own political status. Although the White House and the State Department continued to avoid this issue, increasing pressure from the Senate and House served to raise the issue of self-determination in Washington. For example, Senator Claiborne Pell (Democrat, Rhode Island), on the final international trip of his distinguished Senate career, visited East Timor in May 1996. He reported to Senate Foreign Relations Committee chairman Jesse Helms (Republican, North Carolina): 'When asked how a plebiscite on the issue of independence versus integration would turn out, I was told that over 90 per cent of the people would choose independence and that number would include some who formerly supported integration.'[23]

Later that year, Senator Russell Feingold and 14 others wrote to President Clinton: 'We believe now is the time for the United States to take a leading role in advocating for the right of the East Timorese to choose their own government through a UN-sponsored referendum.'[24] Clinton replied: 'I note with interest your support of a UN-sponsored self-determination referendum in East Timor. I will take your idea into consideration.'[25] Since 1996, roughly a dozen members of Congress and State Department officials have visited East Timor or met with East Timorese resistance leader Xanana Gusmão in his Jakarta prison cell. They invariably came away with a better understanding of the situation and of the rights of the East Timorese people. But often when they got back to 'the swamps of Washington', where *realpolitik*, scandals and special-interest groups are the order of the day, their colleagues paid little attention. Nevertheless, the Senate has officially supported the basics. Senate Resolution 237, introduced by Feingold and Jack Reed (Democrat, Rhode Island) the day after Suharto resigned, was unanimously adopted on 10 July 1998. The Senate called on the president to support democratic and economic reforms in Indonesia and East Timor and to 'work actively, through the United Nations and with United States allies, to carry out the directives of existing United Nations resolutions on East Timor and to support an internationally supervised referendum on self-determina-tion'. Similar wording was approved as report language by the House of Representatives. Although non-binding, these statements made clear that the representatives of the American people believed that people in East Timor should have the same electoral rights as their own constituents.

In 1998, the 'post-Suharto' Habibie government proposed a 'special status' for East Timor, and the self-determination discussion was recast as autonomy versus referendum, a difference mirrored in the executive-legisla-tive separation of powers in the US government. The executive 'realists', including many State Department officials, viewed autonomy as a solution which fitted their world view that powerful governments – like those in Jakarta or Washington – should control their smaller neighbours. Others, legislators whose constituency is voters rather than government and corpo-rate institutions, are more likely to evaluate issues on their specifics. US policy confusion or reversals have often resulted from the debate between these two factions, and policy on East Timor was no exception.

Money talks

US economic ties with Indonesia are largely in extractive (mining, oil and lumber) and labour-intensive (sweatshop) industries. In addition, many weapons and technology companies have profited by selling arms to Indo-nesia. However, at a 1993 press conference President Clinton turned aside the argument that pressuring Indonesia on East Timor and human rights would have an adverse impact on business, realizing that US corporations are engaged in business with Jakarta for mutual profit, a basic fact unaf-fected by Timor policy. Nevertheless, some US companies have direct investment in the Timor Gap oil and gas fields, especially Chevron, Phillips Petroleum and USX/Marathon. Others, especially Freeport-MacMoRan, actively advocated Suharto and Habibie's goals in Washington, including opposition to East Timor-related legislation.

In an unusual reversal of global economics, a local labour struggle helped thousands of US workers to learn about East Timor. The Trailmobile corporation is one of the largest US-based manufacturers of refrigerated tractor-trailer trucks. In 1991 they were bought by the Gemala Group, an

Indonesian conglomerate controlled by the Wanandi family. One of the four Wanandi brothers, Edward, moved to Illinois to manage Trailmobile's factory in Chadeston. Sofian Wanandi, Gemala Group president, was a close Suharto crony trying to develop a tourist industry in East Timor. Jusuf, the third brother, headed Jakarta's Centre for Strategic and International Studies, a think-tank which planned Indonesia's invasion of East Timor and lobbied to gain it international support. Finally, Jesuit Father Marcus Wanandi was assigned by the Indonesian Catholic Church to Dili, where he kept a close eye on Bishop Belo.

When Gemala locked out 1200 workers from Trailmobile's Chadeston plant in 1996, the United Paperworkers International Union members at the plant educated themselves and their community about the Wanandis' connections with Suharto and East Timor. Edward was furious, and demanded (but did not get) an apology. Five months later, the largest lock-out in the USA at the time ended in a victory for the union. The workers credit East Timorese and other solidarity activists for essential support. Trailmobile is an exception – it is more common for a US-owned company to abuse workers and the environment in Indonesia. For several years, US activists have raised these issues at shareholder meetings of Freeport, Texaco, Nike, Chevron, Phillips and other companies which supported Suharto. In 1998, the cities of Cambridge (Massachusetts) and Berkeley (California) enacted selective purchasing laws, barring the local government from buying products sold by companies involved with the occupation of East Timor. The Indonesian economic and political crisis of recent years has heightened American attention to Indonesia. A series of inept International Monetary Fund (IMF) actions, and the looming devastation of structural adjustment, caused many in Congress and elsewhere to become concerned about unqualified US executive branch support for the Suharto-Habibie governments, and for the IMF. Some suggested that human and political rights – as well as economic considerations – be attached to any bail-out. Developments following the 30 August referendum in East Timor (see Chapter 14) served to fuel these recent trends.

The USA discovers East Timor, and then Indonesia

Many of the incremental improvements in US policy since 1991 were achieved due to the ineffectiveness of Jakarta's supporters. Grassroots activists motivated by the moral, political and legal rightness of East Timor's cause have been able to recruit allies in Congress and the media. East Timor has always been a marginal cause in the USA, but has united diverse constituencies: Catholics, Portuguese-Americans, peace and human rights activists, progressives, media critics and others. The Dili massacre, quickly seen as an unprecedented and possibly one-time chance to change US policy on East Timor, happened as many activists who had been working on Nicaragua, Palestine or South Africa were, for different reasons, shifting their focus. The end of the Cold War offered the possibility of dealing with East Timor as something other than a global pawn, and of gaining support from people formerly blinded by anti-communism. The US support for the decades of killing and atrocities in East Timor placed a special responsibility on US citizens and taxpayers.

The East Timor *Action* Network (ETAN) developed in the wake of the Dili massacre to weave these diverse threads and constituencies into an effective political force. Aided by use of the internet, other East Timor support groups and existing human rights and Asia Pacific networks, ETAN rapidly mobilized a small but very active national constituency. ETAN held public meetings at several universities in 1992, organized their first speaking tour in early 1993, and formalized their organizational structure and initial chapters that summer. The film *Manufacturing Consent* (a profile of Professor Noam Chomsky with a segment on East Timor) was invaluable in reaching new activists, although East Timor-specific films like *Death of a Nation* have not been broadcast or distributed to theatres in the USA.

Although the USA has less than a dozen East Timorese residents and the US media tends to ignore events in the Third World (especially when they reflect badly on Washington), ETAN was able to focus its limited resources and begin to shift US policy. It also sensitized thousands of Americans to their own ignorance – if something as devastating as the occupation of East Timor could be unknown to them, how many other atrocities is their own government supporting? Through their struggle, the East Timorese have given US citizens much more than US supporters of East Timor can ever reciprocate.

By 1994, the Indonesian dictator's supporters were bewildered. At a New York conference, keynoted by Foreign Minister Ali Alatas and addressed by at least six former and present US ambassadors to Indonesia, speaker after speaker criticized the constant condemnation of Indonesia *vis-à-vis* East Timor in Washington. Jakarta had all the right connections and was spending tens of millions of dollars on the most prestigious public relations firms in the world, but could not get Congress to listen. They recalled the 1940s, when Indonesian nationalists lobbied to obtain US support for independence from the Netherlands, and lamented that Indonesian leaders had more influence in Washington as a desperate band of exiles than as the rulers of a rich and populous country. Although they could not see the parallels, they were now being outmanoeuvred by a grassroots campaign lacking money, corporate backing and institutionalized political support.

With the help of the US-Indonesia Society, Jakarta initiated a large-scale campaign to get Americans to see Indonesia from their point of view. They also undertook more direct involvement in the US political process, an effort which backfired in the 1996 elections. The Dili massacre and the Nobel Peace Prize award brought East Timor into US popular awareness, but Indonesia remained largely invisible. It was the Clinton-Riady-Lippo campaign scandal, followed by the economic crisis and popular uprisings that led to Suharto's demise, which focused the press and people of the world's third most populous country (the USA) on the fourth (Indonesia).

Conclusion

During the 1990s, US policy on Indonesia and East Timor evolved, under pressure, from unrestricted support for Indonesia's military to political ambivalence and military disengagement. This major shift in Washington's diplomatic and trading relations with Jakarta was one of the factor's which led the Habibie transitional administration to facilitate a referendum on the future status of East Timor on 30 August 1999. The referendum result showed an overwhelming majority of Timorese (78.5 per cent) favouring independence from Indonesia: a result which immediately drew the wrath of the Indonesian military and pro-integrationist militias. The militias were created and controlled by the military to prevent the implementation of a pro-independence mandate and they set about brutally displacing tens of thousands of East Timorese with an estimated 100,000 refugees still captive in camps in West Timor some months after. The extreme violence and havoc wreaked by the military/militias together with sustained lobbying by NGOs and campaign groups on a global scale eventually prompted a belated armed intervention in East Timor by the United Nations. The UN-sponsored International Force for East Timor (Interfet) entered East Timor in September 1999 and led to the withdrawal of the Indonesian military. The militias, meanwhile, were forced to retreat to West Timor and elsewhere, although they continue to make border incursions into East Timor, and threaten and terrorize the local population.

The post-referendum mayhem in East Timor resulted in President Clinton – under considerable congressional pressure – announcing a suspension of military ties with Indonesia on 9 September. By the end of 1999, this announcement was made law when the US Congress passed the Foreign Operations Appropriations Act for Fiscal Year 2000 and the lifting of the suspension was made conditional upon 'the safe return of East Timorese refugees from West Timor, an end to militia violence, and accountability for those responsible for human rights abuses in East Timor and Indonesia'.[26]

ETAN is pressing the US government to maintain this suspension, particularly as traditional adversaries in the Pentagon and Congress are arguing for a 'business as usual' approach to economic and military engagement with Jakarta. There are compelling factors, however, which should dispel such notions of normalization of relations with Indonesia: the virtual imprisonment of 100,000 East Timorese refugees in West Timor; the continued militia activity in East and West Timor; the lack of legal redress relating to human rights abuses perpetrated during Indonesia's 24 year occupation; and the ongoing military oppression and violence within the Indonesian archipelago in regions such as Ambon, Aceh and West Papua.

The Indonesian military continues to operate with impunity in regions pressing claims for greater autonomy or independence and remains a constant threat to the fledgling democracy in Jakarta. The successful prosecution and punishment of those military personnel responsible for human rights abuses could send a clear signal that the practices of the old political order are no longer acceptable in the post-Suharto era. Although the Indonesian parliament is establishing a human rights court to deal with abuses, its mandate will not be retrospective or include crimes committed in East Timor prior to 1 January 1999. ETAN advocates the creation of an international tribunal which would 'focus on atrocities and human rights violations committed during the entire period of Indonesia's invasion and occupation of East Timor'.[27] Such a tribunal – like those examining abuses in Rwanda and the former Yugoslavia – would require the approval of the UN Security Council which has set aside such a move pending the outcome of internal judicial processes in Indonesia. However, ETAN and East Timorese leaders have urged the UN to be prepared to step in should Indonesia's efforts falter or fail to meet international standards.

Washington, too, should be ready to play its part in assisting efforts toward peace and reconciliation in East Timor. The Clinton administration has requested an aid budget for East Timor in the Fiscal Year 2001 which is $15 million less than that allocated in 2000.

Given the US government's military, diplomatic and financial support of the Suharto regime, it should now be prepared to shoulder its responsibilities for supporting vital aid and reconstruction work in East Timor. It is vital, therefore, that the US – and other Western powers – should not now turn its back on East Timor as the territory enters a transitional phase toward independence.

References

1   Kahin, Audrey R. and McKahin, George, *Subversion as Foreign Policy: The Secret Eisenhower and Dulles Debacle in Indonesia* (New York, 1995, The New Press).

2   See articles by Kathy Kadane in *The Washington Post*, 20–23 May 1990.

3   Cable to Canberra from Australian ambassador Richard Woolcott, 17 August 1975, cited in Budiardjo, Carmel and Liong, Liem Soei, *The War Against East Timor* (London, 1984, Tapol), p. 9.

4   Mutual defence agreement between the USA and Indonesia on equipment, materials, and services (agreement effected by exchange of notes signed in Jakarta, 13 August 1958).

5   Hertsgaard, Mark, 'The secret life of Henry Kissinger', *The Nation*, 29 October 1990.

6   Transcript of a lecture by Dr Kissinger given at the Park Central Hotel, New York, 11 July 1995. Audiotape by Amy Goodman (WBAI/Pacifica Radio), transcribed by the East Timor *Action* Network/US.

7   Nixon, Richard M., 'Asia after Vietnam', *Foreign Affairs*, Vol. 46, No. 1, October 1967, p. 111.

8   Hartung, William D. and Washburn, Jennifer, *US Arms Transfers to Indonesia 1975–1997: Who's Influencing Whom?* (New York, 1997, World Policy Institute).

9   UN Security Council Resolution 384 (1975), adopted unanimously on 22 December 1975.

10 Moynihan, Daniel Patrick, *A Dangerous Place* (Boston, 1978, Little, Brown).

11 *Ibid.*

12 Jain, Anurag X. C., 'Senator Moynihan's ode to East Timor', unpublished account of a lecture by Senator Moynihan at Columbia University, New York, on 19 February 1996.

13 Letter from Senator Moynihan to the author, March 1994.

14 Letter from Senator Malcolm Wallop and 51 others to President George Bush, 25 November 1991.

15 This amendment was incorporated into the Foreign Operations Appropriations Act for fiscal year (FY) 1993. The US government runs on a fiscal year beginning in October of the previous year (i.e. FY 1993 begins on 1 October 1992 – even if Congress has not finished their appropriations legislation by then). Legislation establishing guidelines for appropriations is in effect for a single fiscal year. Consequently, it must be re-enacted by Congress every year in order to remain law.

16 Appropriations Committee report to accompany HR 4426, 'Foreign Operations, Export Financing and Related Programs Appropriations Act for FY 1995' approved by the US House of Representatives on 23 May 1994.

17 Nairn, Allan 'Indonesia's killers', *The Nation*, 30 March 1998.

18 Amendment incorporated in the Defence Appropriations Act for FY 1999, HR 3161, passed by Congress on 29 September 1998.

19 The School of the Americas (SOA), a US army facility in Fort Benning, Georgia, has trained thousands of soldiers from Latin America for several decades. Many of the soldiers who committed some of the worst atrocities in El Salvador, Guatemala, Haiti, Colombia and other repressive countries are SOA graduates. A grassroots movement in the USA is trying to close it. Although Indonesian soldiers do not participate in the SOA (it is only for western hemisphere countries), they have received similar training through the IMET and JCET programmes.

20 'International appeal to end military support for Indonesia', *Estafeta* (New York, Autumn 1997, East Timor *Action* Network). The figures are taken from annual reports on world military expenditures and arms exports prepared by the US Arms Control and Disarmament Agency.

21 Editorial, 'Self-defence and reality', *Jakarta Post*, 11 August 1993.

22 President Clinton's press conference at the Jakarta Hilton, 15 November 1994. Transcript by the White House Press Office.

23 Pell, Senator Claiborne, 'Democracy: An emerging Asian value', Report 104-45 to the Committee on Foreign Relations, US Senate, 27 June 1996.

24 Letter from Senator Feingold and 13 other senators to President Clinton, 15 November 1996.

25 Letter from President Clinton to Senator Feingold, 27 December 1996.

26 Fredricksson, Lynn 'We can't stop here: US military assistance to Indonesia remains suspended but for East Timor, refugee return and accountability remain unresolved' *Estafeta* (New York, Autumn 1999, East Timor *Action* Network).

27 Miller, John 'Atrocity investigations in East Timor and the possibilities for a tribunal' *Estafeta* (New York, Spring 2000, ETAN). 4

10

Canberra: Jakarta's Trojan Horse in East Timor

Jim Aubrey

'We would do absolutely nothing.' Australia Prime Minister Gough Whitlam, when asked on ABC television on 4 December 1975 what Australia would do if Indonesia invaded Portuguese East Timor.

Introduction

When the Supreme Commander of the Allied Expeditionary Force, American General (later President) Dwight Eisenhower, entered Buchenwald concentration camp in 1945 and gazed upon the reality of Adolf Hitler's 'final solution' – hundreds of emaciated Jews surrounded by hundreds more who had died in the previous week – he remarked that the only hope to be gleaned from such a devastating sight was that the majority of German people could not have known that this barbarity was taking place. Yet we know that the fate of the Jews was not a state secret, even though the formulation of the 'final solution' was. In contrast to General Eisenhower's assumption about the German people, the Australian leaders and people who turned their backs on East Timor, their Second World War ally, had been fully cognizant of the brutal tyranny and genocide inflicted upon the East Timorese since 1975.

This chapter will discuss the Australian government's (Canberra's) complicity in East Timor's invasion and occupation, with particular reference to crimes against humanity and the right to self-determination. Australia's financial aid to Indonesia and East Timor will also be considered, before discussing the role of Australian leaders, policy makers and some media analysts in perverting the course of justice by aiding and legitimizing the oppressive 'New Order' regime of President Suharto. Diplomatic and material support for Suharto, in effect, undermined and dehumanized the Timorese struggle for justice and freedom, and served to strengthen the

Indonesian hand in the territory. Finally, I will offer an analysis of the role which Canberra has played in East Timor in the post-Suharto era, particularly, following the militia/military backlash to the 30 August referendum vote for independence in the territory.

Australia, Japan and East Timor

After the Second World War, the Australian federal parliament passed the 1945 War Crimes Act, by which military courts were established to apply the judicial process to suspected Japanese war criminals. British and American tribunals were also established to prosecute suspected Japanese war criminals for their maltreatment of Australian prisoners of war. A total of 924 suspects were brought before the Australian tribunals, of whom 644 were convicted and 148 sentenced to death, invariably by shooting or hanging. In effect, the convictions and the harsh sentences meted out to criminals set a precedent for Australia's actions in response to crimes against humanity.

The federal Attorney General and Minister for External Affairs in 1945, Dr Herbert Evatt, stated that 'the Australian government is determined that nothing that can be done to punish those responsible for brutality and cruelty will be left undone'.[1] This viewpoint had bi-partisan support to the extent that it even enjoyed rare parliamentary unanimity. War criminals were prosecuted for abuses that included torture, arbitrary violence, calculated cruelty, ill-treatment of prisoners of war (POWs), extra-judicial killings, ill-treatment of local inhabitants, rape, and massacres of soldiers. Not all of those war criminals executed, however, were found guilty of murder. 'It is our duty,' Evatt stated on 17 September 1945, 'that those who organized the system are punished and that the system itself is completely eradicated.'[2]

Concomitant with these crimes against humanity was the extraordinary sacrifice of the East Timorese for Australia's war effort. Although the Portuguese colony of East Timor was a neutral territory, the East Timorese fought with Australian commandos against the logistically superior Japanese forces during the war, and consequently suffered at least 60,000 fatalities. They provided refuge for the Australian military and fought with the 2/2nd and 2/4th Australian commando companies. The military courts, however, did not prosecute one Japanese soldier for war crimes against the East Timorese, despite the fact that this small territory suffered proportionately twice the fatalities of the Australian military in every theatre of operations during the Second World War.

Post-war Australia recognized, then, that acts of brutality warranted a full judicial response and they acted without equivocation in dispensing justice when Australians were the victims. Bellicose condemnations of Japanese intentions persist to the present – sometimes in the most absurd circumstances. The fact that Japan has never made an emphatic apology for its brutal past has only served to increase the resentment of surviving Australian POWs. There is only occasional consideration given to the current macro bilateral relationship between Australia and Japan, which can arouse memories and emotions of the past, as illustrated in 1997 by the attempt of the executive body of the Australian Capital Territory (ACT) to commemorate a park in Canberra as a peace memorial with the Japanese 'sister city' Nara, naming it the Canberra-Nara Peace Park. 'Given the circumstances of the failure of Japan as a nation to come to terms with its role in World War II, the RSL remains completely opposed to calling the park a "peace" park,' wrote the national president of the Returned Services League (RSL), Major-General Digger James, to the ACT's Chief Minister Kate Carnell.[3] Commonwealth (i.e. central) government pressure resulted in Prime Minister John Howard threatening to withdraw the necessary federal approval for the park if the name was not changed. Even the word 'friendship' was deemed inappropriate, and the ACT executive finally and simply named the site the more innocuous Canberra-Nara Park.

In stark contrast, the Australian government has been quite calculated in tolerating war crimes and human rights abuses directed at non-Australians. In the case of East Timor, Canberra has been supporting autonomy and special status for the territory as part of the Indonesian republic, in spite of the fact that the Indonesians have been responsible for the deaths of 200,000 Timorese since 1975. The Australian government thus approved the execution of Japanese war criminals, but conducted a business-as-usual relationship with Indonesian authorities guilty of similar atrocities, at the same time promoting a policy of 'constructive engagement' and 'quiet diplomacy' – in order to be seen to be safeguarding human rights concerns. The reality is that Canberra has conspired with the Indonesian regime to profit from Timorese resources, as seen in 1991 with the signing of the Timor Gap agreement.

The precedent for ignoring the persecution in East Timor began with Canberra's indifference to the widespread atrocities which attended General Suharto's rise to power in 1965. Previously classified cabinet papers, released in 1997 under the 30-year State Secrets Act, show that the former Minister for External Affairs, Paul Hasluck, persuaded the cabinet to approve secret financial aid to Suharto's anti-communist forces regardless of their widespread atrocities both during and after the 1965 coup. There was some opposition within Parliament House to what was seen as Australia's acquiescence to Jakarta, which was not perceived as being in the nation's interest. Concerning the 1965–66 blood-letting (see Chapter 5),

Kim Beazley, the Labour MP for Fremantle, stated on 19 March 1968 that 'we are friendly towards Indonesia, but I still say that genocide is a crime, and I hope the whole weight of Australia's influence is directed against this extermination. We are never going to escape the price of these crimes. They have a cost.'[4] Albert James, the MP for Hunter, also asked, on 20 March 1969: 'Are we to follow the course that we are now following – to remain silent when barbarity is perpetrated by our friends and to urge military support when it is perpetrated by those who are not our friends?'[5]

Accommodation and collaboration: Gough Whitlam

Deliberate policies to undermine the credibility and legitimacy of East Timor's struggle against the Indonesian occupation were adopted by the successive administrations of Whitlam, Fraser, Hawke, Keating and Howard. With full knowledge of the human rights abuses inflicted upon the East Timorese, Australian leaders and opinion makers chose to offer greater allegiance to the Indonesian oppressors than their victims. When Indonesian soldiers killed five journalists at Balibo in 1975, three of whom were Australian (see Chapter 4), Jakarta took Australian silence as an indication of Canberra's support for the invasion of East Timor. Senator Arthur Gietzelt argued, in April 1976, that the order to murder the newsmen was even picked up on Australian naval radio.[6] Government officials were, therefore aware of the killings at Balibo but failed to condemn (or even avert) them publicly, or the Indonesian invasion of East Timor. Moreover, no immediate, official inquiry was launched into the deaths or their circumstances.

The Australian Ambassador to Indonesia, Richard Woolcott, was more forthcoming on the government's position on the invasion when he stated clinically, in a telegram (later leaked) sent to Canberra in August 1975, that 'we leave events to take their course, and act in a way which would be designed to minimize the public impact in Australia and show private understanding to Indonesia of their problems. I am recommending a pragmatic rather than a principled stand but that is what national interest and foreign policy is all about.'[7] What was an essential and inalienable right to self-determination thus became, in terms of *realpolitik*, an expendable human right for the people of East Timor. President Suharto received the 'green light' for the invasion from the Australian Labour government, and even enjoyed the 'private understanding' of the conservative opposition, as was later divulged by the principal Indonesian figures involved. The Indonesian military had allegedly been involved in clandestine discussions with the Liberal party concerning their position on Indonesia's intentions towards East Timor. Significantly, a conservative coalition was to replace the Labour government a few weeks before the all-out invasion of East Timor on 7 December 1975. The disclosure by the Indonesians of the accommodating nature of their meeting with the new Foreign Affairs Minister, Andrew Peacock, while he was on holiday in Bali in September 1975, was strongly denied by Peacock when he was questioned about the matter in the federal parliament.[8]

An accommodation between Australia and Indonesia, however, later developed into collaboration, when the former Prime Minister Gough Whitlam went uninvited, and ultimately unsuccessfully, to the United Nations in November 1982 to persuade the UN General Assembly to withdraw East Timor from its agenda. Whitlam was Prime Minister from 1972 until 11 November 1975, and is reported as having told President Suharto – at their meeting at Wonosobo, Java, in 1974 – that East Timor would be better off as a part of Indonesia. He stated that East Timor was too small a territory to be independent and that it would not be economically viable as an independent nation.[9] Gough Whitlam's intervention, at the time, begged the question: is East Timor too small a territory to be independent? Its landmass is 14,953 square kilometres; neighbouring states include Brunei at 5765 square kilometres, Singapore at 622 square kilometres and Palau at 1632 square kilometres. An independent East Timor, therefore, is not such a territorial anomaly, that it must accept the demarcation orthodoxy of the one-island argument. The Caribbean nations of Haiti and the Dominican Republic share the same island, Haiti being a former French-speaking colony while the Dominican Republic was a Spanish colony. There is also the more difficult situation in the nation of Papua New Guinea, which shares the same island with the former Dutch colony of West New Guinea, the Indonesian-controlled territory of Irian Jaya.

It is worth recalling one of Whitlam's statements, made during the debates in Parliament House in 1962, over the status of West New Guinea. As opposition MP for Werrima, Whitlam was bemoaning the government's record on West New Guinea:

> On each occasion, self-determination was given no more than a perfunctory nod. It was never in the forefront of our arguments. We always relied on matters of defence, or on the fact that West New Guinea was alien to Indonesia in race, language, history and religion. All the specious arguments were put forward, and the only logical and moral argument was never emphasized. Self-determination is a good argument, and its strength has never yet been put in the UN by this government's representatives... We never pushed self-determination with determination.[10]

In the light of these remarks, one has to question Whitlam's assessment of East Timor's right to determine its own future. When Whitlam visited East

Timor in March 1982 he felt able, after only a week in the territory, to contradict the need for UN food appeals for the Timorese and deny reports of famine and widespread military oppression published by other visitors both before and after his visit.[11]

In 1962, Australia had acquiesced to Indonesia over the territorial status of West New Guinea, and was unwilling to condemn the extremely limited form of self-determination bestowed by Jakarta on West New Guinea and the subsequent annexation of the territory into the Republic of Indonesia as the province of Irian Jaya. The position of Canberra in relation to West New Guinea was a clear signal that Australia would not resist Indonesia's territorial expansionism in East Timor. The Australian Labour party – before, and even during, Whitlam's leadership – had an unequivocal position of support for the right of decolonizing states to self-determination, but Canberra clearly did not apply this policy to East Timor.

In addressing the UN General Assembly in September 1974, Whitlam had again stated that 'refusal to recognize the inalienable rights of all people to freedom and independence produces tension and conflict, not only between the oppressed and the oppressors, but between other nations which become associated or involved in these just and legitimate struggles'.[12] In the overall scheme of geopolitics, Whitlam (and consecutive leaders of the federal government) professed laudatory salutations in the international arena for the fundamental rights of freedom and self-determination, particularly for small nation-states. But when it came to the harsh reality of Indonesian occupation of East Timor, such sentiments were absent. In short, the Whitlam years in office were notable for duplicity, bad faith and collaboration with Indonesia on East Timor.

Aid and trade

Canberra endorsed the new Suharto era with the commencement of a bilateral aid programme and defence aid projects which helped to subsidize Jakarta's ever-increasing military expenditure. There are no official details of spending on aid to Indonesia for the years 1966–70; however, basing an annual estimate for these years at a modest A$10 million (1970–71 being A$15 million), by 1975 Canberra had granted Jakarta A$141 million in bilateral aid. In the period of East Timor's occupation from 1975 to the fall of Suharto in May 1998, Canberra granted Jakarta a total of A$2 billion in various forms of aid.[13]

Far more difficult to ascertain in Australian dollar terms are the Department of Defence contracts for defence cooperation with Jakarta and military training of Indonesian troops. Defence cooperation can include military aid, which again is difficult to estimate financially. However, in the critical period of 1972–80, Australian military aid to Indonesia included 12 GAF Nomad 22B aircraft, 16 Avon Sabre fighter aircraft, two Dakota DC3 aircraft, 12 Bell 47G Sioux helicopters, six Carpentaria-class patrol boats, two Attack-class patrol boats, the provision of training in Australia for 1200 Indonesian armed forces officers, and mapping projects in Sumatra, Kalimantan, West Irian and the Moluccas. The total cost of military aid from Canberra to Jakarta for this period was A\$50.5 million.[14] The deaths of the Australian journalists at Balibo in 1975 (see Chapter 4) had still not been officially confirmed when Canberra announced the second of a three-year military aid programme to Indonesia amounting to A\$25 million.[15] From the very first day of the invasion, in fact, the Australian Foreign Affairs Minister, Andrew Peacock, stated that the government would be ready to provide aid as soon as the fighting had eased.[16]

Since the fall of the 'New Order' regime, there have been some demands within Indonesia for the former president, Suharto, to answer charges of corruption and crimes against humanity. These charges should be pursued, together with an examination of the depth of Canberra's diplomatic and political complicity with Indonesia, which allowed Australia's leaders to aid and abet such a brutal regime for so long, while being in full possession of the facts regarding human rights violations. The genocidal dimensions of the Suharto regime have always been well documented in annual and extraordinary reports by the Catholic Church, NGOs such as Amnesty International and Human Rights Watch, and in the Department of Foreign Affairs' internal reports, regular Department of Defence intelligence reports and Senate enquires.

Canberra's support for Suharto was justified by a convenient 'ignorance' of the facts and was littered with pleas for a more sensitive understanding of 'unique Asian values'. Promoting the cultural relativity argument served to legitimize the 'softly softly' policy of quiet diplomacy and to devalue the universal obligations to defend victims of human rights violations. Jakarta's apologists, therefore, consistently expressed the need for a tolerant understanding of Indonesia's special needs, with genocide being ignored as a somehow acceptable by-product. Moreover, a feature of the policies of successive Australian leaders was their continual attempt to obfuscate the severity of occupation in East Timor. Not even the televised massacre of several hundred youths at Dili's Santa Cruz cemetery in November 1991 persuaded Canberra to deviate from accommodating Jakarta. Indeed, by calling the massacre an aberration, Canberra's policy makers illustrated the entrenched nature of their policy of accommodation and revealed their anxiety not to jeopardize political or commercial interests in Indonesia.[17] Australia's provision of material and military aid to Indonesia thus commenced immediately after the brutal 1965 coup and intensified after Jakarta's invasion of East Timor. The extent of Canberra's support of Indonesia under Suharto therefore showed its disregard for human rights and preparedness to ignore atrocities of genocidal proportions.

From Whitlam to Howard

In 1975, Malcolm Fraser succeeded Gough Whitlam as prime minister, leading a conservative coalition government. While in opposition, Fraser had referred to the East Timorese as 'communists', thereby mischievously delegitimizing their struggle against invasion and persecution and sustaining the policy of betrayal established by Whitlam. Fraser, as with all the leaders of Australian federal governments from 1975–1999, was kept informed about the invasion and occupation of East Timor through Australia's sophisticated defence surveillance network. Bruce Haige, who worked for the Defence Signals Department, recently corroborated this assertion, stating that regular reports on all details of the conflict, including fatality figures, went to the foreign affairs and defence ministers.[18]

Fraser and his colleagues were also kept informed of developments in the conflict through annual reports written by a former Australian consul to East Timor, James Dunn, who was from 1974 to 1985 the Director of the Department of Foreign Affairs advisory body, the Foreign Affairs Group of the Legislative Research Service. These reports gave graphic details of the human rights violations accompanying the invasion and occupation, and included the testimonies of eyewitnesses from interviews conducted by Dunn with East Timorese refugees in Portugal and Australia. Every report contains a detailed description of massacres, torture, famine, imprisonment, arbitrary execution, and the rape and violation of women, pregnant women and young girls. In his 1977 report, for instance, Dunn states that 'the military seizure of East Timor has been a bloody operation, in which atrocities of a disturbing nature have been committed against the civilian population. Indeed, these accounts of Indonesian behaviour in East Timor suggest that the plight of these people may well constitute, relatively speaking, the most serious case of contravention of human rights facing the world at this time.'[19] After reading this report, the Fraser government decided to grant formal recognition of Indonesian sovereignty over East Timor.

Prominent Labour politicians Tom Uren, Ken Fry, Lionel Bowen, Senator Wriedt and Senator Gietzelt, for several years, drew the government's attention to the gravity and scale of the atrocities occurring in East Timor and directed at the civilian population.[20] While Fraser had opted to distance Australia from the East Timorese by branding them 'communists', several parliamentarians had travelled to East Timor in the period before the invasion and offered a more truthful and informed first-hand account of events there. The report of one trip, presented by Ken Fry and Senator Gietzelt to the Labour government and the opposition in September 1975, makes particular reference to the 'communist' bogey:

> We are also satisfied that there is no genuine basis for the charge by the UDT forces that Fretilin is a communist controlled or dominated organization… Their leadership impressed us as being moderate, highly responsible, dedicated and intelligent in their approach. To attribute their success so far to outside influence would, in our opinion, be a grave error of judgement and a misperception of the over-riding grassroots desire for independence from colonial overlords by the indigenous people and their leaders.[21]

Journalist Roger East also stated, in his last report from Dili before his murder (see Chapter 4), that:

> Jakarta has elected to win support from its nervous neighbours by attaching the 'red' label to Fretilin. Visions of Chinese sampans, Hanoi dhows and Russian cruisers riding at anchor in Dili harbour are sufficient for ASEAN states, countering communist insurgencies, to see the threat real and applaud its removal.[22]

Moreover, even though reports of Jakarta's plan to invade East Timor were published in the (Melbourne) *Age* and the *Sydney Morning Herald* in February 1975, the Fraser government had the audacity to state, two days before the invasion on 7 December 1975, that 'the Federal government believes Indonesia may be softening its policy so that East Timor may become part of its territory'.[23] We now know from Hamish McDonald's recent exposé that Canberra not only had advance warning of the invasion, but that Australian officials were meeting with two of the Indonesian architects of the invasion, at times on a daily basis, during 1975.[24]

By 1978 it was estimated, by the Indonesian Foreign Affairs Minister, Mochtar Kusumaatmadja, that the East Timor fatality figure was 120,000.[25] There were also the aforementioned reports from church groups, Amnesty International and other NGOs of dozens of massacres. Some of these reports stated that the civilian population in East Timor living outside the Indonesian-controlled areas was being bombed with napalm on a scale similar to that of the American bombing in Vietnam, and also that thousands were literally dropping dead from the war-induced famine that aid workers had described as being equal to the situation in Biafra. Nevertheless, in 1978, Fraser accorded *de facto* recognition of Indonesia's annexation of East Timor, which by that time had been designated Jakarta's 27th province.

From recognition to expropriation (1979–91)

In 1978, Australia moved from a position of abstaining on the UN General Assembly resolutions which condemned the occupation of East Timor to voting against them.[26] This policy was extended further in February 1979, when Australia became the only state to offer *de jure* recognition of Indonesia's annexation of East Timor. Canberra justified its diplomatic and legal endorsement of Indonesia's aggression toward East Timor by reasserting its view that Timor was an 'unviable state' given the size and population of the territory and, in any event, it was 'geographically natural' that East Timor be integrated into the Indonesian archipelago.[27] However, James Dunn has stated that the real motivation behind Canberra's move to legally recognise the annexation of East Timor was 'to facilitate negotiations with Jakarta on seabed rights and oil exploration in the Timor Gap'.[28] The Australian government wanted to ensure that these negotiations would be conducted on a 'legal' footing to offset the possibility of a third party challenging any agreement brokered with Jakarta under the terms of international law. Nonetheless, Canberra's move to offer *de jure* status to Indonesia *vis-à-vis* its intervention in East Timor was legally flawed. Whilst the UN Security Council and General Assembly resolutions on East Timor did not call explicitly for the non- recognition of Indonesia – which is left to the discretion of individual states – they unambiguously prohibit the use of force in international relations as a principle of international law.[29] Therefore, the basis of Canberra's negotiations with Jakarta on Timor Gap oil exploration – Australia's move to *de jure* status – had no legal foundation.

Canberra's position on East Timor, therefore, remained unchanged when a Labour government came to power in 1983, with Bob Hawke as prime minister. Hawke argued that a refusal to recognize the annexation of East Timor would exacerbate the situation of the East Timorese and close off all channels of communication with Jakarta. The government suggested that those seeking to support East Timor would 'do better to concentrate on helping the province through the provision of development aid and assistance'.[30] However, the apparent prioritization by the Labour government of the humanitarian needs of the East Timorese over non-recognition of Indonesia's annexation of the territory merely served to disguise Australia's own economic interest in East Timor's natural resources. In October 1978, negotiations began between Australia and Indonesia on excavating oil and gas reserves in East Timor's coastal waters, and by 1985 the Hawke administration's discussions with Suharto's regime were considered of 'economic importance to Australia'.[31] By 1986, bids for drilling rights from oil companies had already produced A$31.5 million,[32] compared to a total of A$9 million in aid assistance from the Australian government to the East Timorese between 1975 and 1985.[33] The Timor Gap Treaty, signed by Australia and Indonesia in December 1989, represented a joint enterprise between the two governments to exploit for selfish gain the natural wealth of a brutally occupied territory. As the recognized authority over East Timor in the UN, Portugal attempted to challenge the legality of the treaty in the International Court of Justice, but was unsuccessful owing to Indonesia's non-recognition of the court.

The importance of Indonesia as a major economic force in South-East Asia and trading partner with Australia ensured diplomatic support of Suharto's regime from Canberra. In July 1983, Bill Hayden, the Minister for Foreign Affairs in the Hawke administration, sent a parliamentary delegation to East Timor in the wake of a cease-fire agreement between Fretilin and the Indonesian military leadership in Dili. According to Taylor, the delegation was 'less a commission of enquiry than a goodwill mission' and it viewed East Timor in a 'firmly Indonesian context'.[34] When Bill Morrison, the delegation leader, was questioned on his return to Australia about Fretilin reports of a new offensive by the Indonesian military, he replied that 'certainly nothing we saw, nothing we were told there, gives any credence to that report'.[35] On 17 August, however, reportedly 'heartened by the delegation's supportive approach',[36] Leonardus Murdani, the Indonesian armed forces commander-in-chief, launched a new offensive in East Timor code-named Operasi Persatuan (Operation Unity).

The Canberra government, meanwhile, urged the Australian media to play 'fair' with the regime in Jakarta, and desist from any reportage which might damage Suharto's regime – and, by association, the Hawke administration. In 1981, the Australian Broadcasting Corporation office in Jakarta was closed down after Radio Australia reported a famine in East Timor which was directly related to Indonesia's occupation of the territory. When the office was re-opened in 1990, it was under the watchful eye of the Department of Foreign Affairs in Canberra. Similarly, when journalists filmed the brutal treatment of East Timorese protestors by the Indonesian police during the visit of Pope John Paul II to East Timor in 1989, Australian embassy officials pleaded that their footage should not be used.[37] In February 1991 – nine months before the Dili massacre – Gareth Evans, the Australian Foreign Minister at the time, stated that 'the human rights situation [in East Timor] has, in our judgement, greatly improved under the present military arrangements'.[38] In summarizing this period, Chinkin states: 'It is hard to escape the conclusion that Australia's position on East Timor has been fashioned by expediency and the desire to share in the maritime resources of the territory, rather than by principled application of norms in international law.'[39]

From Keating to Howard

In September 1993, a newly elected Labour leader, Paul Keating, expressly went to Washington at a time when restrictions were being placed upon US defence sales and defence training to Jakarta. Keating urged President Clinton to withdraw human rights considerations from the drafting of economic and defence contracts. In 1995, the Keating government even awarded the Order of Australia to Ali Alatas, the Indonesian Foreign Affairs Minister, at a time when many countries in the world were giving peace accolades to Timorese leaders Bishop Belo and José Ramos-Horta. Then, in December 1995, without any debate in Australia's parliament, the Keating government signed a defence pact with Indonesia, much to the disdain of opposition parties and the general public alike. The current prime minister, Liberal leader John Howard, as Minister for Business and Consumer Affairs in the Fraser government was involved in the confiscation of a boatload of medical supplies which Australian activists had attempted to send to the civilian population of East Timor in 1976.

In August 1998, at a meeting in the UN between Indonesia and Portugal, agreement was reached on 'special status [for East Timor], based on wide ranging autonomy'.[40] The Indonesian and Portuguese Foreign Affairs Ministers, Ali Alatas and Jaime Gama, set a deadline of December 1998 for resolving the dispute over East Timor. The Australian Foreign Affairs Minister, Alexander Downer, called it a 'step forward' and 'great progress' but, at the time, declined any role for Canberra in promoting a just and lasting settlement of the 24-year conflict. Indonesian propaganda depicted the former Portuguese colony as irrevocably divided on the issue of self-determination, and even suggested that the role of the military included protecting the pro-Indonesian integrationists from the East Timorese majority. On several occasions in 1998, Downer too claimed that the East Timorese situation was one of such complexity that self-determination could be more divisive rather than unifying. In 1999, however, the Australian government seemed finally to recognize the gravity of changes taking place across Indonesia and their implications for East Timor. In a letter to President Habibie in January, Premier Howard suggested a reversal of Australia's support for the *status quo* and this made a considerable impact on Suharto's successor (see Chapter 14). Thus, at the eleventh hour, after supporting Suharto 'all the way', the Australian leadership began to abandon a sinking ship.

Conclusion: Complicity, betrayal and damage limitation

Essentially, for Australia's leaders, agreement with Indonesia's 'New Order' regime took precedence over any disagreement. Where there were concerns over Indonesia's human rights record, policies to delegitimize these anxieties were adopted. In this respect, Howard's supine remarks, in Jakarta in 1996, on the issue of human rights violations in East Timor warrant inspection. Howard stated that 'where there were differences and concerns, there should be a sensible dialogue on these, but they should not be allowed to influence or have a negative or deleterious impact on the overall relationship'.[41] Yet, as regards 'the overall relationship', it is important to stress that Australian public opinion clearly supported the UN-supervised act of self-determination for East Timor. A recent television survey before the August 1999 referendum showed an 83 per cent vote of support for East Timor's right to determine its own future.[42] By not immediately supporting this measure, the Australian government had misrepresented the wishes of its people and overruled the needs of the Timorese.

On invasion day, 7 December 1975, a desperate appeal had been published in Australian newspaper reports:

> They are killing indiscriminately. Women and children are being shot in the streets. A lot of people have been killed. We are all going to be killed. I repeat, we are all going to be killed. This is an appeal for international help. We appeal to the Australian people. Please help us! Please!'[43]

Over two decades later at the August 1998 Fretilin plenary held in Sydney, the Fretilin guerrilla leader Mau Hudo Ranka Dalak, on reflecting upon the role of Australia in his country's plight, stated:

> We had hoped Australia was going to be a counter-weight to Indonesian propaganda and power in the international diplomatic arena, however, instead, we were faced with an Australia that was a terrible weight upon us, that weight being the alliance between Jakarta and Canberra.'[44]

In December 1998, the former Australian Prime Minister, Paul Keating, threatened to sue the journalist and film maker John Pilger over accusations that both Keating and the former Foreign Affairs Minister, Gareth Evans, withheld information about further massacres and atrocities which occurred after the 1991 Dili massacre. It is alleged that Philip Flood, the Australian Ambassador to Jakarta, suppressed a report he had written not long after the massacre. This report contained information concerning other atrocities which are said to have occurred after the massacre at the cemetery. The information surfaced at a meeting between Flood and Suharto's son-in-law, Prabowo Subianto, who was the Indonesian special forces (Kopassus) chief at the time. The report was passed on to Canberra almost three years after it was first compiled. Apparently, after having read the report in May 1994, Evans was adamant that no evidence of further atrocities existed, and both he and Keating attacked the credibility of Pilger's revelations (in the film *Death of a Nation*) about these additional atrocities.[45]

Canberra's pivotal role in affording respectability to Jakarta throughout one of the most enduring post-war conflicts and acts of genocide is a sorry indictment of the Australian political class. In this author's view, defending a 'national interest' that condones genocide, complicitly looks the other way, or subverts the struggle of a nation for self-determination is indefensible. As the foreign editor of the *Sydney Morning Herald*, Hamish McDonald, recalls, the Australian government had prior warning of the 7 December invasion and of the 16 October mini-invasion which led to the murder of five Australian based journalists at Balibo, East Timor. The apparent intention of concealing the true fate of the Balibo Five, in addition to the fact that throughout 1975 Australian embassy officials were meeting almost on a daily basis with key Indonesian architects of the invasion of East Timor, warrants a full judicial inquiry into this cover-up. At last – and in the light of new evidence (see Chapter 4) – it would seem that the government has come round to holding a more proper inquiry on Balibo. It is crucial, though, that the new probe gets to the heart of Australia's complicity in this sad affair.

In the closing weeks of the 1998 parliamentary sessions, a motion was adopted in the federal Senate for a new Senate inquiry into the government's record and policy on East Timor, both past and present. In trying to keep pace with the momentum of change in Jakarta, as well as responding to both domestic pressure from the campaigns of Australian activists and the positive policy changes of the Labour party, the government dispatched an Australian Military Attaché to East Timor to review the Indonesian military position and offer various recommendations.

Australia's shifting position toward Jakarta was further evident on 5 January 1999 when the Howard government recognized the East Timorese right to self-determination. This abrupt policy reversal could be seen as a damage-limitation exercise given Canberra's unstinting support of Indonesia throughout the latter's 24-year genocidal occupation. According to Tapol (the Indonesia Human Rights Campaign), however, Australia's belated support for East Timorese independence was the 'final straw' for the Habibie regime[46] and contributed to the dramatic announcement, from Jakarta in January 1999, that a referendum would be held to determine the future of East Timor in August.

The UN-sponsored ballot was held on 30 August in the context of increasing violence in East Timor from pro-Indonesia militias established and guided by the Indonesian military (see Chapter 14). An overwhelming 78.5 per cent of East Timorese, from a 99 per cent turnout, voted for independence, and the militias/military responded to this result by pursuing a carefully orchestrated and premeditated 'scorched-earth' policy, and forcing 'seven out of every eight' people in East Timor to flee their homes.[47] The mayhem and carnage which followed the ballot, together with intense campaigning and lobbying by civil society organizations throughout the world, finally prompted an international reponse to the crisis.

On 19 September 1999, Australia led a UN-sponsored force into East Timor to restore order and ensure the implementation of the mandate for independence. The International Force for East Timor (Interfet), comprised some 7500 troops from 20 nations under the command of Australian Major-General Peter Cosgrove. Ironically, Interfet comprised troops from many of the nations – including Australia – which had facilitated, or been complicit in, the genocide in East Timor. Many of the countries which had provided diplomatic support, material aid and arms to Indonesia were now portrayed in the mainstream media as the saviours of East Timor. This irony was not lost on Indonesia, where most anger was directed at Canberra, its former staunch ally and regional supporter. Canberra's role in Interfet led to 'assaults on Australian personnel and property' within Indonesia, as Jakarta's former ally was considered to have its 'own designs on East Timor's resources'.[48]

Interfet's intervention in East Timor led to the withdrawal of Indonesian troops in October 1999, and it is now incumbent on the international community to actively engage in the reconstruction of the territory. Moreover, Canberra's role in East Timor's persecution should be subject to full accountability, including provision of a compensation package for the illegal exploitation of East Timor's oil and gas reserves in the Timor Gap. Also, codes of conduct must be established for all ministerial departments in order that they are bound by moral and ethical imperatives in the future. The need for such moral safeguards was reinforced by recent comments made by the former Australian prime minister, Paul Keating, in which he stated that 'we are locked for eternity with Indonesia. Our vital interest is in managing that relationship. In three years, Howard has our largest neighbour at our throats.'[49] It is to be hoped that a proper system of checks and balances would prevent Australian leaders from subsidizing brutal military dictatorships in the future.

References

1 *Commonwealth of Australia Parliamentary Debates*, House of Representatives, 1944, p. 2532.

2 *Chronicle of Australia* (London and Sydney, 1993, Penguin Books Australia and Chronicle Communications), p. 601.

3 Green, Gervase, 'War and Peace: how a word upset the PM', *The Australian Age*, 19 April 1997, p. 27.

4   *Commonwealth of Australia Parliamentary Debates*, House of Representatives, 19 March 1968, Vol. 58, p. 218.

5   *Ibid.*, Vol. 62, p. 754.

6   *Commonwealth of Australia Parliamentary Debates*, Senate, Vol. 67, p. 1171.

7   Juddery, Bruce, 'Do not accuse Jakarta: Ambassador', *Canberra Times*, 31 May 1976, p. 1.

8   Fry, Ken, 'Lest we forget' in Aubrey, Jim (ed.), *Free East Timor: Australia's Culpability in East Timor's Genocide* (Sydney, 1998, Vintage Books) gives a comprehensive account of the Peacock affair.

9   Hastings, Peter, *Sydney Morning Herald*, 16 September 1974; Richardson, Michael, *Australian National Times*, 19–24 July 1976, p. 10. In his 1980 book *Suharto's Indonesia*, Hamish McDonald states that after the so-called civil war Whitlam sent Suharto a private message 'saying that nothing he said earlier should be interpreted as a veto on Indonesian action in the changed circumstances', (Melbourne, 1980, Fontana) p. 207.

10   *Commonwealth of Australia Parliamentary Debates*, House of Representatives, 10 April 1962, Vol. 35, pp. 1510–1512.

11   See, for example, reports published in the *Philadelphia Inquirer*, 28 May 1982, and the *Asian Wall Street Journal*, 14 June 1982. Catholic Church sources in East Timor in February 1982 reported that half the population was facing serious food shortages.

12   *Australian Foreign Affairs Record*, Department of Foreign Affairs, Canberra, September 1974, p. 583.

13   Figures provided by AusAID, Canberra.

14   See Waddingham, John, 'Keeping Suharto on top', *Inside Indonesia*, Vol. 2, 1984, p. 34.

15   Richardson, Michael, 'We'll give Jakarta $25m in arms', *The Australian Age*, 8 November 1975, p. 7.

16   See the *Sydney Morning Herald*, 9 December 1975, p. 1.

17   See Aubrey, *Free East Timor*, p. 282.

18   ABC television programme *Four Corners, East Timor: the Final Solution*, reporter Chris Masters, 15 June 1998. See also Van Atta, Dale and Toohey, Brian, 'The Timor papers', *Australian National Times*, 30 May and 6 June 1982; and Munster, George and Walsh, Richard, *Documents on Australian Defence and Foreign Policy*, (Sydney, 1980; though banned at the time, some copies are now publicly available).

19   Dunn, James, *The East Timor Situation: A Report on Talks with Timorese Refugees in Portugal* (Legislative Research Service, Australian Parliament, Canberra, 1977), p. 12.

20   From 1991 there was a bi-partisan parliamentary group called Parliamentarians for East Timor which consistently brought to the government's attention the human rights violations perpetrated in East Timor.

21   Gietzelt, A. and Fry, Ken, 'Report on visit to East Timor, 16–18 September 1975', in Aubrey, *Free East Timor*, p. 39. Ken Fry was also invited to the United Nations in 1976 to address the General Assembly on his view of East Timor. This address is reproduced in *Free East Timor*.

22   East, Roger, in Aubrey *Free East Timor*, p. 29.

23   *Sydney Morning Herald*, 5 December 1975, p. 1. Also see Clark, Roger, 'From Canberra … what we knew', *Australian National Times*, 5–10 January 1976.

24   McDonald, Hamish, 'Revealed: Timor cover-up', *Sydney Morning Herald*, 24 August 1998, pp. 1, 10–11.

25   Taylor, John G., *Indonesia's Forgotten War: The Hidden History of East Timor* (London, 1991, Zed Books), p. 203.

26 Chinkin, Christine, 'Australia and East Timor in international law', in *International Law and the Question of East Timor* (London, 1995, CIIR/IPJET), p. 277.

27 Dunn, James, 'The Timor Affair in International Perspective', in Carey, P. and Bentley, G., (eds), *East Timor at the Crossroads: The Forging of a Nation* (London, 1995, Cassell), p.72.

28 See Chinkin, 'Australia and East Timor', p. 283.

29 *Ibid.*, p. 279.

30 *Ibid.*, p. 277.

31 *Ibid.*, p. 288.

32 Taylor, *Indonesia's Forgotten War*, p. 208.

33 See Chinkin, 'Australia and East Timor', p. 278.

34 See Taylor, *Indonesia's Forgotten War*, p. 138.

35 *Ibid.*, p. 141.

36 *Ibid.*, p. 141.

37 See Pilger, *Hidden Agendas*, p. 271.

38 *Ibid.*, p. 261.

39 See Chinkin, 'Australia and East Timor', p. 289.

40 Le Grand, Chip and Garran, Robert, 'Downer talks up Timor peace', *The Australian*, 7 August 1998, p. 1.

41 SBS and ABC Television news reports, 17 September 1996.

42 The opinion poll was part of the Channel Nine current affairs programme, Sunday 19 July 1998, reporter Paul Ramsley.

43 Richardson, Michael, *Sydney Morning Herald*, 8 December 1975, p. 1.

44 Second Fretilin plenary, 14 August 1998, El Toro Motor Inn, Warwick Farm, Sydney, Australia.

45 Pilger, John, 'Blood on our hands: The betrayal of East Timor', *Sunday Age*, 22 November 1998, p. 25.

46 *Tapol Bulletin*, No 151, March 1999.

47 Taylor, John G., *East Timor: The Price of Freedom* (London, 1999, Zed Books), p. 229.

48 'After murder most foul', *The Independent on Sunday*, 19 September 1999.

49 *The Age*, 4 October 1999.

11

The Local Meets the Global:
East Timor and Ireland's Presidency
of the European Union

Eilís Ward

Introduction

After the fall of the Suharto regime in 1998, the European Union (EU) moved towards a new approach in its relations with Indonesia, including a re-evaluation of its position on East Timor. Following a sustained campaign by the Portuguese government, with the active support of other member states and urged on by civil society campaigns in the member states, the EU had agreed a collective policy on East Timor in 1996. That policy had, amongst other things, called on the Indonesian government to improve the human rights situation in East Timor, and committed the EU to achieving a solution to the problem which accorded with international law and together with the funding of aid projects, bolstered those rights and improved living standards in the territory.

The fall of Suharto and the meltdown of the Indonesian economy in the context of a general economic crisis in Asia during 1998 altered not only the parameters within which the EU viewed issues concerning East Timor, but also how Europe related to Indonesia and the other members of the Association of South-East Asian Nations (ASEAN),[1] among which Indonesia was a major economic player. While Indonesia remained a very important trading partner and investment location for the EU, the immediate objective was to prevent an escalation of the economic crisis and ensure regional economic and political stability. Suharto's demise, however, resulted in some positive changes in the situation of East Timor which necessitated a reconsideration of the EU position on the territory. Significant progress in the UN-sponsored tripartite talks (between the UN, Indonesia and Portugal) on East Timor resulted in the Indonesians accepting the idea of some form of autonomy for the territory. Whilst this was not an ultimate solution in Timorese eyes, the move nonetheless indicated a reversal of Indonesian policy on occupied East Timor. In 1999, the Indonesian government moved even further by agreeing to facilitate a referendum on the future of East Timor under the auspices of the UN on 30 August. The referendum resulted in an overwhelming (78.5 per cent) mandate for independence which prompted a violent backlash by the Indonesian military and pro-integrationist militia groups. The militias were created and controlled by the military to initially prevent the mandate for independence through intimidation and terror, and then following the referendum, to obstruct UN efforts to implement the result. The widespread devastation and violence wrought by the military/militias in East Timor eventually provoked a belated armed intervention by the United Nations. The UN's protracted and ultimately delayed intervention in East Timor, however, through the International Force for East Timor (Interfet), provided the military and militias with the opportunity to methodically and brutally displace tens of thousands of East Timorese (see Chapter 14). Although the Indonesian military eventually withdrew from East Timor following the UN's decision to intervene, there remains the long-term process of recon-struction and redevelopment of the territory and, more immediately, the repatriation of the internally displaced refugees. The EU has a significant role to play here in terms of aid provision, assisting the establishment of an East Timorese government and, importantly, enabling the territory to become a viable self-sustaining economic entity. During the occupation of East Timor, the majority of EU members allowed profitable economic rela-tions with Indonesia to override concerns about human rights abuses in the territory. The EU now has a duty to take responsibility for its past actions with the provision of practical and long-term support for East Timor.

The evolution of the EU's position on East Timor has been slow and uneven. Without Portuguese interest, it is doubtful whether the EU initially would have devoted anything other than cursory attention to the problem. At times, though, other member states played important roles in keeping East Timor on the EU's agenda. When Ireland assumed the six-monthly rotated presidency of the European Union in July 1996, hopes were high amongst activists and others that a significant EU initiative on East Timor would soon follow. It was largely due to the highly successful activities of a small solidarity group that the Republic of Ireland (hereafter Ireland) became identified within the EU as a 'friend' of East Timor. According to Tom Hyland, coordinator of the East Timor Ireland Solidarity Campaign (ETISC), the 'signs' were very good. The Dublin-based government had agreed, in its EU presidential manifesto, to prioritize East Timor during its term. Both the taoiseach (prime minister) and the tanáiste (deputy prime minister) had personally associated themselves months earlier with the need for positive change in the territory. The previous summer, the Minister for Foreign Affairs, Dick Spring, had outlined a detailed and comprehensive policy analysis of Ireland's position on East Timor. This had called for an end to Indonesia's 'illegal occupation' of East Timor and the release of the Timorese resistance leader Xanana Gusmão and other political prisoners, and had proposed, amongst other things, a limited arms embargo against Indonesia.[2] Given Ireland's increasing claim to be a friend of East Timor, such a strong position was perhaps not surprising.

Just days before Ireland took up the presidency, the European Union adopted a common position (CP)[3] on East Timor (see below and Chapter 8). This document had been hammered out over the preceding months, and established, *inter alia*, that any solution to the difficulties in East Timor would have to be both internationally acceptable and based on international law. With the exception of a commitment to providing aid for non-governmental organizations (NGOs) involved in human rights work in East Timor, the common position articulated nothing like the kind of detail set out and called for by Tanáiste Dick Spring. Its adoption presented two possible interpretations of how East Timorese issues might be played out in the EU during the Irish presidency. Firstly, it could have been interpreted as providing a brake on more proactive policies which individual states, such as Ireland, might want to pursue. In other words, the CP was as far as the EU would move for some time. Alternatively, the CP could have been read as providing a basic framework from which the EU could devise further initiatives, such as facilitating the holding of a referendum in East Timor on the future of the territory or shifting the current impasse in other ways. The CP might thus be read as a basic enabling document. For the ETISC, hopes were invested in the second interpretation.

Focus

This chapter will focus on the evolution of Irish foreign policy towards East Timor leading up to and including its period in the presidency of the EU in 1996. It will trace the manner in which the activities of a small solidarity group, the ETISC, formed a bridge between local activism, the Irish state and the global human rights environment via the European Union. It will argue that Ireland's EU membership acted, at that time, as a constraint on its aspirations for change in East Timor, blocking local/national demands which would have gone further than the collective will of the EU allowed. This analysis must be measured, however, against a recognition of Ireland's limits as a small and solo actor on the world stage. As comparatively new policy weapons in the EU's armoury, CPs inevitably pose challenges to analysts. Also, it is important to point out that at the time when research was carried out for this chapter, the CP on East Timor was just a year old.

It will be argued that a source of the constraints which came into play during the Irish presidency was the decision-making structure of the EU foreign policy process, which limited the room to manoeuvre of individual member states. Under the common foreign and security policy (CFSP)[4] of the EU, the principle of common positions was established as a way of creating single collective positions rather than simply coordinating the foreign policies of member states. These collective positions were to be achieved by consensus. No individual state could be forced to comply with a position once it had been achieved, but a decision to go it alone, or to stand outside that position, would be neither politically nor strategically advisable. While changes in the CFSP introduced since the CP on East Timor was agreed altered how decisions were made, the broad thrust of a consensus approach to policy agreement still prevails. These changes, under the 1997 Treaty of Amsterdam, will not alter the CP itself, but they may have implications for how states implement it in the future. Under that treaty, EU member states which disagree on aspects of foreign policy decisions may withdraw from a particular collective action or decision.[5]

This chapter comprises three sections. First, it will establish the manner in which East Timor became a political issue within Ireland. Second, it will examine Ireland's role in the EU – specifically its role in the presidency – in relation to the CP. Thirdly, it will draw some conclusions.

The Irish position on East Timor

Beyond ritualized participation in UN procedures, Ireland, like most other countries in the developed world, effectively ignored the 1975 Indonesian invasion of East Timor and the subsequent fortunes of the occupied territory. Furthermore, at the UN, Ireland's involvement was minimal as abstentionism became the driving policy. Ireland abstained on a UN resolution in November 1976, that condemned the Indonesian invasion and asserted the right of the East Timorese to self-determination. It abstained again on a vote in November 1979, which requested the UN to provide relief within East Timor for refugees and children, and on a vote in November 1981, which – in response to an outbreak of famine – called on the UN humanitarian system to provide assistance to the territory. However, such abstentionism was not unique or unusual, as most other EU (then EC) members also abstained. While Ireland was formally neutral with a reputation for independence, it was in reality firmly allied with the West, and East Timor had become an East/West Cold War issue. The pro-Timor motions, such as both humanitarian motions referred to above, emanated from within the Soviet bloc and were supported by its allies. Portugal was the one European exception to the East/West division, as it supported the pro-Timor side in all votes. In terms of Ireland's world view, however, an abstention can also be read as a position which, by definition, did not oppose Indonesian activities in East Timor.

It was the Santa Cruz massacre, in November 1991, and the subsequent media coverage of this event that provided a significant catalyst for the evolution of a particular Irish position on East Timor. This came about because of two forces. A group of friends, gathered in Dublin to watch a television documentary on East Timor, were so affected by the programme that they decided to take up the issue. By early 1992, the ETISC was well established. The campaign went on to act as an internal force within the Irish policy-making process, pushing East Timor on to the agendas of successive governments, the Irish parliament and officials in the Department of Foreign Affairs. The massacre also provoked the EU member states and the wider global community to respond collectively. This created an external force for change, which was played out in the Irish arena through participation in EU and UN debates. It was, perhaps, through its participation in the EU that Ireland most significantly pressed for change in the Timorese situation in the early 1990s.

Under significant pressure from Portugal, the EU responded quickly to Santa Cruz and a declaration was issued condemning Indonesia for this massacre. East Timor was now an issue within the scope of the EU's foreign policy considerations. Since its accession to the European Union in 1986, Portugal had sought to bring East Timor to the top of the foreign policy agenda. The Santa Cruz massacre turned the tide of world public opinion from indifference to, and ignorance on, East Timor to a more sensitized position. It is from this point onwards, mediated by these external and internal forces, that we can see the development of an Irish position on East Timor, which was part of, and simultaneously more radical than, the slowly evolving policy of the EU.

An examination of Oireachtas (the Houses of Parliament) debates from 1992 to 1996–97 is revealing. In the 1980s, just one parliamentary question was tabled on East Timor.[6] But between 1992 and 1996, a total of 65 questions were tabled in the Dáil (lower house), four motions were passed in the Senate, three detailed statements on East Timor were also delivered in the Senate by the minister for foreign affairs or his representative, and in the Oireachtas Committee on Foreign Affairs (established in 1993) East Timor was debated in detail four times.[7] If Ireland had ignored East Timor in the 15 years following the invasion, it quickly made up for such lack of attention.

However, long discussions in parliament buildings, no matter how passionate, do not necessarily amount to policy. For that, the government had to determine a position which it then would seek to implement and defend internationally. Through statements issued and responses from government representatives to parliamentary questions, it is possible to trace the evolution of a position on East Timor within the Irish administration. This spanned the life of two governments: the Fianna Fáil/Labour coalition of 1992–95 and the Fine Gael/Labour/Democratic Left government of 1995–97. That evolution can be best described as a shift from a position of disengagement, which did little more than support the continued UN-sponsored talks between Indonesia and Portugal, to that described by the Minister for Foreign Affairs in 1995 as representing one of the 'main advocates'[8] of East Timor's struggle in regional and international fora such as the UN and the EU.

It is reasonable to suggest that much of the responsibility for the Irish focus on East Timor rests with the lobbying and networking activities of the ETISC. As a single-issue organization with a non-bureaucratic, flexible operating style, the ETISC successfully became (as it had hoped) an 'irritant' in the body politic of the Irish foreign policy-forming process. It is instructive to ascertain why the ETISC was so successful. Firstly, no opportunities were lost to create public awareness of East Timor. This strategy was described by activists as an end in itself, but also as a means of mobilizing public opinion behind its goals. Achieving these goals required effective public events and educational work in schools, as well as keeping the Irish media constantly attracted to the issue. For instance, during the visit of Australian Prime Minister Paul Keating in September 1993, the ETISC scored a promotional coup by linking Keating's family history and his government's policy towards Indonesia to the oppression of East Timor. Full-page advertisements in the national press argued that, in supporting Indonesia politically and through arms sales, Keating was creating the kind of climate in East Timor which had forced his ancestors to flee Ireland 100 years previously. In addition, a host of alternative media events and the organization of a white carnation protest on the part of sympathetic parliamentarians meant that wherever Keating went, East Timor was never too far away.

A second factor in explaining the success of the ETISC is its non-partisanship. By not identifying with any particular party or, indeed, ideology, and by developing deep relationships with leading members of all the political parties, the ETISC managed to create a concern for human rights in East Timor which generally transcended the adversarial politics characteristic of the Irish and Western parliamentary systems. Finally, the ETISC emerged on to the Irish stage at a time when the domestic foreign policy process was beginning to open up. Representing a small state with a significant overseas development commitment, Ireland's Department of Foreign

Affairs had viewed many non-governmental organizations as 'partners' in policy development and aid disbursement. The same relationship had not existed in relation to foreign policy concerns outside the rubric of development cooperation. But two initiatives opened up the arena somewhat to human rights groups and solidarity organizations in particular. The first was the establishment of the Joint Oireachtas Committee on Foreign Affairs in 1993. The committee was empowered to seek submissions and host delegations from concerned groups or individuals in Irish society on any matter under its consideration. It was also empowered to question officials from the Department of Foreign Affairs in this public arena. From late 1994 into early 1995, in advance of the publication of the white paper on foreign policy in 1996, the Department of Foreign Affairs held a series of public seminars around the country to encourage local and sectoral discussion on aspects of Irish foreign policy. Thus, when Tom Hyland and his colleagues in Dublin formed the ETISC in 1992, they perhaps could not have chosen a better time to set about making Ireland a voice for East Timor. This combination of a receptive environment and a particularly focused and energetic campaign group created a mix which succeeded in linking the local group to the state and to a global community of state and non-state actors, all concerned for human rights in East Timor.

The extent to which Ireland had incorporated East Timor into its foreign policy concerns was perhaps most dramatically illustrated by two newspaper articles on the issue, carried in *The Irish Times* in July 1995. The media debate was opened by a former Minister for State, Tom Kitt (Fianna Fáil), then in opposition, who condemned the coalition government of the day for its failure to act on East Timor. While not using the word 'hypocrisy', Kitt cast doubt on the government's commitment to East Timor because of its failure to initiate concrete policies.[9] Kitt then proposed a wide-ranging ten-point plan of action, which included an arms embargo against Indonesia, the release of all political prisoners and a consideration of the UN Convention on Genocide in relation to Indonesian activities in East Timor. Showing remarkable sensitivity to such criticism, Minister for Foreign Affairs Dick Spring replied immediately, and in great detail, in a personally authored newspaper article. As this article was written in Spring's capacity as Minister for Foreign Affairs, we can surmise that it represented official policy at the time and is worth close examination. According to Spring, the government had consistently condemned Indonesia's actions in East Timor and had gone beyond rhetoric to active international engagement defined by clear objectives. Moreover, Spring went on to commit Ireland to the following aspirations:

- ending Indonesia's illegal occupation of East Timor
- supporting a political solution based on international law and justice

- ensuring that the East Timorese enjoyed their full human and political rights
- ending the supply to Indonesia of arms which could be used as instruments of oppression in East Timor
- gaining the release of political prisoners, including the Timorese resistance leader Xanana Gusmão
- promoting cooperation between Indonesia, the UN and international NGOs on human rights issues within East Timor.[10]

It was this article which caused the well-publicized tension between Spring and Indonesian Foreign Minister Ali Alatas the following September, when the Irish minister walked out of a meeting with his Indonesian counterpart in the UN offices in New York. The meeting had been part of a round of EU/ASEAN talks.[11] Spring claimed afterwards that he had been 'berated'[12] by Ali Alatas; Alatas in turn claimed that Spring's comments had been tantamount to a 'declaration of war'.[13] The row received considerable media coverage in Ireland and led *The Irish Times* to comment that it had left Irish/Indonesian relations 'in tatters'.[14] Whether the claim was true or not, the incident did indicate that Spring's position was not well received by the Indonesians. But what is of greater interest is establishing if and how that position, as specifically articulated in *The Irish Times* article, may have been translated into actual policy initiatives. In order to do this, we need to examine the EU foreign policy process.

Ireland, East Timor and the European Union

As an EU member state, the greater part of Ireland's foreign policy agenda is processed and implemented through multilateral EU fora. In relation to political and security issues specifically, Ireland must take into account its obligations under the CFSP when considering any initiatives or aspirations. Not surprisingly, then, we find that in July 1996, as Ireland took its turn in the chair of the presidency, national policy was inseparable from that which had emanated from within the CFSP decision-making structure. One of the priorities for the presidency was to 'support international efforts to promote a just global and internationally acceptable solution of the East Timor question on the basis of the Common Position'.[15]

The CP was set out in two articles. Article 1 states that the European Union intended:

1. To contribute to the achievement by dialogue of a fair, comprehensive and internationally acceptable solution to the question of East Timor,

which fully respects the interests and legitimate aspirations of the Timorese people, in accordance with international law.

2. To improve the situation in East Timor regarding respect for human rights in the territory.

Article 2 set out the route to realize the goals of Article 1. In this section, it was stated that the European Union:

1. Supports the initiatives undertaken in the United Nations framework which may contribute to resolving this question.

2. Supports in particular the current talks under the aegis of the United Nations Secretary-General with the aim of achieving the solution referred to in point 1 of Article 1, effective progress towards which continues to be hampered by serious obstacles.

3. Encourages the continuation of intra-Timorese meetings in the context of this process of dialogue under the auspices of the United Nations.

4. Calls upon the Indonesian government to adopt effective measures leading to a significant improvement in the human rights situation in East Timor. In particular, by implementing fully the relevant decisions adopted in this connection by the United Nations Commission on Human Rights.

5. Supports all appropriate action with the objective of generally strengthening respect for human rights in East Timor and substantially improving the situation of its people, by means of the resources available to the European Union and aid for action by NGOs.[16]

The CP clearly asserted the international nature of the dispute in East Timor, rejecting claims which Indonesia might make that involvement by any other state was an infringement of sovereignty. It affirmed the supremacy of international over national Indonesian law. Point 2.4 thus asserts this further, by calling on the Indonesian government to implement relevant past decisions on East Timor adopted by the UN Commission on Human Rights. Point 2.1, in supporting the UN framework, implicitly rejected the legitimacy of Indonesian rule in East Timor. UN Resolution 3485, referred to above, had accepted the right to self-determination of the Timorese people. The CP, furthermore, supported the long-standing UN-sponsored talks between Indonesia and Portugal and the intra-Timorese talks between the Timorese and the Indonesian government. Amongst these broad strokes, point 2.5 stands out in its specificity. This section committed the EU to providing aid through NGOs to bolster human rights in East Timor. It was this agenda which Ireland promised to prioritize during its presidency. Did Ireland succeed in this objective, and how was the CP acted on, with or without Irish impetus, during the Irish presidency?

One particular Irish initiative during the round of EU/ASEAN talks held in Jakarta, Indonesia, during July 1996 did not augur well for the presidency. The Irish presidency sought a vote of congratulations for the two new Nobel Peace Prize winners, José Ramos-Horta and Bishop Belo. That attempt was blocked by Germany and no such vote was passed on behalf of the EU. Later, Ireland unilaterally issued its own vote of congratulations. On behalf of the EU, Foreign Minister Spring raised the EU's concerns about human rights during the Jakarta talks, when he referred Indonesia to the CP and the EU's commitment to the achievement, by dialogue, of 'a just settlement which respects the legitimate aspirations of the East Timorese and is in conformity with the Charter of the United Nations'.[17] A second significant initiative during the presidency occurred during the Dublin summit in December 1996, when the European Council adopted a conclusion which reaffirmed the CP and the EU's support for all efforts which could 'contribute to a fair, comprehensive and internationally acceptable solution, which fully respects the interests and legitimate aspirations of the Timorese people in accordance with international law'.[18] Clearly, this did not represent any new initiatives but indicated that, as the Irish presidency came to a close, East Timor was still top of the list of EU foreign policy concerns.

In terms of enacting the CP (as opposed to simply reiterating its intentions), the immediate concern of policy makers in Brussels was to identify acceptable and effective measures which could be put in place. Not surprisingly, perhaps, point 2.5 proved the most attractive starting place. Largely prompted by consistent Portuguese lobbying, a decision was taken to allocate a total of 6 million ECUs over a three-year period to aid NGOs. This required protracted negotiations with NGOs engaged within the area. Healthcare, sanitation and education had been identified by the European Commission as beneficiary areas, but some problems had become apparent. On the one hand, the interests of Jakarta could best be met by channelling aid through, or co-financing, its existing institutions and structures, such as for sanitation and water projects. In terms of conventional aid programmes, such large-scale projects are attractive and easy beneficiaries of funding. On the other hand, the EU did not recognize Indonesia as the legitimate authority in East Timor and the CP made a commitment to fund NGOs rather than the state and its institutions. Furthermore, point 2.5 of the CP clearly envisaged the aid programme as *instrumental* to the enhancement of human rights. To identify projects which had the capacity to absorb the allocated funds, to strengthen 'respect for human rights in East Timor' generally and to improve substantially the situation of those living there in a way that would not legitimize Indonesian rule, was a testing challenge for the European Commission and NGOs in the field. This brief discussion on implementing the aid programme suggests that assistance to

East Timor would continue to be fraught with difficulty until the question of Indonesian occupation was solved. The intention here, however, was to assess how a pro-Timorese presidency of the EU could, or could not, effect change in the territory in the context of the CP.[19] Almost two years after the adoption of the CP, despite the Irish presidency's commitment to the issue, no significant progress was made on the East Timor question. Was the CP itself a problematic document, in that it did not enable the EU to take action? Could Ireland have made greater use of the CP as a potentially powerful instrument for change? In order to understand the picture fully, we need to look at the role and powers of the presidency and the decision-making procedure of the EU under the CFSP.

An important means of achieving the desired single stand of all EU member states on aspects of foreign and security policy is, as already stated, the creation of consensus. All states must be carried forward in the negotiation process and must agree on the details and the thrust of a position before it is adopted. Necessarily, a protracted log-rolling of positions occurs, in which states with the strongest stances must compromise and shift towards a more widely acceptable middle ground. In this sense, the process of forming a common position brings with it an inevitability of acceptance of the lowest common denominator. It is within this context that the presidential office operates. The power of the presidency to set the agenda within the EU is limited by the CFSP itself and by the associated requirement to find 'consensus around which proposals can be built'.[20] Thus, the acquiescence of all member states is required on each issue, no matter how powerfully motivated or engaged any particular presidency may be. The presidency also operates within the troika of the past, current and future presidents, which always contains at least one of the larger EU states, ensuring a coalition of interests at this level. Furthermore, the presidency acts as the representative of the EU on all matters concerning CFSP positions.[21] In other words, on becoming a 'president' of the EU, any particular state must take on board not just its own historic or current policy agenda, but those of other states too. This might include a state agenda that may be entirely contrary to that of the national policy of the president.

This consensual requirement of the CFSP goes some way towards explaining why the CP fell somewhat short of Irish objectives for East Timor, as outlined by Dick Spring in his *Irish Times* article. The constraints of the CP and CFSP partially explain why, as president, Ireland seemed somewhat more silent on East Timor than might have been expected. Both these constraints are very real and, moreover, the secretive nature of decision making within the EU means that we are not privy to information about other initiatives that may not have been adopted. But neither constraint fully explains why no actual policy measures derived from the CP were put in place during the Irish presidency. In retrospect, perhaps, Spring's failure even to refer to East Timor in his keynote address to the European Parliament as incoming president on 17 July 1996 should have been seen as an ominous sign of the many difficulties involved in committing the EU to action (diplomatic, political or commercial) against Indonesia. Additionally, the EU does not move fast in a situation of a long-standing territorial and political dispute which requires careful diplomacy.

Conclusion

We have seen that Ireland developed its own position on East Timor over time, through a national debate involving the media, civil society, parliament, the government and officials in the Department of Foreign Affairs. This involved Ireland identifying with the defence of human rights in East Timor. By 1996, this position had been swept into the collective European foreign policy position, resulting in the CP outlined above. Ireland's stated intention in the presidency was to prioritize East Timor as an issue for the EU. The government expressed satisfaction and pride in its management of the CP;[22] the ETISC also accepted that Ireland managed to 'hold the line' on East Timor during the presidency. A review article of Ireland's presidency, carried in *The Irish Times* early in 1997, reported the ETISC as recognizing that it might have been somewhat unrealistic to expect major initiatives from the government during its tenure. The organization believed that, overall, Ireland had managed the presidency effectively. In February 1997, after the presidential office had rotated to the Netherlands, three young East Timorese activists now living in Ireland personally met Dick Spring to thank him for his efforts.

This chapter has argued that because of Ireland's own, more radical, position on East Timor, the consensus-seeking CFSP offered less than what Ireland alone might have sought on the issue. To claim satisfaction in the context of the CP might thus be to recognize that, in the circumstances, it was as good as could have been hoped for. Satisfaction may arise from a pragmatic acceptance of the limits to political action imposed on the decision-making process of the EU as a single actor on the world stage. That is not to say that Ireland cannot take an assertive lead in exploring every potential which the CP offers for a proactive EU policy on East Timor following Indonesia's withdrawal from the territory. Ironically, perhaps, not being encumbered with the presidency makes this an easier task. In the longer term, however, it is important to keep in mind – when exploring this question – that the overall goal of the ETISC was both simple in aspiration and enormously difficult in application (but ultimately attainable and fulfilling): to keep the issue of East Timor firmly on the international agenda so that it would become untenable for Indonesia not to move towards a resolution. It became clear, too, that Indonesia was not happy with references to human rights during trade talks, but nonetheless often had to put up with these.[23]

In conclusion, the following key points can be extracted from this case study, set in the broader context of how EU policy has evolved since Ireland's EU presidency.

Given the power blocs operating within the EU and the dominance of economic concerns, it may be the case that instead of enhancing the power of a single state to enact its human rights concerns, the office of the presidency may in fact be restrictive – unless, of course, those human rights priorities are shared equally by other member states. These power blocs, informed by economic interests, ultimately produce common positions that, by creating a coalition based on the lowest common denominator, may limit the capacity of individual states to act. The presidency must, by virtue of its office, reflect the lowest common denominator. This point will have implications for advocacy within other EU member states while their governments are part of the EU troika, thereby potentially diluting their position on certain issues.

Since the promulgation of the CP, the Amsterdam Treaty 'opt-out' clause on issues of foreign policy could conceivably allow individual states to withdraw if they do not accept particular actions or initiatives. While this would not necessarily block the general thrust of any common action that might be derived from the CP on East Timor, it could diminish its effectiveness. In any case, the CP has been overtaken by developments in East Timor in 1999–2000.

However, within a broader context and outside the Irish presidential experience, the CP on East Timor could be seen as a potentially powerful enabling document which could be used by NGOs and solidarity organizations in Europe to hold their governments to account on East Timor. Its very vagueness, in a sense, could be used positively. In providing the broad strokes of commitment to improving human rights and in demanding an internationally acceptable solution to the occupation which is based on international law (a recognition of the fundamental illegality of the Indonesian action), the CP set key parameters for activity by member states of the EU. It was then up to the member governments and civil society, at a national and European level, to fill in the details.

Related to the above point, the history of how East Timor evolved as an issue for the Irish government indicates that civil society groups can play a vital role in the formation of foreign policy, both nationally and internationally. At the level of policy input, local lobbying groups and solidarity organizations can help to set a human rights agenda for a state. Ireland's small, open political arena may not be typical, but it nonetheless facilitated the efficacy of the ETISC – and, in 1999, Tom Hyland in effect became a special adviser to the Minister of Foreign Affairs (accompanying him on visits to East Timor) and to the Taoiseach (at the height of the post-referendum crisis). Indeed, the nature of ETISC/Hyland input was further enhanced in that the minister had just been appointed as the EU's special envoy for East Timor, a reward for and illustration of Ireland's acknowledged role of advocate for the cause of the East Timorese. Ireland's leaders used their status on East Timor to lobby world leaders personally to be more proactive and interventionist in resolving an escalating human rights crisis in the territory after the 30 August referendum.

These developments suggest that the potential role of civil society is not just limited to the policy-forming process. At the level of policy output, aid agencies have become partners in or agents of the EU's commitment to strengthening human rights in, for instance, East Timor. At input and output levels, this case study illustrates, too, the importance of coordination among groups in civil society, such as aid agencies and advocacy groups, in providing the detail as well as the broad strokes of commitment to justice and human rights globally.

In relation to human rights issues, it may be the case that advocacy by groups in the 'First World' on behalf of 'Third World' peoples is best understood in terms of bringing about incremental change in the global environment rather than effecting direct change in the target area. The argument that real change must come from within any target group or area has increasing currency today. Such a philosophical and political position has an impact on strategies. A foreign policy of any state which incorporates a human rights agenda as a core value can bring about profound change over time by indirectly sensitizing staff in the target state's embassies to become aware of how their government's actions may, in the long run, involve a cost. It may also serve to strengthen and validate human rights groups active within the target state. Finally, it may serve to normalize the expectation of human rights observance at the level of inter-state and transnational relations.[24]

References

1   The ASEAN group of nations, including Indonesia, is involved in a regular series of trade talks with the EU.

2   Spring, Dick, 'Ireland to the fore in seeking international action on East Timor', *The Irish Times*, 13 July 1995 .

3   Common Position, 25 June 1996, No. 96/407 CFSP, *Official Journal of the European Union*, L168/2, 6 July 1996.

4   The CFSP came about with the Maastricht Treaty of 1992. Article J.2 of that treaty established that, where necessary, a common position on a particular issue area would be adopted and the national policies of all members states would adhere to that position.

5 The Treaty of Amsterdam provides for a 'constructive abstention procedure' whereby states will be allowed to withdraw so long as the issue concerned is not 'fundamental'. In the case of the latter, the consensus rule will still apply. While the elements of the treaty relating to the CFSP indicate some institutional change, they have also been read as indicating that there was 'no consensus as to how to make the CFSP work better', Irish Business Bureau, *European Monthly Newsletter*, June 1997, No. 101, p. 5.

6 In reply to a question from then backbencher John Bruton (Fine Gael), Foreign Affairs Minister Brian Lenihan (Fianna Fáil) stated that the best resolution to the conflict in the region was to be found in the talks between the Indonesians and Portuguese. See *Dáil Debates*, Vol. 373(a), 9 June 1987, p. 915.

7 See Dáil and Senate debates 1992–96 and proceedings of Oireachtas Joint Committee on Foreign Affairs 1993–96.

8 *The Irish Times*, 13 July 1995.

9 Kitt, Tom, 'Spring's East Timor record "disappointing"', *The Irish Times*, 7 July 1995.

10 *The Irish Times*, 13 July 1995.

11 EU/ASEAN talks are conducted in the framework of ASEM (Asia-Europe Meetings).

12 The function of the meeting was to discuss further EU/ASEAN cooperation. But according to Dick Spring, Alatas voiced 'in extreme terms' a complaint that, while other foreign ministers had registered concern at human rights abuses with his government, Spring had gone public. Alatas then, according to newspaper reports, would not accept terms for a continuation of the meeting. 'Spring walked out on Indonesian minister over Timor', *The Irish Times*, 27 September 1995.

13 'Spring attack unacceptable, says Indonesia', *The Irish Times*, 29 September 1995. Alatas stated that Spring had 'refused a meeting with London-based Indonesian minister over Timor', *The Irish Times*, 27 September 1995.

14 *The Irish Times*, 27 September 1995.

15 'Ireland 1996: Presidency of the European Union', priorities for the Irish presidency of the Council of the European Union, 25 June 1996.

16 Common Position of the European Union, 25 June 1996.

17 Press release issued by the Taoiseach's office, presidency of the European Union, 24 July 1996.

18 European Council, Presidency Conclusions, Dublin, 13–14 December 1996.

19 It must also be noted that while any member state holds the presidential chair for just six months, membership of the troika extends share of the leadership role to 18 months.

20 Holland, Martin, *European Union Common Foreign Policy: From EPC to CFSP* (New York, 1995, St. Martin's Press).

21 Edwards, G. and Nuttall, S., 'Common foreign and security policy', in Duff, A., Pinder, J. and Pryce, R. (eds), *Maastricht and Beyond: Building the European Union* (London and New York, 1994, Routledge), p. 100.

22 Shanks, David, 'Lone stance lost to greater agenda', *The Irish Times*, international report on the EU presidency, 12 December 1996.

23 Press statement, the first informal meeting of the heads of government of ASEAN, Jakarta, 30 November 1996. Copy from Department of Foreign Affairs, Dublin. Given that Ireland was speaking on the issue of the CP in its capacity as president of the European Union, the singling out of one unnamed country – presumably Ireland – is interesting.

24 Luard, Evan, *Human Rights and Foreign Policy* (Oxford, 1981, Pergamon Press).

12

East Timor and Western Sahara: A Comparative Perspective

Pedro Pinto Leite

Introduction

In the dynamic of developed and developing world relations, the post-war period has been characterized by the decolonization of Third World countries – the withdrawal of colonial administrations as a direct form of political and economic control – and the assertion of various forms of 'independence' by developing nations. The current levels of poverty and inequality in developing nations reflect the emergence of more insidious but no less effective measures on the part of developed countries, particularly the damaging long-term effects of the debt crisis, to contain the development and independence of Third World nations. Despite the prevailing dominance of the northern over the southern hemisphere, the independent and freely expressed will of people in the developing world must, however, remain a fundamental step on the path to meaningful development. In this context, both East Timor and Western Sahara have shared strikingly similar histories characterised by their struggle for independence and frustrated their aspirations toward decolonization. Although the international community belatedly intervened to help free East Timor in 1999, the situation in Western Sahara remains unresolved.

This chapter explores the similarities and differences in the historical and contemporary elements of the liberation movements in East Timor and Western Sahara, and argues that Western nations have been largely negligent in enforcing the doctrine of international law which asserts the right to self-determination of the Timorese and Sahrawis. There are, though, some positive indicators in the recent initiatives aimed at resolving both conflict situations, and these have provoked greater optimism that genuine self-determination for Western Sahara may become a reality in the foreseeable future following the withdrawal of Indonesia from East Timor.

Comparative overview

The quasi-contemporaneity of the pivotal events which shaped the current occupations of Timor and Western Sahara, and the attendant human rights abuses perpetrated by the occupying forces, induce an easy comparison. But the differences in how the status of both nations has been assessed in a legal context warrant caution in this respect. Both Western Sahara and East Timor are the former colonies of Western nations (Spain and Portugal respectively) and, in the mid-1970s following the withdrawal of the colonizing powers, they were occupied and annexed by neighbouring countries: Indonesia in the case of East Timor and Morocco in respect to former Spanish Sahara. Significantly, both aggressors are Third World countries and themselves former Western colonies which have received support (diplomatic, material, financial and military) from Western nations (particularly the USA) to maintain their illegal occupations. Indonesia was a former Dutch colony and became fully independent in 1954, whilst Morocco secured its independence from France in 1956. Both Spain and Portugal, as former colonial powers in Sahara and Timor, agreed in principle with a planned process of decolonization to facilitate the peaceful transfer of political control to the colonized people. In both cases, a number of factors conspired to prevent the successful completion of this process, most notably the intervention of a third party. Portugal was still regarded by the United Nations (UN) as the administering power over East Timor, whilst an advisory opinion (1975) by the International Court of Justice (ICJ) recognized the right of the Sahrawis to self-determination.

Both East Timor and Western Sahara were occupied in 1975 and since then have suffered various forms of human rights abuses, including torture, disappearances, detention without legal redress, and extra-judicial killings. Indonesia and Morocco have repeatedly been condemned by international human rights bodies and have acted in breach of UN Resolutions 1514 (XV) and 1541 (XV), which make freely expressed self-determination an inalienable right. Despite these flagrant contraventions of the UN Charter and resolutions by Indonesia and Morocco, the dominant Western powers in the UN have been unwilling to act concertedly in upholding the norms of international law in respect of Western Sahara – until recently – East Timor. Portugal has been the more proactive of the two former colonizing powers in supporting efforts toward self-determination in its former colony, as for example when it challenged the legality of the 1989 Timor Gap Treaty between Indonesia and Australia. Spain, however, has been more guarded in its relations with Morocco because of the contested territories of Ceuta and Melilla, which remain under Spanish control despite repeated Moroccan representations to the UN Decolonization Committee.

Origins of the conflict in Western Sahara

Western Sahara, like East Timor, was largely ignored by the Western media in the 1970s and 1980s, when human rights abuses were widespread and the conflict was most intense. The circumstances surrounding the occupation of the former Spanish Sahara by Morocco in 1975, and the subsequent annexation of the territory, have largely remained a marginal concern to the West and its dominant media interests. This has resulted in a lack of awareness in English-speaking countries of the situation in Western Sahara. Located in Northern Africa, bordering the North Atlantic Ocean between Mauritania and Morocco, Western Sahara has an area of 266,000 square kilometres, roughly equivalent to that of Colorado.[1] In 1974, the World Bank labelled Western Sahara as the richest territory in the Maghreb region because of its fishing resources and extensive phosphate deposits in an almost completely desert environment. The Franco regime (1939–75), in association with transnational corporations, invested over $160 million in exploiting the Saharan phosphate deposits in the late 1950s, thereby dramatically reducing the level of nomadism in the region and increasing the capital El Aaiun's population from 6000 in 1959 to 28,000 in 1974.[2]

Influenced by the ideals of pan-Africanism and the anti-colonial movements of the 1960s, such as Nkrumah's in Ghana, the Popular Front for the Liberation of Saguia el Hamra and Rio de Oro (Polisario) was established in 1973 as a guerrilla movement in the Spanish Sahara to liberate their region from the Spanish colonizing power. Named after the two administrative sections into which the Spanish divided the colony, Polisario sought Madrid's compliance with UN resolutions which recognized the independence of Spanish Sahara. Four months after the Carnation Revolution in Lisbon in April 1974, which would heavily influence events in East Timor, Spain announced that it would hold a referendum on self-determination in Spanish Sahara, to be monitored by the UN. Morocco's King Hassan, seizing the opportunity presented by Spanish internal political difficulties, prevailed on the UN to delay the referendum to consider Moroccan and Mauritanian territorial claims over Sahara. In December 1974, the UN General Assembly passed Resolution 3292 XXIX requesting the International Court of Justice in the Hague to give an advisory opinion on the case of Spanish Sahara.

Judicial assessment of Western Sahara

The ICJ's advisory opinion on Spanish Sahara marked an important distinction between the conflicts in Timor and Sahara, as it afforded an international judicial assessment of Moroccan claims to its neighbouring territory. A similar advisory opinion was not requested of the court by the UN in respect to Indonesia's territorial claim over East Timor, although in the context of the ruling on Western Sahara it is probable that Jakarta's sovereignty claim over Timor would have been rejected by the court. The basis of the ICJ's advisory opinion on Western Sahara (16 October 1975) upholds the principles of the UN Charter in respect to the right of peoples to self-determination. Section 55 of the advisory opinion states that:

> The principle of self-determination as a right of peoples, and its application for the purpose of bringing all colonial situations to a speedy end, were enunciated in the Declaration on the Granting of Independence to colonial countries and peoples, General Assembly Resolution 1514 (XV). In this resolution the General Assembly proclaims 'the necessity of bringing to a speedy and unconditional end colonialism in all its forms and manifestations'.[3]

The court analysed Moroccan claims of historical ties with Western Sahara on the basis of an evaluation of internal acts of Moroccan sovereignty and international treaties and acts which the Moroccan government claimed as recognition of its authority and influence over the Sahrawis. The ICJ could not ignore some factual evidence indicating the existence of cultural, religious and political ties between Morocco and the nomadic tribes occupying Western Sahara in the period preceding Spanish colonization, but concluded that it had not 'found legal ties of such a nature as might affect the application of Resolution 1514 (XV) in the decolonization of Western Sahara and, in particular, of the principle of self-determination through the free and genuine expression of the will of the peoples of the territory'.[4]

The court found that Spain had entered into treaties with local tribal leaders during its period of occupation and, therefore Western Sahara was not *terra nullius* (a territory not under the sovereignty of an external power), as Madrid had argued. On the issue of Moroccan and Mauritanian claims to sovereignty over Western Sahara, the court acknowledged that there were historical ties between the territories, but not ties of sovereignty which could overrule Resolution 1514 (XV) regarding the decolonization of Western Sahara and the right of its peoples to self-determination.

If the reasoning of the court's judgement in respect to Western Sahara had been applied to the case of East Timor, there would have been an overwhelming judicial case supporting the freely expressed will and self-determination of the Timorese. Indonesia, as an independent entity, did not exist during the period of Portuguese colonization of East Timor and, therefore, could not viably claim historical ties with the Timorese similar to those forwarded by Morocco as regards Western Sahara. Moreover, as a former Dutch colony, Indonesia has to abide by the delimitation of territorial boundaries accepted by the Netherlands and the colonial frontiers agreed by the two colonial powers. The frontier dividing the island of Timor was agreed by the Dutch and Portuguese in a treaty signed in Lisbon in 1859, and is therefore binding on Indonesia as a state succeeding the Dutch East Indies. Indonesia's territorial claims over Timor were thus even more insubstantial than those of Morocco and Mauritania over Sahara, given both the lack of historical ties between Jakarta and Dili and the UN charter's recognition of peoples' right to freely expressed self-determination.

Occupation and annexation of Western Sahara

In November 1975, a month after the International Court of Justice published its advisory opinion which upheld the Sahrawis' right to self-determination, King Hassan mobilized 350,000 Moroccans across the border into Sahara in the so-called 'Green March'. Hassan intended this mass mobilization southward as a show of defiance against the ICJ's decision and evidence of Moroccan popular support for the annexation of Spanish Sahara. As Spain was determining a new political course in 1975, following 36 years of fascism, it was in no position to challenge militarily the territorial ambitions of Morocco. Spain's hand was forced on the issue of Sahara and the territory was ceded to both Morocco and Mauritania with the signing of a partition agreement in Madrid on 14 November 1975. Neither the UN nor the Organization of African Unity (OAU) – established in 1963 to promote unity and solidarity among African states – challenged the legality of the treaty negotiated by Spain, Mauritania and Morocco, or intervened in response to the Moroccan occupation of Sahara. The UN Security Council, convened at the request of Spain, urged Morocco to withdraw from Sahara following two resolutions which had condemned the occupation, but no effective action was sanctioned when the resolutions were ignored.

Under the terms of the Madrid agreement, Spain withdrew from Sahara in 1976 in return for 33.7 per cent of phosphate mines and fishing rights in Saharan waters for ten years, thereby reneging on its agreement to oversee a referendum on self-determination in Sahara and ensure a peaceful transferral of power. King Hassan invited members of the Yema'a (a 'representative assembly' in Sahara created by Franco in 1967) to convene in the Saharan capital, El Aaiun, for the official handover of power in the territory from Spain to Morocco. Only one in four members of the Yema'a accepted Hassan's invitation and UN officials refused to participate in the ceremony, pressing instead for a referendum in Sahara and continuing to acknowledge Spain as the territory's administering power. Despite the official position of the UN, however, three-quarters of former Spanish Sahara now lay under *de facto* Moroccan occupation, with the remainder of the region controlled by Mauritania.

Occupation and annexation of East Timor

The independence movement in East Timor evolved at a later stage than those organized in other Portuguese colonies, particularly the anti-colonial movements in Africa. In the mid-1970s, however, a clandestine liberation movement opposed to colonial rule attracted widespread support within Timorese society and attempted to seize the opportunity for independence presented by the Carnation Revolution of April 1974. The collapse of the colonial regime in Lisbon transformed the political scene in Timor, and within a month of the revolution two main political groups had emerged. The Timorese Social Democratic Association (ASDT), which later evolved into the Revolutionary Front for the Independence of East Timor (Fretilin), supported self-determination for the Timorese, whilst the Timor Democratic Union (UDT) favoured federation with Portugal. The new Portuguese government promised independence for East Timor, but in the chaotic course of events which followed the revolution, the small overseas province of Timor was not one of Lisbon's political priorities. When some of the UDT leaders organized a coup in August 1974, at the prompting of the Indonesian military, Portugal quickly withdrew from East Timor and a resulting civil war claimed some 1500 lives. By November 1975, Fretilin had won the civil war and also secured a popular majority in local elections.

A significant divergence in the evolution of the independence movements in Western Sahara and East Timor occurred on 27 November 1975, when Fretilin established the Democratic Republic of East Timor, and immediately received recognition of its status from 12 nation-states, though not including Portugal. The life-span of the Timorese Republic was short, however, as Indonesia, in clear breach of the UN Charter, invaded Timor on 7 December 1975. In contrast, when the Polisario Front proclaimed a government-in-exile of the Sahrawi Arab Democratic Republic (SADR) in February 1976, Morocco had already invaded and partitioned the territory with Mauritania, thereby preventing international recognition of the territory as an independent entity before its occupation. The United Nations, though, continued to recognize Portugal as the administrative authority in

East Timor, enabling Lisbon to engineer diplomatic efforts and galvanize international support within the UN and European Union for a resolution to the conflict in its former colony. Indeed, Portugal became actively (albeit belatedly) involved in negotiations with Indonesia on behalf of the Timorese, as Jakarta refused to enter into direct diplomatic relations with the exiled or imprisoned Timorese leadership. The fact that Portugal withheld official recognition of the Republic of East Timor in November 1975 thus continued to have important political and diplomatic implications for the territory.

Human rights abuses

The Sahrawi population in 1975 numbered less than a quarter of a million, and with the enforcement of the Madrid agreement, the area of land controlled by Polisario made the Saharan republic more 'an assertion of faith' than a sustainable entity.[5] The majority of Sahrawis fled the Moroccan occupation forces and were rallied by the Polisario leadership in refugee camps in Tindouf, south-west Algeria, where most refugees now remain. The Algerian government was the strongest regional ally of Polisario and had traditionally supported other African liberation movements. Algeria's ruling party, the Front de Libération Nationale (FLN), had its own grievances against Hassan's conservative monarchy in Morocco, with which it was vying for regional influence, and was therefore strongly supportive of the Sahrawi struggle for independence. Polisario was provided with weaponry, communications and refuge facilities and, importantly, the Tindouf refugee camps were not attacked by Moroccan forces, fearful of provoking the direct involvement of Algeria in the conflict. Between 1974 and 1991, the Moroccan occupation forces increased from 56,000 to 250,000 and its airforce used napalm and phosphorus to displace any civilians who had not already fled to the camps in Tindouf.[6] Although the Polisario guerrillas were heavily outnumbered, they sustained an unconventional desert warfare which necessitated an increased commitment of resources from Morocco and Mauritania to the conflict. In 1979 Mauritania, on the verge of bankruptcy, relinquished its claim on Western Sahara, which allowed Polisario to concentrate on Moroccan-controlled territory.

Amnesty International has been consistently critical of Moroccan human rights abuses, which pre-date the conflict in Western Sahara but have intensified since 1975. An Amnesty report in April 1996 stated that: 'The pattern of "disappearance" of known or suspected political opponents by the Moroccan authorities dates back to the 1960s ... [and] "disappearances" of Sahrawis began to occur at the end of 1975 and continued until the late 1980s.'[7] Amnesty found that 'hundreds of Sahrawis who "disappeared" after arrest between 1975 and 1987 remain unaccounted for' and 'prolonged secret detention, a practice now rarely reported in Morocco, continues to be routine in Western Sahara, where most of those arrested are never put through any legal process'.[8] The fact that the Moroccan authorities refuse to investigate 'disappearances', provide information on detainees or compensate released ex-detainees is also condemned by Amnesty. The human rights group described the treatment of some of those 'disappeared':

> After being arrested by the Moroccan army and other security forces the detainees were taken to secret detention centres in Morocco and Western Sahara, where torture and ill-treatment was routine, especially during interrogation. With few exceptions, those detained were never charged with any offence, brought to trial, or put through any legal process. Some were released after weeks and months in secret detention, and hundreds of others simply 'disappeared'.[9]

Amnesty has also raised concerns that human rights violations have continued to be perpetrated by Morocco despite the presence of the United Nations Mission for the Referendum in Western Sahara (MINURSO) since 1991. Amnesty's criticisms of MINURSO are based on the fact that the mission does not have a comprehensive provision for monitoring the human rights situation in Western Sahara, and also that the limited human rights safeguards contained in MINURSO's mandate are not respected. The lack of an effective international monitoring mission in Western Sahara has enabled the Moroccan military to act with impunity in the region.

Complicity with Morocco and Indonesia

The extent of Western complicity in the Indonesian and Moroccan occupations of East Timor and Western Sahara provides some understanding of how these illegal acts of aggression have been sustained for almost 25 years. A clear example of this complicity is the fact that a few hours before Indonesia launched its invasion of East Timor on 7 December 1975, the US president, Gerald Ford had visited Jakarta and undoubtedly learned of and endorsed Suharto's plans to occupy Timor (see Chapter 9). Suharto was considered a strategically important ally of the West in the Asia Pacific after he deposed Sukarno's anti-colonial regime, which had strongly supported the non-aligned movement and other pro-Third World initiatives. Western nations, particularly the USA and Britain, enjoyed favourable trading relations with Indonesia, particularly in arms, which Suharto required for internal oppression and securing the annexation of East Timor. Consequently, the UN and European Union – largely controlled by Jakarta's trading partners – failed to enforce resolutions condemning the occupation of Timor and demanding Indonesia's immediate withdrawal. As a powerful regional voice and economic force in the Pacific, Australia's support of Indonesia's aggression toward Timor contributed to the grave human rights situation in the territory.

In 1989, Canberra and Jakarta signed the Timor Gap Treaty and agreed a contract with 12 companies, including Royal Dutch Shell and Chevron (British, Dutch and US companies), to extract oil from the coastal waters of East Timor. Portugal challenged the legality of the treaty in the International Court of Justice (ICJ), on the grounds that Australia had negotiated the contract without any form of consultation with Lisbon. The Portuguese argued that excluding their government from the treaty negotiations infringed the rights of the Timorese to self-determination, territorial integrity and sovereignty over its wealth and natural resources. As Portugal was considered by the UN as the administering power over Timor, it argued that its own powers and rights had been infringed and that Australia's negotiation of the treaty thereby contravened existing Security Council resolutions. Portugal carefully delimited the basis of its complaint to the unilateral actions of Australia, in the knowledge that Jakarta had not subscribed to Article 36(2) of the court statute and would thus refuse the ICJ's jurisdiction in deliberating on the treaty. In June 1995, the court found in favour of Australia's arguments, objecting to Portugal's action on the basis that it could not exercise jurisdiction in this case, which would require it to determine the rights and obligations of Indonesia. Although the court's decision ruled against Portuguese claims on the treaty, the judgement went on to recognize Timorese rights to self-determination and territorial integrity as expressed in the UN Charter and Resolutions 384 (1975) and 386 (1976). The judgement was requested to test the legality of the Timor Gap Treaty but, in effect, reinforced the illegality of Jakarta's occupation. The ruling of the International Court of Justice on the treaty in 1995 echoed its advisory opinion in regard to Morrocan claims to Western Sahara in 1975.

The position of Western governments in regard to Moroccan expansionism in Sahara largely mirrored their collaborative approach to relations with Jakarta. Human rights abuses were downplayed or ignored as strategic, geopolitical and economic factors were prioritized. The dominant media interests in the northern hemisphere, reflecting the prevailing new right, monetarist political hegemony in countries such as Britain and the US, largely 'shut out' coverage of the conflicts in Sahara and Timor, as it often seemed 'that a war was only a war by virtue of its being reported'.[10] The media, for example, ignored the fact that in 1981 the US extended $33 million in military credits to the conservative monarchist regime in Morocco and delivered $136 million in arms, whilst licensing the further commercial export of $68 million in arms to Hassan's regime. As a *quid pro quo*, Morocco offered transit facilities to the US rapid deployment force, provided Angola's UNITA rebels (supported by apartheid South Africa and the USA) with military training, and 'quite possibly' served as an arms conduit to UNITA and other US-backed forces in the region.[11] King Hassan also received arms from France, the former colonial power in Morocco and, during the first decade of the conflict, Saudi Arabia provided the monarchy 'with anything between $500 million and $1 billion a year' to bolster the campaign against Polisario.[12]

In the context of Cold War relations, Western Sahara did not emerge as a serious point of contention between the former Soviet Union and the USA. Morocco's interest in Sahara was based in part on the territory's rich supplies of phosphate, which Hassan was eager to bring under his control. Morocco had its own supply of phosphates which it was trading at high prices, and was thus keen to avoid competition from cheaper sources in Western Sahara. For its part, the Soviet Union required a regular supply of phosphates from Morocco and was unwilling to destabilize the region further by intervening in the conflict on behalf of the Sahrawis and thereby threaten phosphate production. According to the Spanish census of Sahara in 1974, the region had a population of 74,000, making it one of the least-populated territories in the world and thus unlikely to engage the serious support of Western powers or the Soviet bloc against 27 million Moroccans. Soviet pragmatism on the matter was reflected in Moscow's agreement to finance a Moroccan phosphate mine in 1978 at a cost of $2 billion.[13]

The withdrawal of Mauritania from the conflict against Polisario in 1979 and the Sahrawis successful containment tactics prompted Morocco to construct a 2250-km-long defence wall between 2.7 and 4.5 metres in height, protected by minefields and advanced electronic equipment supplied by the USA and France. The aim behind the wall's construction was to protect Morocco's important phosphate regions from attack by Polisario guerrillas and exclude Sahrawis from habitable areas which sustained their campaign.

In 1980, 26 nations recognized the Sahrawi Arab Democratic Republic at an Organization of African Unity conference in Freetown and, in November 1984, Polisario scored another diplomatic victory when it was accepted as a full member of the OAU. In 1980–81, severe food shortages in Morocco – caused by drought – forced the government to increase food imports, a measure which saw the country's foreign debt reach unmanageable levels. The war in the Sahara was costing Morocco over $1 million a day and lack of success in the conflict began to create tensions within the military. Morocco's internal political difficulties, its spiralling foreign debt and increasing diplomatic isolation on the Saharan question – it left the OAU following the SADC's acceptance as a full member – forced Hassan to enter into peace negotiations with Polisario under the auspices of the UN. In 1988, Morocco and Polisario agreed a peace plan which would facilitate the holding of a referendum on the future of Sahara: voters would choose between independence and integration with Morocco. The main difficulty in administering the referendum, however, has been in agreeing voter eligibility, given that the last census in Sahara was taken in 1974 and the Moroccan government had initiated an aggressive policy of transmigration whereby 200,000 of its subjects had already settled in Sahara. In 1991, a UN settlement plan was agreed which established the United Nations Mission for the Referendum in Western Sahara, and included a cease-fire between Morocco and Polisario effective from 6 September 1991.

Western Sahara: an important test for the UN

The situation in Western Sahara over the past decade has been characterized by disagreements over the voting constituency in the referendum, with Morocco settling its citizens in the region in an attempt to swing any future vote toward integration. The settlement plan included the proclamation of an amnesty for political prisoners, but although over 300 Sahrawis who had 'disappeared' for up to 16 years were released, Amnesty International claims that 'hundreds of other "disappeared" remain unaccounted for' and has heavily criticized MINURSO for 'being a silent witness to blatant human rights violations in Western Sahara' since the implementation of the cease-fire.[14] The transitional period outlined in the 1991 implementation plan was postponed repeatedly on the recommendation of the UN secretary-general, reportedly because of the difficulties in identifying those eligible to vote in the referendum. A referendum planned for January 1992 was rescheduled as Moroccan repression against Saharans intensified, and international observers were banned from Saharan territory. The MINURSO plan for voter eligibility was to draw up an electoral register based on the Spanish census of 1974, whereby a large number of Sahrawis could not vote but, in exchange, all Moroccans who arrived in the territory after 1976 would also be ineligible.

Difficulties over voter registration prevailed until 1997, when an agreement on implementing the settlement plan was brokered by James Baker, the UN Secretary-General's personal envoy to Western Sahara and a former US Secretary of State, after talks in Houston. The agreement had three main stages: first, the United Nations High Commission for Refugees (UNHCR) in partnership with MINURSO would register those refugees in Algeria, Mauritania and other areas who were prepared to return to

Western Sahara, with the establishment of an identification commission to compile lists of eligible voters; second, the repatriation of as many as 120,000 eligible voters and their families would begin by road and air from the refugee camps to UNHCR reception centres for the referendum vote; third, the UNHCR would concentrate on rehabilitation measures and the monitoring of returnees.[15] On the basis of this three-phase implementation plan, the referendum was scheduled for 7 December 1998, but yet again the deadline for the vote was postponed because of registration irregularities.

The referendum has recently been postponed until 2002[16], which has necessitated an extension to the UN mandate for MINURSO and increased the costs of the military and civilian elements of the UN's mission in Western Sahara. In a recent report to the UN Security Council concerning the implementation of the settlement plan for Western Sahara, UN Secretary-General Kofi Annan outlined the current strength of the UN mission in the territory: 229 troops, 81 civilian police officers, and 30 identification commission members with responsibility for registering voters and processing appeals from those excluded from the provisional voting lists.[17] The mounting expense of this operation is increasing pressure on the Secretary-General from UN members to complete the referendum process successfully without continued extensions to MINURSO's mandate. The Secretary-General secured $52.1 million to maintain the mission in Western Sahara until July 2000, although, by 15 October 1999, there was a total of $71.2 million in unpaid contributions to supporting MINURSO operations from UN members.[18] Moreover, Kofi Annan has requested that 36 additional identification commission members with 'corresponding numbers of United Nations registration/appeals officers and other personnel' be sent to Western Sahara to ensure that voter lists are completed to the satisfaction of all parties to the referendum.[19]

The strengthening of the mission in Western Sahara has been necessitated by the overwhelming number of appeals received by the UN during the voter registration process. By 18 September 1999, MINURSO had received 79,125 appeals – the vast majority of these from Moroccans – which represents a massive administrative challenge to UN staff, who have to cross-reference files, analyse the basis of each case and organize appeal hearings.[20] Ahmed Boukhari, the Sahrawi representative to the UN, has stated that 'Morocco is determined to kill the referendum by using the appeals weapon'[21] and cites previous delays to the consultation process caused by Morocco's failure to engage fully with the voter registration procedure. This growing frustration with Moroccan attempts to 'run down the clock' on the UN's mission in Western Sahara has resulted in a new political initiative in the USA. In July 1999, a US-Western Sahara Foundation was established with the support of members of Congress, ambassadors, media representatives and former UN diplomats who had served with MINURSO. Congressman Joseph R. Pitts called for the self-determination of the Sahrawi people at the launch of the foundation, and pointed out 'that a failed Western Sahara peace plan represents a failure not only for the parties concerned but for the international community and the United States'.[22]

New King in Morocco: positive change or status quo?

The establishment of the foundation coincided with the death of King Hassan, aged 70, on 23 July 1999. Described in an obituary by *The Economist* as 'the Arab world's ruthless manipulator',[23] Hassan had personally pursued Morocco's territorial designs on Western Sahara; it was hoped that his successor, King Mohammed VI, would adopt a more constructive approach to the Sahara situation. King Mohammed's first speech to the Moroccan people as monarch was positive in so far as it included a commitment to the 'protection of human rights', although he accused Morocco's 'enemies of going to great lengths to ensure that this referendum fails'.[24] Early signs suggest that Mohammed's accession to the monarchy in Morocco has not resulted in any immediate change of position on the referendum in Western Sahara. Moreover, Amnesty International's 1999 report states that 'hundreds of Sahrawis and some Moroccans remain unaccounted for', whilst 'reports of torture and ill-treatment continue to be received'.[25] Repressive measures taken by Moroccan occupation forces against Sahrawi demonstrators in September and October 1999, included excessive violence and dozens of arrests amid reports of torture and ill-treatment.[26]

The new monarchy of Mohammed VI has been characterized by an ambiguous mix of political reform, policy innovation, renewed energy in the crown's role and continuing human rights abuses which were so prevalent during the reign of his father, Hassan II. In November 1999, however, Mohammed appeared to make a public break with the past when he dismissed Driss Basri, the minister for the interior since 1979 and notorious hardliner who was closely implicated in the repressive practices of the Hassan regime. Basri's dismissal was one of several changes in key government positions made by Mohammed through royal appointments which have enabled him to install his favoured personnel into state ministries. There are concerns that, like Hassan, the new king is asserting the monarchy as the dominant policy making body in Morocco at the expense of the government led by prime minister Abderrahmane Youssoufi. Already, in his short reign, Mohammed has been extremely active politically and launched royal commissions on individual rights, investment, education, poverty and social problems. These new initiatives are being viewed in some quarters as deliberately designed to undermine the government which, by comparison, seems 'timid, passive and unimaginative'.[27] Mohammed appears to be 'modernising the monarchy without calling its continuity into question'[28] whilst the government is either unwilling or unable to challenge the traditional political role play and court hierarchy associated with the Hassan era.

Nonetheless, there have been some positive developments in the context of human rights with the establishment by Mohammed of an arbitration commission in August 1999 to assess compensation claims for material and psychological damage suffered by victims of "disappearances" and arbitrary detention. The commission started work in September 1999 and received some 3,900 applications by 31 December although the latest Amnesty International Report (2000) claims that the Moroccan authorities have still not provided details of 'disappeared' Sahrawis.[29] The new king has, however, established a royal commission to examine the grievances of Sahrawis in the wake of the September/October 1999 crackdown on Sahrawi protestors and recently opened dialogue with the Algerian government, which remains a key player in the Western Sahara situation. Recent direct negotiations between the Polisario Front and the Moroccan government sponsored by the UN have not produced a breakthrough though and, with the postponement of the referendum until 2002, it seems that an early solution to the Saharan situation is unlikely.[30]

The UN Committee against Torture and the UN Human Rights Committee have 'recognised positive steps taken by the Moroccan government in the field of human rights' in 1999 but have urged the administration:

- to intensify investigations into the whererabouts of all persons reportedly missing,
- to release any persons who may be still held in detention, to provide lists of
- prisoners of war to independent observers, to inform families of the location of the
- graves of disappeared persons known to be dead, to prosecute those responsible
- for the disappearances or deaths, and to provide compensation to victims or their
- families where rights have been violated.[31]

Clearly, there is scope for further reform and movement toward democracy in Morocco and this process must include the above items. Amnesty International has welcomed the fact that the change in monarchy has resulted in greater openness in Moroccan society, freedom for the press, and less restricted political and NGO activity, but remains concerned about human rights abuses and impunity for the military and security forces. Amnesty has focused, particularly, on the human rights situation in Western Sahara in 1999, which 'continued to lag a long way behind that in Morocco itself, with regard to freedom of expression and association'.[32] Thus, as with East Timor, there remains an urgent need to maintain international pressure on Morocco to apply international standards in human rights to the situation in Western Sahara.

Economic pressures on Indonesia and Morocco

Many of the social, economic and political factors which have beset the Moroccan government over the past two decades were also evident in the crisis which finally resulted in Suharto's resignation in May 1998, after 32 years in power. The annexation of Western Sahara and East Timor by Morocco and Indonesia, respectively, served to create internal difficulties and increase external diplomatic pressures on the occupying powers. Suharto's regime, particularly, was regularly condemned overseas by the international network of campaigning organizations for East Timor established after the 1991 Dili massacre. Also, diplomatic pressure from within the European Union, largely driven by Portugal and more recently Ireland (see Chapter 11), and the weakening support from Washington in the face of economic uncertainty in South-East Asia, raised questions about Suharto's ability to maintain order and stability in the archipelago for inward investors. Private capital and Western allies were prepared to tolerate human rights abuses in Indonesia and East Timor as long as Suharto could ensure economic growth and contain social unrest through military repression. During the 1990s, however, workers' protests and land disputes became regular occurrences, and riots targeted at Christian and Chinese communities created greater social fragmentation. A series of crises in 1997–98 finally made Suharto's position untenable: disastrous man-made forest fires with resulting wide-spread environmental damage; the serious collapse of the economy, which unnerved investors and devalued the rupiah; allegations of business irregularities and corruption directed at Suharto and his family; student-led demonstrations sparked by sharp increases in food and fuel prices; and continued repression and human rights abuses reported in East Timor.

King Mohammed's monarchy in Morocco will continue to be tested on similar socio-economic issues to those which finally undid Suharto in Indonesia. Morocco's external debt in 1994 was $22.5 billion and serviced by a third of all exports, which totalled $4 billion in the same year.[33] Unemployment is on the increase and the migration of around 1 million Moroccans per year to urban areas has led to housing and sanitation problems. The heavy reliance of Morocco's economy (46 per cent) on agricultural produce makes it vulnerable to droughts, and in 1995 the GNP dropped by 4 per cent because of harvest failure. Mohammed will have to consider the economic consequences of a resumed war with the Polisario Front should Morocco fail to respect the referendum process in Western Sahara.

Morocco has stalled the implementation of the UN peace plan since its agreement in 1991, and enhanced diplomatic pressure is required to ensure that the new monarchy facilitates the holding of a referendum in 2002. The recent referendum process in East Timor was largely made possible through a concerted international campaigning effort and the (belated) involvement of key regional and international actors. Similar action is needed to ensure a fair and free referendum in Western Sahara, otherwise continued Moroccan prevarication on the consultation process will inevitably force the withdrawal of the UN mission. It is important, therefore, that UN members see the settlement plan in Western Sahara through to its conclusion and avoid the mistakes made in East Timor regarding the provision of security both during and after the consultation process. The terror and mayhem wrought by the pro-Indonesia militias in East Timor following the referendum there on 30 August 1999 should not also be visited on the Sahrawi people, if or when they are allowed to determine their future in a popular mandate.

Conclusion

Following the collapse of the Suharto regime, a 'transitional government' led by former vice-president Habibie was quickly established, with a cabinet containing many of the ministers who had served under Suharto. According to Tapol, the Indonesia Human Rights Campaign, Habibie was the presidential choice of 'constitutional fixer' General Wiranto, the former Commander-in-Chief of the Indonesian armed forces (ABRI), mainly because 'Habibie would be much easier to control as he lacked a power base'.[34] Habibie inherited the economic difficulties and social upheavals which underpinned Suharto's downfall, and without a popular mandate or widespread support in the country he was always unlikely to improve conditions for the millions living in poverty throughout the archipelago.

The power vacuum resulting from Suharto's downfall, though, created the opportunity for the establishment of political parties and greater freedom for the press in preparation for free legislative and presidential elections in 1999. The June 1999 elections saw the political demise of Habibie, whose Golkar party became a minority force in the Indonesian people's consultative parliament (MPR), and frustrated – at least temporarily – Wiranto's political aspirations. In October 1999, the MPR elected the respected Muslim leader Abdurrahman Wahid as the president of Indonesia, and he immediately appointed his defeated electoral rival Megawati Sukarnoputri (leader of the Indonesian Democratic Party – Struggle) as Vice-President. Wahid has inherited the serious social and economic problems created by his predecessors, and will have to contend with the ever-looming threat of the military.

Habibie's downfall was largely precipitated by events in East Timor, which continued to influence international opinion toward Indonesia. In January 1999, Habibie unexpectedly announced that he would facilitate a referendum on the future of East Timor to be held in August. Accords agreed between Indonesia and Portugal in May 1999 allowed the Indonesian military to provide security both during and after the referendum, which was held on 30 August. The referendum resulted in 78.5 per cent of an almost 99 per cent turnout supporting independence, despite the threats and violence of pro-Indonesian militias formed under the auspices of the Indonesian military (see Chapter 14). The militias/military responded to the mandate for independence by pursuing a 'scorched-earth' policy and forcing the mass displacement of the East Timorese. The UN's completely inadequate security provisions for the referendum ensured that the military/militias could freely expedite what was clearly a preconceived strategy for preventing the implementation of a vote for independence.

The belated intervention of a UN-sponsored force (Interfet – the International Force for East Timor) finally led to a withdrawal of Indonesian troops from East Timor in October 1999, and in the same month the MPR ratified the referendum result. Whilst East Timor now faces a massive reconstruction programme and begins to contemplate building a future as an independent state, it will require the sustained support of the international community to recover from a 24-year genocidal occupation. An analysis of the situations in East Timor and Western Sahara clearly highlights the limitations of the UN in acting effectively without the support of its most powerful member states. In both cases, economic and strategic considerations have overridden respect for human rights and international law. The UN has an obligation to ensure that human rights are enforced universally – in the First and Third Worlds – irrespective of the primary interests of its member states.

References

1 *The World Guide 1997–98* (Instituto del Tercer Mundo, 1997), p. 479 of the English-language version (Oxford, New Internationalist Publications). Background information on Western Sahara is also available on website (http://www.odic.gov/cia/publications/factbook/wi.html).

2   *Ibid.*

3   Rigaux, François, 'East Timor and Western Sahara: A comparative view', in *International Law and the Question of East Timor* (London, 1995, CIIR/IPJET), p. 169.

4   *Ibid.*, p. 172.

5   Harding, Jeremy, *Small Wars, Small Mercies* (London, 1993, Viking), p. 118.

6   *Ibid.*, pp. 117–118.

7   'Human rights violations in Western Sahara', Amnesty International report (MDE, 29 April 1996), p. 3, available on website (http://www.amnesty.org/ailib/aipub/1996/MDE/52900496.htm).

8   Amnesty International press release on Western Sahara, 18 April 1996, p. 1, available on website (http://www.amnesty.org.uk/press/morocco_apr18.html).

9   Amnesty International report, 29 April 1996, p. 4.

10 Harding, *Small Wars, Small Mercies*, p. 133.

11 *Ibid.*, p. 135.

12 *Ibid.*

13 *Ibid.*, p. 116.

14 Amnesty International report, 29 April 1996, pp. 6–9.

15 'UNHCR Western Sahara information update', 14 January 1998, p. 3, available on website (http://www.unhcr.ch/news/media/wsa01-13.htm). For regular weekly updates on Western Sahara access *Africa News On Line* on website (http://www.africanews.org/north/westernsahara/stories/19971013_feat1.html).

16 *Le Monde Diplomatique*, February 2000.

17 Report of secretary-general on the situation in Western Sahara, 28 October 1999, United Nations (http://www.arso.org/S-99-1098e.htm).

18 *Ibid.*

19 *Ibid.*

20 *Ibid.*

21 *Western Sahara Weekly News*, 31 October – 6 November 1999 (http://www.arso.org/01-e99-44.htm).

22 *Western Sahara Weekly News*, 25–31 July 1999.

23 *The Economist*, 31 July 1999.

24 *Western Sahara Weekly News*, 25–31 July 1999.

25 *Amnesty International Report 1999* (London, 1999, Amnesty International Publications), p. 252.

26 *Western Sahara Weekly News*, 31 October – 6 November 1999.

27 *Le Monde Diplomatique*, 'Is Morocco really changing?', February 2000.

28 *Le Monde Diplomatique*, February 2000.

29 *Amnesty International Report 2000* (London, 2000, Amnesty International Publications), p.171.

30 *The Guardian*, 'Western Sahara talks falter', 16 May 2000.

31 *Amnesty International Report 2000* (London, 2000, Amnesty International Publications), p.173.

32 *Ibid.*, p.173

33 *The World Guide 1997–98*, p. 401.

34 *Tapol Bulletin*, No. 147, p. 5, July 1998. This issue details the downfall of Suharto and the prospects for the future in Indonesia beyond the 1999 elections.

13

South Africa's Transition: Lessons for East Timor?

Adrian Guelke

In December 1996, South Africa's constitutional court certified that the country's new constitution, which had been drawn up by the representatives elected in South Africa's first non-racial democratic general election in April 1994, was in accordance with the constitutional principles which the parties had agreed should be embodied in the constitution. This was the second draft submitted to the court as it had referred parts of an earlier draft back to the representatives in September 1996. The approval of the constitution set the seal on the country's miraculous transition to democracy that began with President de Klerk's announcement on 2 February 1990 that he was lifting the ban on the African National Congress (ANC), the Pan-Africanist Congress (PAC), the South African Communist Party (SACP) and a number of other prohibited organizations. Further, he announced that the ANC's Nelson Mandela was to be released from prison.

One can point to earlier developments that contributed to de Klerk's speech of 2 February 1990. The reason this speech has been singled out is not merely because of its huge implications in the context of a system as authoritarian as that of apartheid South Africa, but because of what it represented in terms of South Africa's relations with the outside world. There had been reforms and modifications of apartheid before this. What was different this time was that the South African government was accepting that the country would have to be governed in terms of the norms of the international community. In effect, South Africa's defiance of world opinion in relation to the principle of self-determination was at an end. Naturally enough, within these parameters the ruling National Party wished to negotiate the best deal it could for itself. That led to conflict before agreement was finally reached with the ANC, towards the end of 1993, on the basis of the transitional arrangements for the country.

South Africa exemplifies the role that the international community is capable of playing in bringing about change in situations where there is a clear violation of its basic norms, such as that of self-determination. Of course, the international community (acting through the United Nations) is frequently a disappointment in this respect, as was the case of East Timor during Indonesia's occupation of the territory. The individual states that make up the United Nations all too often find reasons of *realpolitik* not to accept their responsibilities in these cases. And that is another lesson of the South African transition. If the question of apartheid had simply been left to governments, the pressure on the political establishment in Pretoria would never have developed to the extent that it did. The opposition of ordinary citizens in dozens of countries across the world ensured the engagement of governments. Certainly, there were parallels with East Timor here – not least in September 1999, when global public opinion pressured UN member states to intervene to arrest escalating carnage and destruction (see Chapter 14).

World opinion was by no means the only factor for the big change in South Africa, and by itself would never have been sufficient to have brought about such a fundamental shift in political power in a country as large as South Africa. Among other important factors in bringing about the change were a major demographic shift, the structural weakness of the economy, the mobilization of opposition to apartheid within the country, and the end of the Cold War. Each of these factors deserves a brief elaboration.

Under apartheid, South Africa was a white-ruled state, notwithstanding the claim of the ideology to provide the basis for the self-determination of all of the country's so-called population groups. The proportion of whites in the population was consequently critical to the functioning of apartheid. Between 1910 and 1960 there was relatively little change in the white proportion of the country's total population: it remained at roughly the 20 per cent mark. However, after 1960 the white share of the population began to decline sharply so that, at the point of de Klerk's speech, it stood at a little over 13 per cent, with projections that it would fall below 10 per cent around the millennium. At the same time, a sharp increase was occurring in the African share of the total population.

Coinciding with this demographic shift was a change in the structure of the economy, with mining and agriculture losing their dominant positions and a move to manufacturing and commerce. The change enhanced the bargaining power of black workers, since both manufacturing and commerce invested far more in the skills of the workforce than mining and agriculture had done. As significant as this change in the structure of the economy was its inability to adapt to oil crises in the 1970s which meant that the economy remained overprotected. The failure to restructure was reflected in low economic growth, generally below the increase in the population. As a consequence, there was a stagnation of real per capita incomes, and average per capita incomes in 1990 were lower than those in 1970.

Opposition to the regime was reinvigorated by the decolonization of Angola and Mozambique consequent upon the Portuguese revolution of 1974. In particular, the internal opposition derived considerable inspiration from South Africa's failed Angolan intervention that had pitted South African against Cuban troops. Moreover, grievances over educational policy led to a revolt by secondary-school pupils in Soweto in June 1976; this quickly developed into a full-scale uprising against the government in which thousands died. Faced with a crisis of governability that it was unable to end through the adoption of repressive measures, the regime was forced into making concessions. However, it found that each fresh concession empowered its opponents further, necessitating still more of the same.

De Klerk's actual decision to liberalize the South African political system was strongly influenced by the fall of the Berlin Wall. He believed that the ANC would be severely embarrassed politically by its relationship with the SACP, in the light of the discrediting of communism as a system. De Klerk hoped that by liberalizing in the immediate aftermath of the collapse of communism in Eastern Europe, the National Party would be able to take maximum advantage of disarray in the ANC camp over its links with the SACP. This proved to be a miscalculation. In fact, the effect of the collapse of communism was to reduce the salience of the ANC's relationship with the SACP, so that the continued alliance between the two parties largely ceased to draw hostile comment either from Western governments or the Western media. Further, the discrediting of communism as an economic model provided the ANC with a ready pretext for abandoning commitments that were an obstacle to its development of good relations with major business corporations. Consequently, de Klerk's hopes that he would be able to construct an alliance capable of challenging the ANC electorally in one-person one-vote elections were confounded.

While external pressures certainly played a part in persuading the government to liberalize the political system, it is easy to exaggerate the actual economic impact of sanctions imposed by South Africa's main trading partners. In particular, South African studies suggest that their impact on the country's trade with the outside world was very slight. Much more important than the economic impact of sanctions was their political effect. In fact, of the various sanctions designed to isolate apartheid South Africa, the ones that had the most powerful influence on the situation were those with symbolic rather than real importance for people's lives.

Measured by their influence on both white and black public opinion in South Africa, the most effective sanctions imposed on the country were the sports boycotts. An indication of this was the prominent role that the issue played in the referendum among whites in March 1992, when de Klerk sought and secured endorsement for continuing the process of reform. The threat of a resumption of the sports boycott in the event of rejection of de Klerk's plea for support featured strongly in the 'yes' campaign. By coincidence, a South African cricket team was taking part in the cricket World Cup at the time of the referendum. It featured prominently in the campaign: an advertisement urging white voters to endorse de Klerk's reforms contrasted the success of the South African cricket team in Australia with a picture showing broken stumps and an overgrown cricket pitch as a way of highlighting the consequences of a 'no' vote.

A factor that helped to magnify the impact of international opinion on the regime was the stance taken by the main opposition political movement (the ANC) on international norms, including most particularly the question of self-determination. For example, the ANC did not fall into the trap of laying claim to neighbouring territories on the grounds of geography or their historical links with the country. Thus the ANC, while refusing to recognize the independence of Bantustans established under apartheid, did not attempt to suggest that the former high commission territories of Lesotho, Botswana and Swaziland should form part of a new South Africa. There were temptations to do so, deriving from the fact that – in the 1950s – migrant workers from these territories had often supported and sometimes even became members of the ANC. However, the ANC recognized that if it adopted policies that ran counter to international norms, it would put at risk support for its cause and weaken the appeal of anti-apartheid movements in other countries. Unfortunately, in government the ANC has been less principled in its foreign policy than it was as a movement in exile. Thus for two years after Mandela's inauguration as president, South Africa continued to recognize the Republic of China (Taiwan) as the government of China. Recognition of Beijing materialized as Mandela came reluctantly to appreciate that not having diplomatic relations with one of the veto powers in the UN Security Council might have consequences seriously detrimental to South Africa's security. For a time, it seemed as if Taiwan's cheque-book diplomacy would carry the day.

Morocco and Indonesia have also sought to influence the country's stance on the issues of Western Sahara and East Timor in a similar manner, though slightly less lavishly than Taiwan. The impact of foreign donations to the ANC on the government of national unity's foreign policy did not go unremarked. In December 1995, under the heading: 'For sale SA's diplomatic relations',[1] the *Weekly Mail and Guardian* carried a swingeing attack on the effect of ANC fundraising on the conduct of foreign policy. The article mentioned Taiwan, Morocco and Indonesia, as well as speculating that South Africa's disastrous 'softly softly' policy towards the Nigerian military regime had its roots in financial backing received by the ANC from previous rulers of Nigeria. It also noted Mandela's revelation, in May 1995, that the ANC had received substantial donations from the Indonesian government, though Mandela did not give any details of the sums involved. The context in which Mandela had made this admission was criticism of his trip to Indonesia in 1994, during which he had refused to speak out over human rights questions despite the South African government's commitment to give priority to human rights in the conduct of its foreign policy.[2]

In September 1996, a Fretilin delegation led by José Ramos-Horta visited South Africa at the invitation of the ANC. Mandela gave Ramos-Horta an assurance that donations by the Indonesian government to the party would not make it a 'hostage' of South African foreign policy.[3] However, when the question of Indonesia's conduct in East Timor came up in the United Nations Human Rights Commission, South Africa abstained, a stance criticized by the chair of the South African parliament's committee on foreign affairs, Raymond Suttner.[4] A further complicating issue in relations between South Africa and Indonesia were losses suffered by a South African charitable enterprise, the Foundation for Peace and Justice (FPJ), as a result of its dealings with an Indonesian bank, Bank Putera Sukapura. The FPJ was associated with a leading figure in the ANC, Allan Boesak, who was already in deep trouble as a result of accusations that he had misappropriated funds the FPJ had received from Scandinavia. Bank Putera Sukapura was closely associated with the family of President Suharto. The losses arose as a result of the bank's false assurances of the creditworthiness of an Indonesian company that was to have advanced a loan to the FPJ for major building projects. To make matters worse, at the time the loan was being arranged, it was in contravention of the ANC's policy on financial sanctions. Despite the potential for embarrassment to both the ANC and the government, Mandela had taken up the issue with President Suharto in an attempt to recoup the money that the FPJ and other non-governmental organizations had lost as a result of the collapse of the loan, but without any success.[5]

This was the somewhat inauspicious background to an official visit by Mandela to Indonesia in July 1997, his third trip to the country during the 1990s. In the course of this visit, Mandela met the imprisoned East Timorese leader Xanana Gusmão. By agreement between Suharto and Mandela, the Indonesian government made the announcement that the meeting had taken place after Mandela's return to South Africa. Mandela described his meeting with Gusmão as part of a UN initiative to resolve the conflict being undertaken by the secretary-general, Kofi Annan, when he separately briefed Ramos-Horta and the Portuguese president, Jorge Sampaio, on his meetings in Indonesia. Confusion then arose over whether Mandela had written to President Suharto calling on him to release all jailed political leaders, including Gusmão. The Indonesian government denied receiving such a letter. It then transpired that the letter had mistakenly been delivered to the Portuguese embassy in Pretoria. The contents of the letter, highlighting Mandela's call for the release of prisoners, had subsequently been leaked to the press in Lisbon. The breach of confidentiality angered Mandela. He blamed the Portuguese embassy in Pretoria for the disclosure and expelled the Portuguese ambassador over the affair.[6] The Portuguese government deplored South Africa's action, but rebuffed opposition demands for retaliation. The spat between the two countries overshadowed Indonesia's belated acknowledgement of receipt of the Mandela letter.

The row between South Africa and Portugal was a setback to the prospects of successful mediation in the conflict by Mandela. The possibility that, in the words of the Johannesburg newspaper, *Business Day*, 'the world's most admired head of state'[7] might add further lustre to the country by helping to bring to an end one of the last conflicts arising out of the colonial era had aroused considerable interest in the issue of East Timor in South Africa. However, a measure of disillusionment set in after the dispute with Portugal and the failure of the Indonesian government to act on Mandela's initiative, reviving fears that Mandela was being used to lend respectability to the regime in Jakarta, especially in the light of the invitation to Suharto to visit South Africa in November 1997. These fears have been somewhat allayed by the fact that Mandela has continued to speak out on the question of East Timor. In September 1997, he had a meeting with Bishop Carlos Belo, who had earlier turned down an invitation to discuss the issue with the South African president. After his meeting with Bishop Belo, Mandela told a news conference that the basis of his approach was that Indonesia should accord autonomy to East Timor, and that responsibility for a solution lay with the leaders of East Timor and the Indonesian government.

The most negative factor regarding South African mediation is the part that money has played in the relationship between the ANC and the Indonesian government; the most positive factor is the support in South Africa for international norms as a result of the country's own experience. In general, the South African case has provided a helpful precedent for those campaigning on the issue of East Timor. Eventually, the cost of being out of step with world opinion came to be too much for the South African regime and, in the end, the need to normalize its relations with the rest of the world brought far-reaching change in the way the country was governed. The point of principle in the South African case was the denial of voting and effective citizen rights to a majority of the population. In the case of East Timor, it was the demand that the people of East Timor should be allowed to decide their own political future in free elections. Both cases stand out as fundamental and unambiguous violations of the principle of self-determination, as it has been interpreted by the international community. Since those campaigning for East Timor have prevented the normalization of Indonesia's relations with the rest of the world, the Suharto regime was constantly forced on to the defensive over the issue, and this pressure has helped to bring about a dramatic reversal in the policies of Indonesia, as occurred in the South African case.

As a matter of fact, it is quite evident that the Indonesian regime failed to normalize its occupation of East Timor, despite the long passage of time since its brutal intervention to prevent East Timor's independence. Also, just as anti-apartheid campaigners were aided by the internationalization of the situation in South Africa, so the campaign for a free East Timor benefited from a high international profile. Again, just as the award of the Nobel Peace Prize to Archbishop Tutu underscored the hostility of the world towards apartheid and symbolically drove home the message to whites that South Africa would not escape pariah status as long as apartheid remained on the statute book, so the award of the Nobel Peace Prize to Bishop Belo and Ramos-Horta in 1996 underlined the impossibility of the Indonesian government persuading the outside world to accept the annexation of East Timor as a *fait accompli*. This constant drip of international rejection eroded Indonesian obduracy over East Timor and led to striking policy changes. This suggests that symbolic protests can be as effective as economic sanctions, if not more so, since their impact is often more direct than a fall in income, the latter being a compound of many different factors.

As in the case of apartheid in South Africa, non-governmental organizations rather than governments played the larger role in keeping the issue of East Timor alive, especially in periods when power realities appeared to favour the status quo. Both the Suharto regime and the old National Party government relied on Western governments turning a blind eye to their violations of human rights for Cold War considerations. Contrary to de Klerk's expectations, the end of the Cold War worked to the advantage of the ANC. The same factor has impacted upon Indonesia, with the East Timorese and opponents of the Suharto and Habibie regimes as the beneficiaries.

Another noteworthy topic is the role now being played by the Truth and Reconciliation Commission in examining South Africa's past violations of human rights. It is essential not to draw too many lessons for East Timor from this aspect of the South African transition. For one thing, it is a bit early to draw definite conclusions about the value of the Truth and Reconciliation Commission for South Africa itself. In particular, despite the positive view that has generally been taken of the work of the commission in the way it has been reported outside the country, it is far from clear that the revelation of the details of atrocities is in fact contributing to a healing process in South Africa, as the proponents of this mechanism had hoped. It is worth noting, however, that Bishop Belo – in a February 1999 address to a public meeting in Sydney – suggested that a South African-modelled truth and reconciliation commission would be of great benefit to East Timor. Belo stated that 'The effort being made in South Africa to create a public debate on reconciliation is a great step forward', and added that 'Their [South Africa's] Truth and Reconciliation Commission is a very open process ... allowing ordinary South Africans to recount their stories in a public way. I think we in this part of the world have a lot to learn from this process.'[8] The fact that Belo was raising the issue of a truth commission for East Timor provided some indication of the progress made toward finding a solution to the conflict in the territory.

The establishment of a truth commission, however, rested on a settlement to the conflict in East Timor, and a clear commitment from the government in Jakarta to adhere to the norms of international law. In 1998–99, the focus on the central issue of the manifest illegitimacy of the occupation of East Timor was productive in securing concessions from a cash-strapped Jakarta, notably the announcement by the former president, B. J. Habibie, that Indonesia would accept the independence of the territory if it was the favoured option of the majority of Timorese.[9] Now, following a brutal military/militia backlash against the result of the 30 August referendum on the future of East Timor (see Chapter 14), consideration may be given to constructing a way forward for the East Timorese and those responsible for past policies and actions, as was done in South Africa through the offer of amnesties in return for truth.

References

1   *Weekly Mail and Guardian* (Johannesburg), 8 December 1995.
2   'Mandela's strange links to human rights abuser', *Weekly Mail and Guardian*, 26 May 1995.
3   'Mandela placates East Timorese from his bed', *Weekly Mail and Guardian*, 20 September 1996.
4   *Business Day* (Johannesburg), 25 April 1997.
5   'Boesak, Mandela and the 40 million dollar fiasco', *Weekly Mail and Guardian*, 5 May 1995.
6   'Ambassador expelled over media', *Business Day*, 5 August 1997.
7   'Mediating in East Timor', *Business Day*, 24 July 1997.
8   Miller, John M., ETAN, 25 February 1999 (http://www.etan.org).
9   For a full analysis of the Habibie statement and its implications for East Timor, see *Tapol Bulletin*, No. 151, March 1999.

14

Conclusion: East Timor After Suharto – A New Horizon

Paul Hainsworth

Introduction: Indonesia – from Suharto to Habibie

On 21 May 1998, Suharto resigned dramatically after over 3 decades as president of Indonesia. The immediate context to his resignation was the economic crisis that swept through the Asian regional economy and severely hit the fragile construct of Suharto's highly personalized, weakly structured 'crony capitalism'. Massive devaluation of the Indonesian currency, widespread rioting and civil unrest (which soon left over 1200 dead), growing opposition within civil society to authoritarian rule and devastating environmental problems all hastened Suharto's downfall.[1] Amidst the escalating crisis, then, underlined by an ebbing away of confidence in Suharto amongst military élites, political supporters, Western backers and business investors, the reins of government were handed over swiftly, albeit to Suharto loyalist and Vice-President B. J. Habibie. The fall of Suharto, however, opened a window of opportunity for democratic change in Indonesia and East Timor, not least since the deteriorating economic situation, continuing unrest and burgeoning movement for reform acted as constraints upon the new government's freedom of manoeuvre.

The first few months of Habibie's presidency witnessed some significant political developments. These included releases of political prisoners, the drafting of legislation for the registration of (hitherto proscribed) political parties, a national human rights plan developed in consultation with the United Nations Commission for Human Rights (UNCHR), arrest and suspension of several members of the military special forces (Kopassus) for their role in kidnapping political activists, investigations into unlawful state killings in East Timor and Irian Jaya (see Chapter 5), and the establishment of a fact-finding team to probe the systematic rape of ethnic-Chinese Indonesian women during the May 1998 rioting. In addition to these measures, Habibie apologized for past military excesses and the new regime was notable for greater press freedom, political discussion and a more flourishing civil society. Multi-party parliamentary elections were scheduled for June 1999, with a presidential election to follow a few months after. The successful – free and fair – conduct of these polls would undoubtedly be a measure of Indonesia's democratization process.

However, despite a discernible liberalization, the trappings of the *ancien régime* remained essentially intact, with a continuing, strong role for the armed forces (ABRI), a lack of independent investigating and judicial mechanisms, the retention of repressive, draconian legislation on the statute books and impunity for human rights violations was still the order of the day. Indeed, in the summer of 1998, Habibie, whilst urging restraint from those forces policing demonstrations, also instructed the military to be tough with any 'disruptive forces'.[2] In this respect, on 7 September, Amnesty International summed up the situation as follows: 'In general, ABRI continues to regard human rights as something to be traded off against stability and economic prosperity rather than as a fundamental principle underpinning long-term security and development.'[3] Moreover, as Budiardjo points out in Chapter 5, the military – notwithstanding some apparent internal divisions – remained attached to its 'special role' (*dwifungsi*) within the Indonesian state and society, and this reality is likely to impede the prospect of transition to a more democratic future.

Nevertheless, it became increasingly evident that economic prescriptions for the revival of Indonesia would be bound up with the broader issue of societal reform. As Hubert Neiss (Asia director, International Monetary Fund) explained: 'We have to recognize that the economic measures will only work and be really effective if there is political stability.'[4] In a similar vein, Amnesty International's Asia-Pacific director, Rory Mungoven, called for a rounded approach to Indonesia's problems:

> Distortions in Indonesia's economy cannot be addressed in isolation from distortions in its political and institutional life. This is why the [proposed] IMF rescue package must be complemented by broader reforms which strengthen the rule of law, government accountability and respect for human rights... Indonesia's long-term stability and development would be better served if tensions in society were aired and addressed rather than bottled up to the point of explosion.[5]

Clearly, these strictures applied to the Indonesian occupation of East Timor, which was estimated to be costing the cash-strapped Jakarta regime about $1 million per day and considerable loss of military lives and prestige, as well as provoking a barrage of embarrassing criticism globally.

East Timor under Habibie

As within Indonesia at large, the transition of power from Suharto to Habibie ushered in a whirlwind of developments in and relating to East Timor. These developments were, simultaneously, promising and destabilizing, contributing to an ambivalent mix of advances on the diplomatic and constitutional front and, more worryingly, continued human rights abuses, hardship and uncertainties on the ground. On the one hand, East Timorese society shared in the broad post-Suharto mood of greater democratization and political openness. According to one visiting journalist (*The Irish Times*'s Conor O'Clery), for instance, the political climate had changed since Suharto's fall, with less surveillance of visitors in evidence, and more open dialogue and the holding of student demonstrations.[6] Also, several observers pointed to the vibrancy of the student movement as a renewed force for change in East Timor, echoing the broader student impetus for reform within Indonesia. Again, East Timor experienced a flourishing of organizational activity, in the form of new or reconstituted/returning political parties and structures, representing youth, women, students and pro-referendum elements. The openness and greater resort to public discussion was evident in the so-called 'dialogues' (public meetings) which took place in the post-Suharto period. The East Timor Human Rights Centre (ETHRC), based in Melbourne, noted 'an unprecedented atmosphere of freedom and opinion in East Timor'.[7]

However, on the other hand, the Habibie presidency was characterized by ongoing repression. As Amnesty International explained, in November 1998, despite a more open political climate in East Timor there were 'serious human rights violations, including arbitrary arrests, incommunicado detention, "disappearances" and unlawful killings by ABRI, in the context of operations' against the East Timorese resistance movement.[8] In the second half of 1998, the ETHRC recorded 28 extra-judicial executions, 149 arbitrary detentions and 183 cases of torture and ill-treatment.[9] Indeed, abusive practices – including rape and humiliation of Timorese women by the military – marked both the Suharto and Habibie presidencies. Moreover, the army maintained an undiminished presence in East Timor, notwithstanding propaganda exercises and subterfuge designed to imply the contrary.[10] Further repression occurred as increasingly the military began arming, training and subsidizing pro-integrationist militias, whose violence and intimidatory activities also led to considerable population displacement as threatened Timorese sought refuge beyond their homes and villages. As diplomatic moves accelerated at the UN and at government levels (see below), one effect was to create more uncertainty and tension on the ground between pro- and anti-integrationist forces. Thus, according to the Indonesian Human Rights Commission, at least 50 people died during clashes between pro- and anti-Jakarta groups in the territory over the six-month period leading up to early February 1999.[11] One of the worst atrocities inflicted upon the East Timorese took place in Liquisa in April 1999. At least 25 civilians were massacred by the Red and White Iron – a pro-integrationist militia – with participation and complicity from Indonesian military forces. Subsequent violations and killings by the militia occurred whilst the Irish Foreign Minister, David Andrews, was visiting East Timor (see Chapter 1). As Andrews explained: 'We saw for ourselves that the army and police were letting all this happen. It is clear that this is an attempt to derail the tripartite peace process [see below].'[12]

In addition to the physical violence, poverty, unemployment and health and nutrition deficiencies remained part of the Timorese daily reality. In March 1999, for instance there were increasing reports of a 'pending food and health disaster' in East Timor.[13] According to Dan Murphy, a doctor working in the territory, 50 to 100 people were dying there every day from curable diseases, such as malnutrition, diarrhoea and tuberculosis, or in childbirth.[14] Again, the critical situation was summed up by the East Timor *Action* Network (ETAN) in the USA, as follows: 'Foreign and East Timorese health care workers, aid workers, and journalists report serious food shortages and a mounting health care crisis with few doctors and limited medicines available.'[15] Unsurprisingly, the future of healthcare was one of the key issues being debated constructively in the various Timorese/NGO/solidarity meetings taking place across Australia, Portugal and elsewhere, organized to discuss the needs of East Timor, both immediate and in the event of constitutional change. Other crucial areas for discussion and consideration included agriculture, education, the environment, structures of governance and gender relations.[16]

Habibie's millstone: Re-imagining Indonesia's relationship with East Timor

The upsurge in pro-integrationist paramilitarism and the general anxiety in the pro-Jakarta camp in 1998–99 could be seen as directly related to the acceleration of political and diplomatic developments, as the Habibie regime began to reassess its policy on East Timor amidst increasing international criticism of Indonesia's occupation of the territory, continuing domestic economic problems and ongoing pressures for change from the Timorese and across the archipelago. As Carey explained, the Suharto regime's intractability on East Timor gave way to a Habibie government which was, at least, 'more accommodating than its predecessor in offering cosmetic change' for the territory.[17] Within weeks of taking up presidential office, Habibie had announced special-territory status for East Timor, allowed an amnesty for 16 prominent Timorese political prisoners and was even mooting the possible release of Xanana Gusmão, the leader of the East Timorese resistance movement. However, such status was a long way from self-determination via a free and fair referendum, and it still involved recognizing Indonesia's overall authority. John Pilger suggested critically that special status was merely 'a Vichy arrangement run by quislings'.[18] Indeed, special status for the disputed territory of Aceh in northern Sumatra has not prevented massive killings and human rights abuses by the Indonesian military. On the broader diplomatic front, meanwhile, UN-sponsored talks on East Timor (started up in 1992) continued to engage Indonesia and Portugal, but East Timorese spokespersons were excluded from these particular discussions on their future. Lisbon, in effect, was negotiating on their behalf.

Nevertheless, amidst the continuing economic crisis, diplomatic activity and civil unrest, the Habibie administration began to respond to the growing pressures for change on East Timor. In fact, by mid-1998, the media reported that officials in Dili were 'engaged in active official and unofficial dialogue with the independence movement'.[19] By early 1999, the Habibie regime was seen to be offering considerably more than special status or autonomy for East Timor within the Indonesian state. Following a cabinet meeting in January, Foreign Minister Alatas (a longstanding exponent of East Timor's absorption by Indonesia) and Information Minister Yunus Yosfiah both floated the possibility of some form of independence. According to Alatas: 'If they want their freedom they are welcome to it ... it is only fair and wise and even democratic and constitutional to suggest to the [new Indonesian parliament] to allow East Timor to separate from Indonesia in a dignified and good manner.'[20] Yosfiah added that, whilst a strong measure of autonomy was the preferred Indonesian governmental option, a suggestion would be made to parliament to 'release East Timor from Indonesia' if that was the preferred option of the Timorese.[21] The head of the armed forces, General Wiranto, appeared to throw his indispensable authority behind the new line: 'We have always pulled together to do the best for East Timor ... if it is now decided that East Timor is no longer part of Indonesia, of course ... we will comply with it.'[22] Understandably, these statements were interpreted widely as a very significant development in the debate about the status of East Timor although, given the experience of occupied East Timor, there was also scepticism and a distinct absence of euphoria from Timorese spokespersons as to the sincerity of the Indonesian authorities.

Nevertheless, Tapol, the Indonesia Human Rights Campaign, referred to the Indonesian government announcement as 'a thunderbolt': 'The economic meltdown and the worsening political crisis have forced Jakarta to re-assess its East Timor policy.'[23] Reporting on the new situation, *The Guardian*'s correspondent, John Aglionby pointed tellingly to 'a U-turn that would have been unthinkable before autocratic President Suharto was forced from office',[24] whilst *The Independent*'s Richard Lloyd Parry alluded to 'a further capitulation to international pressure'.[25] According to Lloyd Parry, the statements from top-level Indonesian sources represented 'a turning point in one of the world's most tragic and vicious small wars'.[26] Again, the apparent attitudinal thaw was seen as 'the result of a combination of foreign lobbying, pressure from within the Indonesian government and Jakarta's desperate economic plight'.[27] Moreover, *The Financial Times*'s Sander Thoenes suggested that 'it has become more difficult for Indonesia to hold out against international criticism of its policy towards the territory as economic crisis has forced the government to rely more on foreign aid'.[28]

Certainly, a seemingly abrupt change of heart from Australia, Suharto's staunchest ally and apologist on the East Timor question, contributed to the strategic reassessment in Jakarta. According to one informed assessment, Habibie's sudden decision was 'triggered' by a pre-Christmas letter from Australian Prime Minister John Howard, forewarning of a shift from supporting Indonesia's occupation to favouring self-determination in East Timor.[29] Tapol, too, described the Australian move as the 'final straw' for Habibie.[30] This *volte-face* must surely have come as a shock to the Indonesian authorities, given – as Aubrey explains in Chapter 10 – Australia's *de facto* and *de jure* support for East Timor's occupied status. As John Pilger suggests: 'Of all those who sustained Suharto in power, perhaps the most shameless was Australia, an accessory to genocide.'[31] Amongst the Australian government's measures of support for Suharto, Pilger lists three: Foreign Minister Gareth Evans's minimizing of the 1991 Santa Cruz massacre as an 'incident'; Prime Minister Paul Keating's haranguing of the US Senate Foreign Relations Committee for voting in 1993 against selling arms to Indonesia; and the 1995 agreement to help train Kopassus, Indonesia's élite corps, responsible for a catalogue of human rights abuses in East Timor.[32]

At the time of Suharto's fall, the Australian government was reported as being 'nervous'[33] about the collapse of the regime, and arguably Canberra's new line on East Timor could be seen as a belated attempt at damage limitation, as well as a vote for stabilization and conflict resolution. Nevertheless, a telling comment was made by Marcus Einfield, ex-president of the Australian Human Rights Commission: 'When democracy does come … what will [Indonesians and East Timorese] think of Australia which … stood by in silence for over 20 years as the poor grew poorer and thousands of East Timorese were murdered, raped and oppressed.'[34] In addition to the revised (and welcome) stance from Canberra, the (post-Cold War) criticisms from Western backers and persistent pressures from the UN, the European Union (EU) and the international community also played their part in encouraging change – once the Indonesian regime and economy were in downfall mode. As the journalist John McBeth explained, the resignation of the former president was the watershed factor:

> Suharto's fall has clearly changed the way Indonesian society views East Timor. Gone is the nationalist rhetoric which dismissed any notion of secession. In its place, there is now an almost resigned attitude that if the East Timorese don't want to be part of Indonesia, then it would be better to cut them free.[35]

Again, as Australian journalist Mark Baker pointed out, in an August 1998 interview with Ramos-Horta:

> What began as a frisson of excitement with the disintegration, in May, of the loathed Soeharto [Dutch spelling] regime, has grown steadily into a conviction that there is now an unstoppable momentum towards change and democratisation in Indonesia that must lead to the end of two decades of repression in East Timor, and an occupation that has claimed the lives of an estimated 200,000 Timorese.[36]

A key player here on the government side was President Habibie's foreign policy adviser, Dewi Fortuna Anwar, who depicted East Timor as an embarrassment to and drain upon Indonesia. For Anwar, the transition provided a 'whole new prism through which we see the issue'.[37] Such an open admission from regime spokespersons would have been unimaginable under Suharto. In the post-Suharto context, however, it was part of the re-imagining of Indonesian-Timorese relations and symptomatic of the quest of some policy makers to work towards a face-saving resolution in East Timor, in order to free up the regime to tackle the broader issues of economic reconstruction, political reform and territorial stability in the rest of the archipelago. As one Indonesian diplomat is reported to have said, alluding to an infamous portrayal of Indonesia's East Timor problem by Foreign Minister Ali Alatas: 'This has been more than a pebble in our shoe. It's been a millstone around our neck.'[38]

East Timor, then, had been part of Indonesia's problem, but in rapidly changing circumstances it now had to be part of the solution. In fact, for years the East Timorese resistance, diaspora and global solidarity movement had speculated upon whether change in East Timor would spark a wider movement for reform or revolution in Indonesia, or vice versa. With Suharto's resignation, the struggle for self-determination in East Timor entered a new phase: what had not seemed immediately possible hitherto suddenly emerged as a tangible prospect. Undoubtedly, the status of East Timor was becoming progressively negotiable in the period leading up to the June 1999 legislative elections in Indonesia. More than at any time since the 1975 occupation, self-determination for East Timor emerged as a realizable objective.

The transfer of Xanana Gusmão from Cipinang prison to house arrest in January 1999 – an intensely, internationally lobbied-for step – enhanced this prospect. The move confirmed Indonesia's recognition of his pivotal role in negotiations on East Timor's constitutional status, and the resistance leader was seen widely as the most authoritative voice for progress and reconciliation, the Nelson Mandela figure of East Timor.[39] According to one sympathetic view: 'Xanana Gusmão could help the Indonesians leave the territory without losing face, and guarantee stability in the region. He has the capacity to understand all the sensibilities involved, both internally and on the international scene.'[40] (Like Mandela, he was soon – in December 1999 – to be awarded the European Parliament's Sakharov Prize for his contribution to human rights.)

However, in early 1999, the Habibie regime – although seeming to favour a face-saving withdrawal – was not yet reconciled to a referendum on East Timor's constitutional position. According to Alatas, this step 'practically and politically could not be accepted … it would lead to conflict or civil war'.[41] Shortly afterwards, Alatas reiterated that position: 'What we have in mind is very wide-ranging autonomy. A referendum is a recipe for civil conflict.'[42] Nevertheless, the momentum was now with the forces for agreement and change and, in March 1999 in New York, the UN-brokered talks process yielded further significant developments. The Indonesian and Portuguese negotiating teams now agreed to a ballot on autonomy. East Timorese living all over the world would participate. This would thus involve a consultation process within East Timor and also with the approximately 30,000 East Timorese residing in places such as Australia, Portugal and Macau, other parts of Europe and North America. The Indonesian Foreign Minister, Alatas, was still reluctant to call the ballot a referendum, but this could be seen as a face-saving exercise. For all intents and purposes, a vote against autonomy would be taken as a vote for independence. Pro-independence groups were reported to be cautiously optimistic, and Xanana Gusmão issued a statement welcoming Indonesia's acceptance of 'a form of consultation which respects basic democratic and representative principles', whilst the Portuguese Foreign

Minister, Jaime Gama, called the agreement 'a turning point'.[43] The UN talks process yielded up further fruits in New York in April and May 1999, when the following 30 August was agreed as East Timor's consultation day. At the same time, the Indonesians accepted the need for UN monitors, although this fell short of a peace-keeping force.[44]

Developments at the diplomatic level contrasted with uncertainties in East Timor: the arming of paramilitary elements, a deficit of confidence-building measures (such as genuine reductions of troops), the reluctance of Indonesia to engage in direct discussions with legitimate Timorese spokespersons and the resistance to change from the pro-integrationist camp all served to complicate any movement towards a just and peaceful solution. Additionally, there were concerns within the Indonesian state apparatuses that constitutional change in East Timor might open up the floodgates to secessionist forces across the archipelago. The arming of local paramilitaries could be seen as a reaction – manifest on the ground, but orchestrated by military élites – against the rapid course of developments concerning East Timor's constitutional status. It could be seen, too, as part of a wider strategy (articulated – and denied – on high) to portray the territory as verging on the brink of civil war and therefore incapable of managing its own affairs. There were ominous parallels here with the 1975 period, when Indonesia had manipulated a nascent, post-colonial situation in East Timor to 'justify' invasion and takeover.[45] According to *The Guardian*'s Martin Woollacott, ABRI 'continues to play the game at which it has become adept, that of fomenting and encouraging violence so that it can then appear as the only force able to impose law and order'.[46] It is clear that the sponsoring of paramilitary activity represented an irresponsible and dangerous step, at a time when the people of East Timor needed a measured and reflective period of transition in the changing circumstances of the new post-Suharto era. As the overseas development agency CAFOD had explained earlier, in a memorandum to the UK House of Commons Foreign Affairs Committee:

> It is significant and positive that for the first time for many years a space for genuine dialogue has been opened up between the Indonesian government and civil society in East Timor. Such openings, however, are fragile and need support and reinforcement from the international community if they are to lead to lasting understanding and agreement.[47]

In reality, the rapid succession of events in Indonesia in 1998–99 took by surprise many observers of and participants in the 'East Timor question'. Whilst change was certainly expected at some time in the future, it was not anticipated to come quite so quickly, even though attention has often focused on the regional comparison of the Philippines and the dramatic demise of the Marcos regime. In an August 1998 interview, however, José Ramos-Horta expressed a new sense of confidence that, within 'a year or two from now', there would be a non-violent solution – albeit not 'a definite one' – with peace and stability forthcoming in East Timor:

> Frankly, it's only in the last few weeks that I have really felt this way... I was always confident that we would go back, but it was more like a philosophical approach than a practical one. Now, yes, I believe we really can do it.[48]

Practical proposals for the future of East Timor were formulated in the National Council of Maubere Resistance (CNRM)'s peace plan, which Ramos-Horta presented to the European parliament in 1993. The plan comprised three elements. First, confidence-building measures were deemed necessary to promote a spirit of trust and goodwill between Indonesia and East Timor. These measures included considerable troop reductions, release of political prisoners, demilitarization of heavy weaponry, access to East Timor for UN specialized agencies, freedom for political activities, and the establishment of an independent human rights commission. Second, following the implementation of stage one, the plan called for an autonomy phase, based upon free and fair (UN-supervised) elections to a new territorial assembly, and the removal of all remaining Indonesian troops. It was anticipated (and laid down) that the autonomy period would last from five to ten years. The third phase consisted of a UN referendum on the question of self-determination for East Timor.[49]

The referendum thus was an objective, but not an immediate one. Understandably, therefore, there were concerns amongst supporters of self-determination that the Indonesian abrupt 'take-it-or-leave-it' attitude to autonomy – as exhibited, notably, by Foreign Minister Alatas in early 1999[50] – might be counterproductive to the process of securing a better future for East Timor if the conditions for peaceful change were not forthcoming on the ground. The prospect of a sudden withdrawal might create problems as well as resolving them (see below). Both President Habibie and his foreign policy adviser (Dewi Fortuna Anwar) seemed also to be coming round to a position of 'dumping' East Timor at all costs. Addressing the Indonesian Chamber of Commerce and Industry in February 1999, Habibie said: 'From January 1, 2000, we don't want to be burdened with the East Timor problem.'[51] Against this approach, Bishop Belo, 1996 Nobel laureate and head of the Catholic Church in East Timor, served as a prominent voice supporting a period of negotiated autonomy and reconciliation prior to any referendum on self-determination. Inadequate preparation and education for change and the disruptive consequences of arming pro-Jakarta paramilitaries were two principal anxieties in this context. However, if such difficulties could be overcome[52] and the mechanisms and conduct of the consultative ballot or referendum worked out satisfactorily, then the East Timorese people could begin to aspire towards a more just and peaceful homeland. Under the terms of the final tripartite agreement, signed in New York on 6 May 1999, the following wording was agreed upon: 'Do you accept the proposed special autonomy for East Timor within the Unitary State of the Republic of Indonesia?' or 'Do you reject the proposed special autonomy for East Timor, leading to East Timor's separation from Indonesia?' As the East Timor Human Rights Centre optimistically concluded: 'For the first time in its long and difficult struggle for peace, East Timor is hopeful that a political solution, leading to independence from Indonesia, is possible.'[53]

The August 1999 referendum and its aftermath

For several years hitherto, East Timor had been depicted as a territory 'standing at the crossroads' of change and, with the onset of the August 1999 ballot, this description was particularly apt. Clearly, the moral and political 'war' had been won by the East Timorese as Indonesia, in economic and social crisis, finally had to come to terms with its international pariah status and the sheer unfeasibility of occupying East Timor and brutalizing its people. Whatever the semantic, face-saving wranglings over terminology, it was clear that the East Timorese were now to be given an important say on their future. The UN-brokered agreement between the Indonesian and Portuguese governments provided this.

The voter registration process was to be managed and monitored by the UN – in the form of UNAMET (the United Nations Assistance Mission in East Timor), with participation from locally and internationally recruited individuals and volunteers. Crucially, though, security throughout the pre- and post-registration and voting periods was to remain in the hands of the Indonesian military. Unsurprisingly, given the latter's human rights record in East Timor, there were widespread misgivings about this arrangement. Nevertheless, the view of many, including Xanana Gusmão, was that the Timorese may not again – soon or perhaps ever – be given such an opportunity to express their opinion. Thus, arguably, it was important to proceed with the referendum, despite reservations about the conditions on offer and the security arrangements. UNAMET spokesperson David Wimhurst also pointed to a 'moral obligation to allow the people of East Timor to vote. If we give in to thuggery, then democracy fails.'[54] In any case, the UN Secretary-General was authorized (via the terms of the agreement) to postpone or cancel the vote if the level of intimidation and harassment of registrees/voters was deemed to be preventing a free and fair ballot.[55]

In the event, it was a testimony to the courage and determination of the East Timorese people that they completed the registration requirements (in difficult circumstances, with the militias active and threatening) and that around 98 to 99 per cent turned out on (a relatively peaceful) 30 August, with an overwhelming 78.5 per cent of them voting for separation from Indonesia.[56] However, despite the margin of success for anti-integration sentiments, the results were not accompanied by any proportional outpouring of euphoria or victory celebrations. Indeed, the pro-integration militias – such as Aitarak, Besi Merah Putih and the Nahidi Suai – had always threatened not to accept a vote against Jakarta's authority and, increasingly, the collusion and interdependency between the military and the militias became all too apparent as East Timor was plummeted into crisis. The dramatic and draconian reaction to the referendum result should not, therefore, be seen as a sudden and casual reaction to unwanted constitutional change by the regular and irregular security forces. Rather, it was premeditated and had been planned for months as a contingency operation: this was the logic of the military's arming and training of the militias. According to Tapol, pro-independence activists and human rights workers had seen leaked copies of a detailed plan to wreak havoc and had 'warned the UN authorities of impending disaster but they were ignored'.[57]

The next phase, in fact, was characterized by a military/militia 'scorched-earth' policy of killings, abuses, lootings, burnings and massive population displacement (both internally and to West Timor and other parts of Indonesia). For instance, over the month or two after the referendum, around 230,000 persons were estimated and reported to have been removed by the Indonesian military/militias to camps in West Timor, and about 200,000 fled to the mountains and interior in East Timor to escape carnage and destruction in Dili and elsewhere. Thousands were declared killed and/or unaccounted for, following reports and testimonies from witnesses, survivors and refugees. Some of the pro-integrationist forces also speculated on repartitioning the border between West and East Timor, to the latter's disadvantage. The military/militia backlash could be seen as an attempt to thwart the verdict of the people and punish them for wanting to turn away from Indonesia's jurisdiction. Also, it represented the bruised and humiliated reaction of a military (and its supporters) used to ruling with impunity in East Timor, counting ruefully its own casualties since 1975 and fearful that the East Timorese 'model' might inspire other disaffected parts of Indonesia.

As the violence and destruction continued and escalated throughout the next few weeks, the military/militia strategy was to try – with some success – to intimidate UNAMET and international monitors and observers out of East Timor, whilst simultaneously targeting suspected pro-independence elements, including Catholic clergy, nuns, aid workers and missionaries.

Bishop Belo was forced to flee the country following attacks upon his home and congregation. Moreover, as in 1975, it suited the Indonesian authorities to talk up again the danger of a civil war in East Timor in order to portray the military as would-be saviours. However, with the world's media very much focused on the crisis and the Falintil pro-independence resistance movement refusing to be drawn into this scenario, such claims were seen to be hollow – as were the unsubstantiated suggestions that the ballot had been rigged in some way. Also, although the political authorities in Jakarta were reluctant to criticize their own military for failing to maintain order in East Timor, it was clear to the international community that some differences of interpretation on East Timor were evident between political and military élites. In particular, President Habibie and his close advisers were conscious of the growing international diplomatic, economic and interventionist threats and pressures (including the imposition, in mid-September, of a European Union temporary arms sales embargo) on Indonesia if it continued to preside over massive human rights abuses and a rejection of the people's freely chosen wishes in East Timor. Indeed, it was these considerations and the blatant unwillingness of the military/militias to recognize the popular verdict that forced Habibie, again in September, to accept reluctantly the logic of external intervention in the form of Interfet.

Interfet (the International Force for East Timor) was the UN-sponsored body, comprised of troops (around 7 to 8000 in all) drawn from several countries, given the task of restoring order and creating a peaceful situation in the beleaguered territory. Initial threats against it from the militias came to nought although, forced to operate elsewhere, the militias continued to target and terrorize East Timorese in the refugee (in effect hostage) camps of West Timor and beyond, which were largely closed to Interfet, outside human rights monitors and investigative journalists. Interfet's presence and the grudging Indonesian military acceptance of external peacemakers was accompanied by the relatively swift withdrawal of Indonesian armed forces, now renamed TNI (Tentara Nasional Indonesia), from East Timor.[58] Again, as Tapol explained: 'Never in the history of the [Indonesian] Republic has the TNI been so discredited.'[59]

In October 1999, the Indonesian people's consultative parliament (MPR), newly elected in June that year, formally accepted the result of the referendum in East Timor. This decision was further consolidated by the demise of Habibie (clearly damaged by the overall developments in East Timor) as, in the same month, the MPR elected the respected Muslim leader Abdurrahman Wahid as the new president of Indonesia. Wahid, of ailing health and eyesight, promptly selected as vice-president his defeated rival (and one-time coalition partner), Megawati Sukarnoputri, head of the Indonesian Democratic Party – Struggle (PDI) – and daughter of the former President Sukarno (himself deposed by the Suharto coup in 1965). Together, albeit with some misgivings, they accepted the East Timor referendum result. Wahid even suggested that the troubled territory of Aceh in northern Sumatra might enjoy a referendum, as in East Timor, and this was coupled with an initial measure of demilitarization in the province. Moreover, General Wiranto was promptly replaced as Defence Minister by a civilian – although Wiranto remained publicly supportive of the new Indonesia rulers, who also promised to welcome Xanana Gusmão formally to Jakarta in the weeks ahead. Gusmão had eventually been released from prison following the referendum and, after a short spell of sanctuary in the British embassy in Jakarta, had begun to lobby worldwide for support and relief for his country. In East Timor, the UN Security Council prepared (in late October) to replace Interfet by a bigger (around 11,000 troops) and more long-term force to help protect the people as the territory evolves towards full independence over the next two to three years, with all expectations that the East Timorese themselves would put up a provisional executive with Gusmão in the lead role.

The role of the international community thus proved decisive in the post-referendum period. Shocked into action by the unfolding of the crisis in East Timor, leading member states of the UN were unable to stand by, in the last resort, and see the indigenous people slaughtered for simply expressing their opinion through a free ballot, consented to and initiated by the Indonesian state. One of the cruel ironies of this situation was that some of the countries now seen as saviours of East Timor, through their belated interventionism, were *de facto* past guarantors of the Suharto dictatorship and Indonesian occupation of the territory. Indeed, given the previous record of UN member states' inactivity on implementing the resolutions against the post-1975 occupation of East Timor, it is little wonder that the Indonesian authorities, especially the military, doubted the developed world's political will to intervene in 1999. It is arguable whether this 'eleventh hour' interventionism would have taken place at all without the strong chorus of outrage and condemnation from civil society around the globe.

A central theme of this book has been that international pressures for change and redress in East Timor have played a significant and supportive part in the struggle to achieve self-determination for East Timor. This again proved to be the case at the height of the post-referendum backlash. Massive and targeted lobbying, letter writing, phoning, faxing, e-mailing, holding of vigils, demonstrating (notably outside embassies and home government/parliament buildings), public meetings, NGO and solidarity group activities, popular mobilization, boycotting, parliamentary questioning and so on testified to the depth of feeling and concern for the Timorese people and cause. The extensive media coverage of the unfolding violence and the presence and testimonies of international observers also helped to spotlight the stark nature of Indonesian rule and contributed towards keeping the East Timor question centre stage. As UNCHR leader Mary Robinson explained, on 23 October 1999:

> The awful abuses committed in East Timor have shocked the world. It is hard to conceive of a more blatant assault on the rights of hundreds of thousands of innocent civilians... Action, when it came, was painfully slow; thousands paid with their lives for the world's slow response... It was the tide of public anger that stirred world leaders to intervene.[60]

With international peacekeepers and aid agencies in East Timor involved in the process of relief and reconstruction, it is crucial not to lose sight of the problems to be resolved. For instance, the militias need comprehensively disarming to prevent further intimidation; all reluctantly displaced persons need to be assured of safe return; and those guilty of human rights abuses need to be held accountable. As regards the last point, impunity has been a regrettable feature of Indonesian rule and this practice, more than anything, has encouraged human rights violations. A lesson of the East Timor struggle is the need to accelerate the ratification process to set up an international criminal court, with teeth, to deal promptly and authoritatively with human rights abuses and crimes against humanity. Its launch would serve as a warning to would-be human rights abusers in similar situations to expect to be pursued in the courts. Other voices have called for the UN to be given its own permanent military/security capacity to intervene swiftly in situations such as happened in East Timor, Kosovo and the African Great Lakes region. This would entail moving away from the doctrine of national sover-eignty in order to address human rights crises more quickly.[61] External forces were reluctant to move decisively on East Timor and send in peacemakers without the consent of the Indonesian president. As Mary Robinson *inter alia* noted (above), the delay cost lives and led to further suffering.

In the interim, a UN commission of inquiry was approved to investigate the violations of human rights but, in the view of one informed observer, 'it is by no means certain that it will be able to uncover the truth or bring those responsible to justice'.[62] Ramos-Horta, too, was known to be unhappy with the composition of this body and other related aspects. In a keynote speech following the signing of the New York tripartite agreement on East Timor, Ramos-Horta had called for justice for his people: 'Justice is not revenge. Without justice there cannot be reconciliation.'[63] Speaking in London (alongside Ramos-Horta) in October, Xanana Gusmão ruled out a blanket amnesty for those responsible for the recent violence against the East Timorese and called for a war-crimes tribunal.[64] Ultimately, it is up to the people of East Timor and their democratically elected representatives as to how they treat momentous and difficult questions of impunity, redress, retributive justice, reconciliation, forgiveness, victim support, compensation and reconstruction of lives. The establishment of the truth, though, is surely central to these deliberations, and the international community will certainly have a voice here, especially given the current transitional and supervised status of East Timor and the universal dimensionality surrounding such issues and human rights. In practice, truth commissions and peace and justice structures are increasingly familiar institutions in various societies as they move through the transition from conflict to reconciliation. Such a body might concern itself with not only the recent violations in East Timor, but also with accounting for Indonesia's record in the territory since 1975. However, as Guelke points out (Chapter 13), there are no easy or prescribed answers to these questions. Each society in the throes of change has to work through its own problems and legacy in order to reach a better future.

East Timorese leaders appealed to Western governments and the international solidarity movement to maintain the political and economic pressure on Indonesia, notably to ensure a safe and swift return of refugees and investigate war crimes. Addressing particularly the international solidarity movement, Xanana Gusmão was fulsome and constructive in his tribute:

> Your role in helping us to pressure governments was magnificent. We won in this difficult struggle. We won with you... Yesterday we fought as activists. Now we will fight in other ways – in a way that will start cultivating the seeds of freedom, independence, justice, democracy and development.[65]

It is essential, therefore, that global solidarity continues and the international community also plays its part in assisting, financing and protecting the East Timorese at a promising, but difficult, time in their nation's history. Obviously, this means international peacekeepers in East Timor in the short term, to prevent any recurrence of the post-referendum mayhem and a return to the horrors of the past.

The immediate task of managing East Timor's transition from occupation to independence lay now with the United Nations Transitional Administration for East Timor (UNTAET). This body, replete with international peace-keeping troops, was expected to last for two to three years and had the job of building up East Timor's new institutional and working structures virtually from scratch, after years of repressive military occupation and an embittered scorched earth finale from retreating military and pro-integration militias. Criminal justice, policing and security, human rights protection, health care, education, (re)construction of infrastructure, housing, food and water, essential services, a vibrant media and civil society, and – not least – the return of the refugees: the list was endless and the problems were immediate. Moreover, there were criticisms that aid money, promised from the developed world for reconstruction, was slow in materializing whereas, in effect, nothing less than a new 'Marshall Plan' was needed if the territory was to be in a position to redress the legacy of Indonesian occupation.

Furthermore, in the view of many East Timorese, the above problems were compounded by a consultation deficit, a marginalization process on the ground: lack of ownership of their own peace, reconciliation and reconstruction process was an increasing complaint in the early phase of UNTAET management. Some observers pointed, in fact, to an excess of big, international NGOs (BINGOs), some of which had insufficient knowledge of and sensitivity to local needs and culture. Ultimately, the success of the transitional period would depend upon sufficient resources being available to finance the new East Timor and on successful cooperation between UNTAET and bodies such as the CNRT, the Catholic church, and indigenous and international NGOs. At the same time, cross-border incursions by pro-integration militias, in 1999–2000, served as a bitter reminder of the violence visited on East Timor. Also, at time of writing, the conditions inside the militia-controlled refugee camps in East Timor remain harsh, with death, killings, harassment and disease reported to be prevalent. Meanwhile, the resolution of the aforementioned problems of impunity remain central to the reconstruction of a new East Timor. Here, the international community has an important role to play, if the democratic government in Indonesia is unable to hold its military and militia to account for widespread human rights abuses in East Timor. Of course, any UN prospective investigation, tribunal and prosecution for war crimes, crimes against humanity or genocidal actions – all listed under the regulations that set up UNTAET – would have to be sensitive to the wishes of the East Timorese people and the standing of their peace and reconciliation process. Nevertheless, having failed this people for so long, the international powers and community as a whole now have an opportunity and a responsibility to make some amends, and help promote a new horizon, a lasting peace and justice in East Timor[66].

References

1   See, for instance, Liddle, R., 'Indonesia's democratic opening', *Government and Opposition*, Vol. 34, No. 1, Winter 1999.

2   Indeed, on 12 June 1997, the day after Habibie had called for restraint from the security forces, ABRI brutally dispersed a peaceful East Timorese protest in Jakarta, leaving over 25 demonstrators in need of hospital treatment. Cf. Amnesty International, *Indonesia: An Appeal for Restraint to the Indonesian Forces*, 12 May 1998.

3   Statement/information from Amnesty International, London, 7 September 1998.

4   *Far Eastern Economic Review*, 4 June 1998.
5   *International Herald Tribune* (Europe), 27 January 1998.
6   *The Irish Times*, 26 November 1998.
7   East Timor Human Rights Centre (ETHRC), *Escalating Violations in East Timor: Is a Peaceful Solution Possible?*, annual report of human rights violations in East Timor 1998, ETHRC annual report (Fitzroy, Australia, 28 February 1999, ETHRC). See also *Tapol Bulletin*, No. 151, March 1999.
8   Amnesty International, *Fear for Safety/Arbitrary Arrests/Unlawful Killings: East Timor*, Urgent Action 299/98 (London, 20 November 1998, Amnesty International).
9   ETHRC, *Escalating Violations in East Timor*.
10 Indonesian claims to have reduced the number of troops in East Timor could be seen as an orchestrated publicity exercise. Official figures of around 13,000 troops were seen to be wide of the mark and more realistic levels would be in the 18,000 to 21,000 range, including about 2000 'irregulars'. See *The Independent*, 30 October 1998; *CAAT News*, No. 152, November 1998; *The Observer*, 24 January 1999.
11 *International Herald Tribune*, 6 February 1999. See also ETHRC, *East Timor: Building on Freedom … the Newest Nation Demands Justice*, ann 40/ report, (Fitzroy, March 1999, ETHRC).
12 *The Guardian*, 19 April 1999; see also Amnesty International, *East Timor: Paramilitary Attacks Jeopardize East Timor's Future* (London, 16 April 1999, Amnesty International).
13 *Sydney Morning Herald*, 10 March 1999.
14 *Ibid.*
15 Statement by the East Timor *Action* Network (USA), 12 March 1999.
16 In recent years, the question of gender relations has belatedly begun to get more attention as Timorese women have highlighted the gender deficit in various aspects of the East Timorese struggle. See, for instance, contributions by Ines Almeida and Milena Pires in *Timor Link*, February 1999, and by the representative of OMT (Organizacão da Muhler Timor/The Timorese Women's Organization) in *FITUN Bulletin*, No. 17, 1998.
17 *Timor Link*, August 1998.
18 *New Statesman*, 30 October 1998.
19 *The Independent*, 26 July 1998.
20 *The Guardian*, 28 January 1999.
21 *The Irish Times*, 28 January 1998.
22 *The Times*, 29 January 1999.
23 *Tapol Bulletin*, No. 151, March 1999.
24 *The Guardian*, 28 January 1999.
25 *The Independent*, 28 January 1998.
26 *Ibid.*
27 *Ibid.*
28 *The Financial Times*, 28 January 1999.
29 *Far Eastern Economic Review*, 11 February 1999.
30 See *Tapol Bulletin*, No. 151, March 1999.
31 *New Statesman*, 29 May 1998.
32 *Ibid.*
33 *The Independent*, 16 May 1998.
34 *Ibid.* It should be pointed out, of course, that – since late 1998 – the Australian government had begun to play a more positively proactive role in East Timor's future and had

suggested setting up a 'contact group' to contribute towards the transition to autonomy or self-determination. Certainly, geographically and financially, Australia is well placed to make a development aid contribution to East Timor, as well as providing peacekeeping forces for any UN operation. Indeed, in April 1999, Australia promised A$ 20 million to help finance the 30 August consultation (or referendum) on East Timor's status. Within civil society, alongside specifically East Timor-focused bodies (e.g. the ETHRC and the East Timor Relief Association), organizations such as Caritas and the Australian Council for Overseas Action have already contributed much to support East Timor and will no doubt continue to do so.

35 *Far Eastern Economic Review*, 21 January 1999.

36 *The Age* (Melbourne), 15 August 1998.

37 *Far Eastern Economic Review*, 11 February 1999.

38 *Ibid*.

39 See *Timor Link*, February 1999.

40 Roque Rodrigues (CNRT National Executive Committee), in *ibid*. See also reference 41 below.

41 *The Guardian*, 28 January 1999.

42 *International Herald Tribune*, 3 February 1999. See also 'Indonesia is confused about what to do with East Timor, leaving the territory frightened and uncertain about its future', *The Economist*, 13 February 1999.

43 *The Guardian*, 13 March 1999. See also the statement by the East Timor *Action* Network (USA), 'East Timor will have its referendum on self-determination in all but name', 12 March 1999.

44 *Le Monde*, 25–26 April 1999; *The Guardian*, 29 April 1999.

45 See, for instance, Carey, Peter, 'East Timor: Third World colonialism and the struggle for national identity', *Conflict Studies*, No. 293/294, October and November 1996; Dunn, James, *Timor: A People Betrayed* (Sydney, 1996, ABC Books); Taylor, John G., *Indonesia's Forgotten War* (London, 1991, Zed Books, and Leichardt, Australia, 1991, Pluto Press).

46 *The Guardian*, 30 January 1999. See also the EHTRC *Annual Report 1999*, which suggests that the arming of the militias 'seriously undermines the sincerity of the Indonesian government's commitment to finding a peaceful solution'.

47 CAFOD (1998) 'Memorandum submitted by CAFOD' to the Foreign Affairs Committee first report, *Foreign Policy and Human Rights*, Vol. III, Appendices to the Minutes of Evidence, House of Commons, Session 1998–99, June (submission), p. 308. CAFOD is the overseas development agency of the Catholic Bishops Conference of England and Wales.

48 See the extensive interview by Mark Baker in *The Age* (Melbourne), 15 August 1998.

49 For fuller details of the peace plan, see 'The CNRM peace plan' in *East Timor: Nobel Peace Prize. Lectures Delivered at the 1996 Nobel Peace Prize Awarding Ceremony* (Lisbon, 1997, Editions Colibri). As regards the CNRM, the word Maubere in the title means 'son of Timor' (from Mambai *mau bere* – my brother/my friend), cf. Carey 'East Timor' in *Conflict Studies*. Estêvão Cabral (*FITUN Bulletin*, No. 16, 1997) provides the following explanation: 'The term Maubere comes from the Mambae language and the name is usually attributed to men. This term was used by the Portuguese colonialist in East Timor to refer to East Timorese in disparaging tones. It was reclaimed by Fretilin and reasserted as an emblem of a distinct East Timorese collective identity.' Cabral also points out, in Chapter 6, that the umbrella CNRM was replaced in 1997 by the CNRT,

the National Council of Timorese Resistance, with Xanana Gusmão elected as its president.

50 See, for instance, *International Herald Tribune*, 28 January 1999; *The Irish Times*, 28 January 1999.

51 *International Herald Tribune*, 12 February 1999.

52 Subsequent regime comments tried to be more reassuring, suggesting a 'reasonable' delay before Indonesia unburdens itself of East Timor. See, for instance, *Far Eastern Economic Review*, 25 February 1999. Note also, though, the comments by Dewi Fortuna Anwar (in *International Herald Tribune*, 17 February 1999), supporting a rapid withdrawal: 'I tend to believe the longer we leave the situation, the more difficult it will be to resolve... The most important thing at the moment is to ensure disarmament among the East Timorese.'

53 ETHRC *Annual Report 1999*.

54 *The Independent*, 27 August 1999.

55 *The Irish Times*, 7 May 1999. For a full presentation and analysis of the argument between Indonesia and Portugal, see *Timor Link*, No. 47, June 1999.

56 Taylor, John G., 'Introduction', in Taylor, *East Timor: The Price of Freedom* (London, 1999, Zed Books).

57 *Tapol Bulletin*, No. 154/155, November 1999.

58 In April 1999, the armed forces' name was changed (by General Wiranto) from ABRI back to TNI (Tentara Nasional Indonesia). The latter name was used in the early years of the republic. See *ibid.*, p. 18.

59 *Ibid*.

60 *The Independent*, 23 October 1999.

61 See, for instance, Palmer, John, 'The UN must stand up and be counted', *Red Pepper*, October 1999, p. 11.

62 Conor Foley, Amnesty International (UK)'s East Timor crisis response director, in Foley, Conor, 'East Timor crisis response', *The Newsletter* (Amnesty International internal newsletter), November 1999, p. 1.

63 State of the World Forum, Belfast, 7 May 1999.

64 *Tapol Bulletin*, No. 154/155, November 1999, p. 21.

65 *CIIR News*, November 1999, p. 2.

66 For further on recent developments see *Inside Indonesia*, No 61, January-March 2000 and No 62, April-June 2000; *Maubere* (Newsletter of the East Timor Ireland Solidarity Campaign), May 2000; *Tapol Bulletin*, No 157, April 2000 and No 158, June 2000; *Timor Link*, No 48, December 1999 and No 49, May 2000.

Index of Names

Index of Places